Colora

Robert S. Lorch

Colorado's Government

Structure, Politics, Administration, and Policy

FIFTH EDITION

University Press of Colorado

Published by the University Press of Colorado
P.O. Box 849
Niwot, Colorado 80544

The University Press of Colorado is a cooperative publishing enterprise supported, in part, by Adams State College, Colorado State University, Fort Lewis College, Mesa State College, Metropolitan State College of Denver, University of Colorado, University of Northern Colorado, University of Southern Colorado, and Western State College.

Library of Congress Cataloging-in-Publication Data

Lorch, Robert Stuart, 1925–
    Colorado's government: structure, politics, administration, and policy /
Robert S. Lorch. — 5th ed.
      p. cm.
    Includes bibliographical references and index.
    ISBN 0-87081-245-9 (cloth). — ISBN 0-87081-220-3 (pbk.)
    1. Colorado — Politics and government. I. Title.
JK7816.L67 1991
320.9788 — dc20   91-21556
                                                         CIP

The paper used in this publication meets the minimum requirements of the American National Standard for Information Sciences—Permanence of Paper for Printed Library Materials. ANSI Z39.48–1984
   ∞

10 9 8 7 6 5 4 3 2 1

DEDICATED TO THE PEOPLE OF COLORADO

Contents

Colorado's Government

A Compact Political History of Early Colorado

CHAPTER OUTLINE

Terra Incognita
Louisiana Purchase
Pike
Long
Fremont
Mexican War
First White Settlers
Beaver Hunters and Trading Posts
Gold
Civilization

Government Comes to Colorado
Territorial Government
Statehood
The Constitutional Convention of 1874
Railroads
Indians
Cattle
Colony Towns
Silver
The Twentieth Century

It is sometimes said that political scientists should study the present and leave the past to historians. But almost everything, really, is rooted in the past. Therefore, political scientists have to intrude on the territory of historians to look into the social and political past in order to make sense out of the present — for, as historians are first to insist, the present is but an extension of the past.

The first problem is where to begin our quick sketch of the Colorado story. Shall we begin with admission of Colorado to the Union in 1876? Or with the discovery of gold in the 1850s? Or with the Louisiana Purchase some two hundred years ago? Or with the Spanish explorations nearly five hundred years ago? Or with the Indians whose earliest record in Colorado goes back to the Basket Makers of the Mesa Verde two thousand years ago? Or with the migration of Asians to the New World fifteen or twenty thousand years ago? Or with the formation of Colorado when it rose out of the ancient sea millions of years ago? A geologist's history would surely differ from a political scientist's history, but what has affected Colorado more than her geology, geography, and topography?

Any political history of Colorado should certainly be a history of the people who have lived here and who has lived here longer than the Indian — the Apaches, the Pawnees, the Comanches, the Utes, the Cheyennes, the Kiowas? But unfortunately they kept no written record of their adventures and of their national existence in the region we now call Colorado. As for Caucasians, the Spanish explorers were the first to keep written records in the territory that is now Colorado. Later, after the United States paid $15 million for the Louisiana Purchase, the administration became curious about what had been bought and sent Zebulon Pike, Stephen Long, John Fremont, John Gunnison, and others out west to look. Much of what we now call Colorado was included in the purchase.

TERRA INCOGNITA

For a couple of hundred years after Spain took possession of Mexico in the late fifteenth and early sixteenth century, Colorado was unknown territory to the north of Mexico that the Spanish expected one day to investigate. A sudden impulse to explore this vast terra incognita occurred when rumors reached the Spaniards that there were in that area seven large and immensely wealthy cities known as the Seven Cities of Cibola, so rich that the doors of the houses were studded with jewels. These rumors were brought south by Cabeza de Vaca and by a black man named Estevan who had returned to Mexico in 1536 after wandering about in the unknown territories.

The viceroy of Mexico decided to send a reconnaissance party to check the truth of these rumors. He sent Friar Marcos de Niza and several others, including Estevan. On this scouting trip Estevan was killed by Indians, but not before sending word to Friar Marcos that he had found one of the Seven Cities of Cibola. The friar and his men climbed a hill and looked at the distant "city" Estevan had reported and were impressed by its size. Rather than risk being killed himself, Friar Marcos led his party back to Mexico, where he gave glowing (but poorly documented) testimony to the actual existence of the Seven Cities of Cibola. Unfortunately, his only evidence was

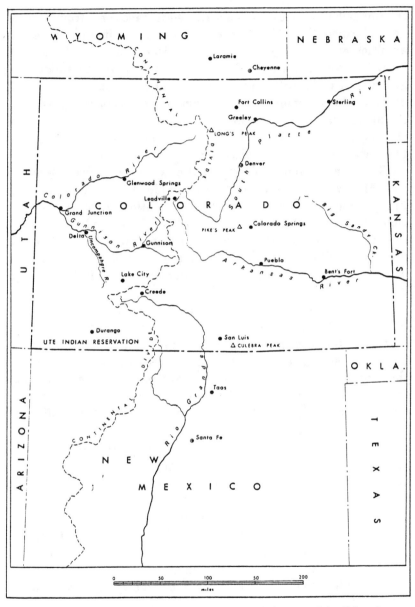

This map shows some locations important in the early history of the Colorado area before 1900.

the somewhat dubious message alleged to have come from Estevan before he died. Friar Marcos's reports, which still further stirred the ambition of the viceroy, motivated the viceroy to dispatch the great Francisco Vasquez Coronado with a strong party to subdue the Seven Cities of Cibola and bring back treasure. It was a splendid party of 260 horsemen, many of them young cavaliers representing the noblest families in Spain. There were flags, swords, crossbows, shields, and suits of gilded armor glinting in the sun. Coronado took Friar Marcos along to show the way.

The expedition meandered about in what we today call Arizona, New Mexico, Texas, Kansas, and Colorado. They plundered many Indian villages but never found the Seven Cities. It was a grand tour, well recorded by Pedro Castenada, whom Coronado brought along to keep a journal of daily events. One important thing Coronado unwittingly did was show Indians an animal they had never seen before — the horse, which was to change the plains Indians' way of life.

In 1609 Juan de Onate planted a colony that became the city of Santa Fe. For the next couple of hundred years Santa Fe was the northernmost outpost of the Spanish empire; there was apparently little interest in what lay beyond. It is true that some Indians whom the good people of Santa Fe had enslaved and converted to Christianity grew tired of being slaves and Christians and ran away to the north. It was said that the runaways liked to go especially to El Cuartelejo in what is now southeastern Colorado (later to become the site of Bent's Fort), and the Spanish periodically sent troops to retrieve them. Juan Archuleta led one such expedition to El Cuartelejo. If Coronado was not the first Spaniard to set foot in what is now Colorado, then it was Archuleta.

In 1706, Juan Ulibarri, who was hunting runaway Indian slaves in the direction of El Cuartelejo, heard disturbing news from Apache Indians about recent battles with Pawnees in the north. The Apaches said the Pawnees were armed with French firearms, evidence that the French were beginning to make an appearance in the neighborhood.

The French had some right to be in the area; through Robert La Salle in 1682 they had laid claim (loudly so) to all the land drained by the Mississippi River and its many tributaries. Probably not even France had a clear idea what a vast piece of real estate had been claimed. The Mississippi drains much of the American Midwest as well as all of the plains, even reaching deep into the Rocky Mountains to the Continental Divide — in short, everything from the Alleghenies to the Rocky Mountains. For a long time no one knew much about the geography and boundary lines in the area of Colorado, although in 1739 two French explorers, the Mallet brothers, traversed Colorado and gave the Platte River its name. The Spanish had a vague sense that all territory north of Santa Fe was within the Spanish orbit, while the French had a vague notion to the contrary. So for many years there was difficulty between the Spanish and the French across the plains of North America involving Indians allied to one side or the other. The conflict appeared to be resolved when France gave the entire province of Louisiana, including such diverse points as eastern Colorado and the city of New Orleans (much to the distress of the French colonists of that city), to Spain. This gave Spain undisputed (except, of course, by Indians) authority over the whole of what we call Colorado.

Still, Spain paid little attention to the area. There was some prospecting for gold and other metals, but not much. Juan Rivera led some miners from Santa Fe into the La Plata Mountains (which he named) in 1765, but Spain's main interest in Colorado had to do with California, not Colorado itself. San Francisco, founded by the Spanish in 1776, was threatened by the English and the Russians coming down the Pacific Coast, and the Spanish wanted to open an interior road between New Mexico and San Francisco. Two Spanish friars, Fathers Dominguez and Escalante, were commissioned to explore this possibility. They reached western Colorado and pressed on to Salt Lake before they were forced by weather to return home. Spanish explorers had a fortunate habit of keeping meticulous records of their journeys, and Father Escalante's journal provides the first extensive description of Colorado, including parts of the stream beds of the Los Pinos, Animas, Dolores, San Miguel, Uncompahgre, Gunnison, Colorado, and White rivers.

About this time the Comanche Indians under Chief Greenhorn were becoming a thorn in the side of the Spanish. Juan Bautista de Anza, founder of San Francisco, set out in 1778 north from Santa Fe into Colorado to smash the Indian troublemakers, who might interfere with overland communications. With the help of Utes and Arapahoes, he defeated the Comanches, killed Chief Greenhorn at the base of Greenhorn Mountain, and marched eight or nine hundred miles through Colorado to deal with any other nuisances.

LOUISIANA PURCHASE

In 1800 much of the land so expertly pacified by de Anza was given back to France through the efforts of Napoleon. Although this came as a relief to the French colonists in Louisiana who had been agitating for a return to French rule, it had little immediate effect on Colorado. However, the long-range effect was monumental. Three years later, the Americans, who needed access to the mouth of the Mississippi, bought the entire Louisiana province from France (although France had promised the Spanish in 1800 never to surrender Louisiana to any other power).

Approximately one-third of the present state of Colorado was acquired with the Louisiana Purchase: the part north of the Arkansas River and east of the Continental Divide. That one-third includes the whole Front Range, from the present city of Pueblo up to the Wyoming border, and the plains eastward. Most of the population of present-day Colorado is concentrated in this area, in Pueblo, Colorado Springs, Denver, Boulder, Fort Collins, Greeley, Sterling, Julesburg, and Burlington. The other two-thirds of Colorado belonged to Spain until 1821, when Mexico won her independence; Mexico held the area until it was ceded to the United States as a consequence of the Mexican American War of 1848 and the annexation of Texas in 1860. Yes, for a couple of years a strip of south and middle Colorado was part of the Republic of Texas.

Much of the Louisiana Purchase was blank space on the map, blank space that teased President Thomas Jefferson. No one had the time or resources or even the inclination to draw definite boundaries. The whole area was regarded as a hopeless wilderness. Jefferson moved at once to find out what was there, especially as he was being criticized for having paid so much ($15 million — perhaps several billion dollars in today's equivalency) for what was believed to be a wasteland. In 1804 he sent Captain Meriwether Lewis, Lieutenant William Clark, and a party of about forty men across the continent by way of the Missouri River to Oregon. Their report seemed to Jefferson to justify the purchase.

PIKE

Two years later, in 1806, Lieutenant Zebulon Pike and a party of twenty-two men were sent to explore the sources of the Arkansas River. The Arkansas was a controversial river: while the Spanish were certain that the boundary line of the Louisiana Purchase ran along the Arkansas, the Americans were not convinced. Pike's mission was, in part, to secure sufficient knowledge of the southeastern boundary of "Louisiana" to enable the United States government to arrange for a definite line of demarcation between American and Spanish territory. Pike traveled along the Arkansas, which flows out of the Colorado Front Range at Pueblo, some forty miles south of the peak later to be named after him. Pike himself named it Grand Peak and was impressed with it, even trying to climb it. It was then the last week in November, snow was already waist high in the mountains, and the effort failed. He did manage to reach the top of Cheyenne Mountain and was mightily impressed by the scenery from there. It being nine degrees below zero, his party returned to the Arkansas River, pursued it up to the present Cañon City, and penetrated a short way into the Royal Gorge, which they finally decided was impassable.

Meanwhile, the Spaniards had heard of Pike and were looking for him. Pike made the mistake of proceeding into the San Luis Valley south of the Arkansas, which the Spanish firmly claimed as their own. He was captured by a troop of Spanish soldiers and taken to Santa Fe, then to El Paso, then to Chihuahua. He was finally released in 1807. He lost all his maps, so his exact route in Colorado is hard to follow today. In 1819 the United States and Spain concluded a treaty that officially set the boundary between the United States and Spanish possessions along the Arkansas River in Colorado.

LONG

In the same year, 1819, Major Stephen H. Long was sent with a party of naturalists, topographers, geologists, and others to explore the country north of the Spanish possessions. The expedition was forced to stop for the winter on the Blue River in Kansas; here their horses were stolen by Pawnee Indians. By June 1820, Major Long and his party had gotten new equipment and pushed on. They entered Colorado on a route up the South Platte. Long's first view of the mountains was from near St. Vrain's fort. The peak that he first saw towering above the clouds he named after himself, a vanity of which Pike had not been guilty. Long's expedition examined the mountains and the plains that lie along their base from the South Platte to the Arkansas River. The journal of the expedition, written by Dr. Edwin James, deals mainly with Indian tribes, animals, geology, botany, and general facts about the country. It was Dr. James, incidentally, who first climbed Pikes Peak. But neither the official name Grand Peak, which Pike gave it, nor the name James' Peak was to endure. Early residents of Colorado habitually called it Pikes Peak, and that is the name that finally stuck. Dr. James did, however, have one of Colorado's finest mountains named after him.

Long made disparaging observations about eastern Colorado and the plains, from the Front Range of the Rocky Mountains to the Missouri River. He said the area was worthless for agricultural purposes; on his map he labeled it "The Great American Desert," leading people to think it resembled the Sahara. Thus he did much to hold back settlement of the West.

FREMONT

The next important expedition into Colorado organized by the United States government was sponsored by the U.S. Topographical Engineers and was entrusted to Colonel John C. Fremont. He entered Colorado three times: in 1842, 1843, and 1845. The Pathfinder, as Fremont was known, was looking for a route for a railroad through the central Rocky Mountains to the Pacific, an enterprise that excited the whole nation. His first two trips were concentrated in the northern and western part of the state. On his second trip he was accompanied by William Gilpin, who in later years became the first governor of the Colorado Territory. His third trip was in the southern part of the state, where he gathered data for military use in case of war with Mexico. While he himself explored along the Arkansas River boundary, he sent a detachment from Bent's Fort to find a suitable military road into New Mexico.

In 1848 Fremont, having resigned from the military, led an expedition financed by railroad interests to find a central route across the Rockies. He thrashed about in the middle of winter through the Wet Mountains and the Sangre de Cristos and tried to cross the Continental Divide (against the advice of Indians and trappers) by following the Rio Grande rather than going through Cochetopa Pass. It was a disastrous trip in bitter cold and deep snow. One-third of his thirty-four men died. On Fremont's fifth trip (also privately sponsored) he explored the same general area but took the safe way through Cochetopa Pass. He followed the route down the Gunnison River previously charted that year (1853) by Captain John Gunnison, who was also making a railroad survey, although Gunnison was working for the government rather than for private interests. Fremont left a narrative of his explorations.

MEXICAN WAR

The military data gathered by Fremont on his third trip, in anticipation of war with Mexico, were used a year later in 1846 when the war began. Colorado was a staging area for the drive by General Stephen W. Kearny south to Santa Fe. Kearny gathered his forces south of the Arkansas River near Bent's Fort (which was north of the river in the neighborhood of present-day La Junta). Bent's Fort itself, which had been established many years before as a trading post by the Bent brothers, was now taken over by the government for use as a military hospital and storehouse. Kearny with his Army of the West marched to Santa Fe with little resistance. From there he marched on to California.

FIRST WHITE SETTLERS

The war ended in 1848 after two years. The Treaty of Guadalupe Hidalgo gave the United States possession of the southwestern part of our present nation, including about two-thirds of the present state of Colorado: those areas south of the Arkansas and west of the Continental Divide. The scattered inhabitants of this region were so isolated from the heart of affairs in Mexico that many of them possibly did not even realize that political changes had occurred. At this time (the 1840s) the only white settlers in the territory now called Colorado were a few independent trappers, traders, adventurers, and employees of the American Fur Company. There were a few "civilized" Indians and Mexicans in the southern portion, and bands of "savages" (as they were then called) who roamed the plains (Pawnees, Cheyennes, Arapahoes, Utes, and Comanches, among others). None of these people are known to have had knowledge of the existence of precious metals beneath the soil.

In 1852 and 1853 Mexican colonists established four towns on the Culebra River: San Luis, San Pablo, San Acacio, and Chama. These were the first permanent settlements in Colorado. The original settlers were Mexicans who, in 1843, before the Mexican American War, had tried to settle near the present town of Antonito but were driven away by Ute Indians. Not deterred by the results of the war, they tried again to settle on the Culebra River, this time successfully. These pioneers built low adobe houses with dirt floors and gravel roofs. At Conejos in the 1850s they built the first church in Colorado: Our Lady of Guadalupe.

In this period there was a great rush of people across the plains to California, beginning with the California gold discoveries of 1848. But the tide of people flowed around Colorado rather than through it. It was much easier to go across Wyoming to the north or through Raton Pass to the south than to try to cross the perilous mountains of Colorado. Practically no emigrants from the East, except for hunters and traders, settled in Colorado until 1859, when gold was discovered.

BEAVER HUNTERS AND TRADING POSTS

Long before the precipitous growth of Colorado that began in 1859 when gold was discovered, this territory was a favorite area for fur gathering. At first, beaver fur was the most valuable product. Early in the century it was fashionable in the East and elsewhere to wear top hats covered with beaver pelts, and so there were a handful of people in Colorado and throughout the West who hunted for beaver. They were a somewhat reckless breed of men who lived a lonely and dangerous life. It required only some traps, a gun or two, and a horse to go into the fur business. Trappers in southern Colorado would gather as many pelts as they could and take them to Taos, the main fur-trading center on the Santa Fe Trail.

Many trading posts were established in Colorado, most of them set up by such great trading companies as the British-owned Hudson's Bay Company, John Jacob Astor's American Fur Company, and the Rocky Mountain Fur Company. Near the present site of Delta, Fort Uncompahgre was built on the Gunnison River by a trader named Antoine Robidoux. In the northwestern corner of Colorado, Fort Davy Crockett on the Green River was used for trading pelts. Near the present town of Platteville, Fort St. Vrain was established by a businessman named Ceran St. Vrain. Nearby was Fort Vasquez, built in 1837 and now partially restored. Farther south on the South Platte River were Fort Jackson and Fort Lupton (1836). Near Pueblo were Gantt's Post and Fort Pueblo (1842). And on the Arkansas River near the present town of La Junta was the famous Bent's Fort built by William Bent about 1832. William was one of four brothers who, with Ceran St. Vrain, did a successful business as Bent, St. Vrain & Company. Bent's Fort, now restored for Colorado's centennial, became a model for many other forts and posts. It was well situated on the Santa Fe Trail to serve both the beaver pelt and buffalo robe business. Its adobe walls were from two to four feet thick and fifteen feet high. It was rectangular, measuring about 180 feet by 135 feet. After southern Colorado became the property of the United States, new forts were built in that area, including Fort Massachusetts, in 1852, near Mount Blanca. Soon Fort Garland replaced Fort Massachusetts six miles south. For a while Kit Carson served at Fort Garland as Indian agent.

When beaver hats lost popularity around 1830, beaver hunting became less profitable. About the same time, buffalo hides gained popularity as a raw material for coats, sofas, rugs, and blankets. The great forts along the Front Range, such as St. Vrain's and Bent's, were in part a response to the buffalo hide business. Hides, being large and bulky, required warehouse space and protection pending shipment via the Oregon Trail to the north or the Santa Fe Trail to the south. Most buffalo hunting (unlike beaver hunting) was done by Indians, who brought hides to forts and posts and traded them for looking glasses, finger rings, wristbands, ear bobs, beads, bells, axes, knives, kettles, blankets, and whiskey. Indians were not permitted to buy whiskey, but one buffalo robe was approximately equal in value to one pint.

GOLD

The first American gold rush was not in California nor in Colorado but at Auraria, Georgia, in 1833. The name *Auraria* means "gold" in Latin. On June 22, 1859, some educated Cherokee Indians from the gold regions of Georgia on their way to California camped near the present site of Denver. One of them, Lewis Ralston, tried his hand at panning gold on a branch of Clear Creek. He found a little, and the creek, which runs through Arvada near Denver, was named Ralston Creek in his honor. The Indians went on to California, then made the long return trip to Georgia. They didn't forget Colorado. Eight years later in 1858 another Cherokee expedition came west under the leadership of Green Russell, a white man married to a Cherokee woman. They numbered about seventy and were joined by another thirty-four men near Ralston Creek.

This group prospected for gold intensively, but the men were deeply disappointed by failure to locate a spot that produced a satisfactory return for their efforts. By July most of the party was ready to go home. All but Russell and twelve others departed. The thirteen persisted and eventually found gold on Dry Creek (which runs through present-day Englewood) about five miles from its confluence with the Platte, near the present site of Denver. News of Russell's discovery reached the East and caused a sensation. Glowing accounts spread all over the world of the richness of the gold strike. By October people were beginning to arrive at the scene to lay claims. Many settled on the Platte near the mouth of Cherry Creek. By October 30, so many had arrived that a need for government was apparent, and on that date a mass meeting was held. They decided to found a town on the west side of Cherry Creek where it meets the South Platte, and they named it Auraria.

By November, William Larimer, an experienced town promoter, had arrived at Auraria from Kansas. He promptly laid out a new town directly across Cherry Creek and called it Denver, after James W. Denver, governor of the Kansas Territory. (The Denver area was then part of the Territory of Kansas.) Auraria and Denver were rivals facing each other across Cherry Creek until they united in 1860. Other towns were founded in 1858, including Boulder, La Porte (near Fort Collins), Fountain City (at the site of present-day Pueblo) on Fountain Creek where it meets the Arkansas, and El Paso (near the site of present-day Colorado Springs).

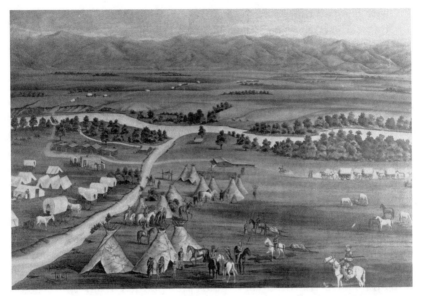

Denver was founded in 1858 where Cherry Creek meets the South Platte River.

Four hundred people wintered in the region in 1858–59. By spring, as soon as the weather permitted, adventurous spirits from all over the world set out for Colorado. Parties assembled at different points along the Missouri River, supplied themselves with equipment for gold hunting, gulch mining, and pioneer life, and set out for the Pikes Peak gold regions (as the area was then called), to the distress of Indians who disputed the white man's right to cross these vast domains.

The great rush to Colorado was spurred not only by reports of gold strikes but by the great depression of 1857. Masses of unemployed people headed for Colorado with the bright hope of instant prosperity. In March 1859, a Kansas City newspaper carried these unsympathetic remarks about the migration to Colorado:

Only think of 100,000 persons scattered over a few miles of territory, digging, and tearing up the ground in search of wealth. Eating greasy meat, sleeping on the cold ground, in rain, snow and hail, hot and cold, wet and dry — up early and late — striving like giants to turn upside down the earth for the sake of gain, away from the cheering hearthstone, joyous laugh and happy home, among wolves and savage beasts, working out their lives for naught, when,

with one-half that energy, industry and perseverance, at home on
their farms, they would have full pockets, good health, be with their
family and friends, enjoying happiness, comfort, and peace.

The bubble of hope soon burst. The immigrants found little gold.
Many, disheartened and disgusted with the prospector's life, started
back home across the prairies in a kind of stampede. Along their line
of retreat across the plains they met thousands of hopefuls en route
to the land of gold. To these they told the story of failure and disaster,
and these stories stemmed, and even turned, the tide of immigration. Going to Colorado they had painted "Pikes Peak or Bust" on
their wagons and "Pikes Peak Humbug" returning.

Some stayed and found gold, including George Jackson and John
H. Gregory. Gregory's discovery on May 6, 1859, was an important
event in the nation's history. He discovered the first gold-bearing
lode in Colorado (a lode is a vein of ore in the ground that must be
mined); before his discovery, gold was panned from the creeks.
Gregory's lode was truly remarkable in its richness. The discovery
of so much wealth (to which he laid claim, of course) dazed him. He
is alleged to have said with a faraway look in his eyes, "My wife will
be a lady and my children will be educated." Jackson's discovery,
near the present site of Idaho Springs, was not like Gregory's lode
but was a placer — the richest placer yet discovered. A placer is a
valuable mineral deposit contained in sand or gravel, usually found
along the banks of streams. The news of these discoveries spread
throughout the civilized world and soon thousands of prospectors
were busy with pick and pan in the gulches. By the spring of 1860
there were over twenty thousand inhabitants in the territory.

CIVILIZATION

Already in 1859 some signs of civilization were appearing in
Denver. Colorado's first schoolteacher, Owen J. Goldrick, arrived in
Auraria on October 3, 1859. It is said he entered town wearing a silk
top hat, a black broadcloth suit, and white kid gloves, seated on a
filthy freight wagon and driving an ox team with a bullwhacker's
whip. He passed his silk hat to get his salary in advance and then
opened the first school. It was a mud-roofed cabin, but the settlers
were so proud of it that they met the next incoming wagon trains

with the cry, "We've got a school!" The following year the territorial legislature created the University of Colorado at Boulder, though it was 1877 before the first building was completed and put to use. This was Old Main, still standing and still useful. Church services were begun in Denver in 1859. Eighteen-year-old William Larimer, son of the founder of Denver, reported that the first service was held in one end of a cabin while at the other end gambling was going on and the jingle of money formed the background to Mr. Fisher's preaching. Theater came to Denver in October 1859 when Colonel Thorne's Star Company from Leavenworth, Kansas, played "Cross of Gold" at Apollo Hall. The *Rocky Mountain News* was founded by W. N. Byers in April 1859 after he secured a shipment of a press across the plains.

By spring 1859 Denver had about three hundred log huts. After a summer and fall of feverish activity, buildings were rising, some substantial brick structures were to be seen, and trains of prairie freighters were arriving and departing every day. Clark, Gruber and Company established a mint for coining gold. Banks were formed, a chamber of commerce founded, and in the environs farming by irrigation was getting started to provide vegetables, corn, grain, potatoes, and other produce.

GOVERNMENT COMES TO COLORADO

The sudden appearance of people and business in Colorado, especially in Denver and the adjacent Front Range, and throughout the area from north to south and deep into the mountains, produced an obvious need for some kind of government to protect property and personal rights and to bring law and order. There was need for local authority close to the people and for a general government over the whole region. Within one year the population (excluding Indians, who had their own tribal government) had gone from essentially nothing to many thousands. Within that year, almost before these thousands had unhitched their wagons, there was a call for creation of a new state. Without any authority to do so, the population of the area gathered and elected in the winter of 1859 a delegate to Washington (Hiram J. Graham), who promptly lobbied to have a bill introduced into Congress establishing a territorial government for the Pikes Peak region. The bill was defeated. At a second meeting in Auraria on April 15, 1859, the people proposed creation of the State of Jefferson and called for a constitutional convention to meet in June. The call said in part: "Government of some kind we must have, and the question narrows itself down to this point: Shall it be government of the knife and revolver or shall we unite in forming here in our golden country, among the ravines and gulches of the Rocky Mountains, and in the fertile valleys of the Arkansas and Platte, a new and independent State?"

However, during that particular spring and summer when so many miners were returning home disillusioned, momentarily stemming the tide of immigration, the enthusiasm for state government died down in favor of a territorial government established by Congress. The question of state versus territorial government was submitted to the people for a vote on September 5, 1859, and the state idea lost. Promptly, a move was made to set up a territorial government. A territorial constitution was ratified and R. W. Steele was elected governor without Congressional authority. Boundaries of the territory were drawn embracing all of present Colorado plus a slice of what is now Wyoming and Utah.

All this was illegal, or perhaps extralegal would be a better term, for the people lacked authority to form a territorial government. The United States Congress had, in fact, specifically voted against a separate territorial government for the Pikes Peak region. Folks in the region set up their government anyway and proceeded to pass laws and elect officers as though all were perfectly proper, despite the fact that the area was actually already subject to existing territorial government properly set up by Congress. In fact, four legal governments had jurisdiction over what is now Colorado: Kansas, Utah, Nebraska, and New Mexico. Denver was in the Kansas Territory, Boulder was in the Nebraska Territory, and their territorial governments were seated hundreds of miles away. Governor Denver had dispatched officials to the Pikes Peak region, and the Pikes Peak region had elected a delegate (A. J. Smith) to the Kansas territorial legislature, but such arrangements had proved unsatisfactory. The extralegal Jefferson Territory thus went into business. A general assembly was elected, which met at Denver on November 7, 1859, and went to work passing laws, incorporating cities, and setting up counties. Denver was incorporated and twelve counties established.

More important to the settlers than the extralegal territorial government were extralegal local governments set up by people wherever a few inhabitants needed law and order. To govern the miners who thronged the slopes, gulches, and valleys along Clear Creek and elsewhere, rigid laws were required. Officials elected by the citizens and commissioned by distant territorial governments were unable to enforce the law in this wild country. Instead, *miners' courts* enforced the law of *miners' meetings*. Miners' meetings, composed of all inhabitants of a district, enacted civil and criminal codes, defined boundaries, prescribed duties of officers, and elected officers. Laws were based upon similar enactments in California and Nevada framed earlier by miners in those older mining areas. The officers included a president, judge, sheriff, collector-surveyor, and recorder, who was also secretary and treasurer of the district. No distinctions of sex were made.

The first miners' court was organized in the Gregory district. With the discovery of other rich lodes, the organization of other districts followed rapidly. Farmers also needed protection of property rights, and they formed *claim clubs*. The land claims of members were filed with the recorder of the claim club, thus clarifying who owned, or claimed, what until regular government was established. The extralegal acts of these miners' courts, miners' meetings, claim clubs, and of the illegal Territory of Jefferson itself were eventually confirmed and made legitimate by the legal Territory of Colorado government when it was established in 1861 by an act of Congress.

TERRITORIAL GOVERNMENT

When Congress took up the bill to create the legitimate territorial government, members debated what name to give the government that had been calling itself the Territory of Jefferson. The idea of calling it the Territory of Idaho was popular until someone suggested it be called Colorado, after the great river that has its source not far from present-day Glenwood Springs. Some were not sure such a magnificent name should be wasted on the Pikes Peak region. Finally, the name Idaho was struck from the bill and Colorado written in. On February 28, 1861, in the closing hours of his term in the White House, President James Buchanan signed the bill, and the Territory of Colorado came to life at a crucial moment in

American history. A few days later President Lincoln was inaugurated. He appointed Major William Gilpin of Missouri, a man who knew Colorado and had accompanied Fremont in 1843, to be the first governor of the territory. While Gilpin crossed the plains to take up his new office in the spring of 1861, Fort Sumter was fired on and the Civil War began.

On May 27, 1861, Major Gilpin arrived in Denver. In July a supreme court was organized. In August a general election was held, and H. P. Bennet was chosen delegate to Congress. A census was taken shortly after that, showing a population of 25,331 for the territory and around 3,000 in the City of Denver. On September 9, 1861, the First Territorial Legislature met in Denver and divided the territory into seventeen counties: Arapahoe, Boulder, Clear Creek, Conejos, Costilla, Douglas, El Paso, Fremont, Gilpin, Huerfano, Jefferson, Lake, Larimer, Park, Pueblo, Summit, and Weld. Colorado City (near present-day Colorado Springs) was selected capital of the territory because of its central location.

There is no space here to describe at length Colorado's participation in the Civil War. Briefly, a troop of Colorado volunteers met an army of Texans in Apache Canyon at La Glorieta Pass. Major John M. Chivington (who later played a role in the massacre of Indians at Sand Creek) led the Colorado troops to victory. The Battle of La Glorieta, sometimes called the Gettysburg of the Southwest, ended the Confederate threat in the region. Unfortunately, Governor Gilpin got himself into trouble because of his enthusiasm. Armies cost money, and there was no money authorized to pay the Colorado volunteers. Gilpin solved the problem simply: he issued drafts on the Treasury of the United States, and these illegal promises of payment were accepted by Colorado merchants. For this indiscretion Gilpin was removed from office. President Lincoln replaced him with Dr. John Evans of Chicago, a friend of the president's. Evans was a man of distinction and accomplishment — a physician, the editor of a medical journal, and a founder of Northwestern University at Evanston (named after Evans), Illinois. In Colorado he became one of the founders of Denver University.

Colorado City, the territorial capital, was the site of the Second Territorial Legislature on July 7, 1862. The legislators did not care for the quality or quantity of accommodations in Colorado City,

William Gilpin, first governor of the Territory of Colorado.

however, and adjourned to Denver, a two-day, seventy-mile trip to the north. In Denver the legislature declared nearby Golden to be the capital of the territory, which it remained until, by popular vote in 1867, Denver was chosen to be the capital city.

STATEHOOD

Colorado probably could have become a state in 1864 if it had wanted to. Congress passed an enabling act that year, giving the people of the Colorado Territory the right to enter the Union as soon as they wrote a constitution and accepted it by popular vote. The vote, however, went against statehood, partly because the people didn't want to assume the tax burden of supporting the apparatus of a state government. While Colorado remained a territory, the federal government paid the expenses of government. Also, a bitter fight within the Republican Party between Jerome Chaffee and Henry Teller — over which one of them should be a United States senator from the new state — produced votes against statehood. Colorado remained a territory for slightly more than another decade, owing in part to a political tangle too complex to describe here that involved the competing ambitions of Colorado politicians, as well as President Andrew Johnson's doubts about whether Colorado's delegates to Congress would, if the state were admitted, support him. Three times during the decade, Johnson vetoed admission of Colorado to the Union. Colorado's boom was petering out in the sixties, and this, too, cooled enthusiasm for statehood, both in Colorado and in Congress. For several years Colorado had remained fairly steady in population: there was about the same number of people in 1865 as there had been in 1860. In the early 1870s population boomed again, business flourished, and in 1875 Congress passed another enabling act.

Again the process of constitution making was embarked upon. There was some lingering unhappiness in Congress about the wisdom of passing this enabling act and opening the door to Colorado statehood. Some senators had been looking at 1870 census figures, which showed a population of only 40,000 in Colorado. It was difficult for Jerome Chaffee, Colorado's representative in Washington, to convince them that the population in the territory had increased to 150,000 in just four years.

Some senators and representatives from the eastern seaboard states were apprehensive about the growing influence of the West. They denounced Colorado as lacking in substantial resources except gold, the remaining amount of which was no longer impressive, and some profligate scenery. Historian Frank Hall reports that a fair idea of the sentiments of these congressmen, whom Governor Gilpin liked to call the "salt water despots," is reflected in a periodical of the time (which he did not cite):

> There is not a single good reason for the admission of Colorado. Indeed, if it were not for the mines in that mountainous and forbidding region, there would be no population there at all. The population, such as it is, is made up of a roving, unsettled horde of adventurers who have no settled homes, there or elsewhere, and they are there solely because the state of semi-barbarism prevalent in that wild country, suits their vagrant habits. There is something repulsive in the idea that a few handfuls of rough miners and reckless bushwhackers, numbering less than a hundred thousand, should have the same representation in the Senate as Pennsylvania, Ohio and New York, and that these few thousands should have the same voice in our legislation and administration of the government, as the millions of other States. A territorial government is good enough and effective enough for such unformed communities, and to that they should be confined for a generation to come. (Frank Hall, *History of the State of Colorado,* Volume 2, Chicago: The Blakely Printing Company, 1890, p. 271.)

THE CONSTITUTIONAL CONVENTION OF 1874

It is worthwhile for political scientists to take a look at how the state constitution of 1874 was made. That constitution remains the basic law of Colorado today, although it has been amended many times over the years.

A constitutional convention met in Denver in December. Delegates, thirty-nine in all, came from all over the Colorado Territory. Traveling at that season was difficult. The state-to-be was large — more than a hundred thousand square miles — traversed by ranges of snow-covered mountains, many of them passable only at widely separated points. Many members had to travel hundreds of miles over such terrain to attend the convention (as Congress was later told).

Some people in the Colorado Territory still feared that a state government would impose intolerable tax burdens, discouraging existing and prospective settlers. The convention therefore had reason to design a government that was as frugal as possible, and yet one equipped to handle the growth that was sure to come. This concern with cost and frugality was especially timely because the nation was in a depression called the Panic of 1873, at its worst in 1874. As if depression were not enough, an infestation of grasshoppers had wrought havoc to farmers. The convention opened in the midst of depression and devastation. There was yet another concern haunting delegates: would their efforts come to naught? Two previous constitutions had been drafted. One was defeated by the people; one was adopted by the people but later aborted by presidential veto, even after the state (erroneously assuming it was in the Union by virtue of adopting a constitution) had elected two United States senators, who went to Washington expecting to be seated in the Senate. What unforeseen disaster might lie in the path of the efforts of this present convention?

Under the leadership of the president of the convention, Joseph C. Wilson of the town of El Paso (near present-day Colorado Springs), the convention did its work in eighty-five days. The convention subdivided itself into twenty-four committees to draft separate articles of the constitution. When a committee was ready with a draft, the draft was laid before the entire convention for debate and approval. Every member of the convention was a member of from two to four of these panels. The convention was besieged with petitions and remonstrances from special interests, particularly about corporations, water rights, railroads, schools, fees, and salaries of officials. Most members were Republicans; fourteen were Democrats. Three were Spanish-speaking, two of them requiring an interpreter to participate; two members were German-speaking.

The convention was guided by the United States Constitution and the constitutions of the already admitted states of the Union. In broad outline the Colorado Constitution resembles that of other states. It is, however, much longer and more detailed than the United States Constitution, and it is often said that much was put into the constitution that should have been left to ordinary legislation. The Colorado Constitution was written in an era of corrupt legislatures, when long constitutions were in vogue: drafters of state constitutions wanted to do everything possible to limit the mischief-making powers of legislatures. This spirit of distrust of legislatures contrasts diametrically with the faith in legislatures that prevailed during the first fifty years of our national life. The original Colorado Constitution ran about twenty-three thousand words, while the

United States Constitution, and the constitutions of states admitted in the first years of the Republic, ran about four thousand.

Three of the liveliest issues before the convention touched the subject of religion. First, whether to mention God in the preamble. Some delegates pointed out that the United States Constitution does not acknowledge God. The pro-God lobby prevailed, and the constitution begins, "We the people of Colorado, with profound reverence for the Supreme Ruler of the Universe . . ." Next, there was controversy over how to tax church property: whether to tax it like all other property or to exempt it. It was finally decided to exempt from all taxes property used exclusively for religious worship, for schools, and for charitable purposes. Third was the issue of whether to permit use of public funds to support parochial schools. This emotional issue carried overtones of north-versus-south Colorado sectionalism, owing to the predominance of Spanish and Catholic culture in the south; delegates were concerned that aid to parochial schools would not only undermine the idea of public schools but would cause an unfair drain of public money to the southern part of the state. The convention wrote a prohibition of aid to parochial schools into the constitution.

Other subjects were hotly debated, none more bitterly than the question of how to regulate and control corporations, especially railroads. Issues relating to taxation of mining properties, water rights, and use of forests were heatedly argued. One can imagine how vigorously lobbyists representing those concerns made their views known to the members of the Colorado constitutional convention.

The constitution drafted by the convention was submitted to the people on July 1, 1876, and passed four to one. On the first day of August (a date now annually celebrated as Colorado Day), President Ulysses S. Grant proclaimed Colorado a state of the Union. Colorado was nicknamed the Centennial State because it was admitted just one century after the United States declared its independence.

No specific date marks the end of the early history of Colorado. Certainly no history of early Colorado should be concluded without mentioning the development of railroads in the state, the boom in silver mining and later gold, the planting of colony towns, the "cow kingdom" on the plains, and the fate of Indians. These were among the forces that left their mark on Colorado, geographically and culturally. There are good books on these subjects and on other matters dealt with here. A sketch follows.

RAILROADS

It is hard to overestimate the role of railroads in the birth of Colorado. In 1864 the American Union was divided east and west. In the far west were the states of California, Oregon, and Nevada, separated from the eastern states by vast plains, deserts, and mountains almost wholly undeveloped. No railroad crossed the continent; the western terminus was St. Joseph, Missouri. In 1858, the year of the Colorado gold strike, stage coach service from St. Joseph to California was established. The overland journey took twenty-five days through Indian country. Congress gave millions of acres and millions of dollars to the railroad companies to build a railroad coast to coast.

For practical reasons the coast-to-coast line was not put through rugged Colorado but followed the easier route across southern Wyoming through Cheyenne. In 1869 the Union Pacific line was completed. A railroad through Cheyenne was not a railroad through Denver, however, and Colorado boosters feared Colorado was being left to wither on the vine, to be a sideshow on the national stage until rail connections were made. Concerned businessmen in Denver, frightened by the prospect of decline, mounted a heroic campaign to collect money to construct a line connecting Denver and Cheyenne. "Pay or Perish" was the slogan. By spring 1870 the line was completed by the Denver Pacific Railway; by summer of the same year the Kansas Pacific had run a line across the plains from Kansas City to Denver.

As the Kansas Pacific tracks were laid westward, General William J. Palmer arrived in Colorado to find the best route to Denver. On this pathfinding mission, Palmer came to the village of Colorado City near Pikes Peak. He was thrilled by the great peak, the Garden of the Gods, the Seven Falls, the Monument Valley. When the Kansas Pacific was finally completed to Denver, Palmer seized upon the Pikes Peak area as his home. He built a castle in Glen Eyrie near the Garden of the Gods and lived there until his death in 1909.

General Palmer had a great deal to do with spreading a network of railroads through the wild mountains of Colorado, making permanent many towns that had hitherto been temporary and vastly improving the economy of the state by making possible the shipment of heavy machines, tons of ore, and other materials and people across and through the state. General Palmer is especially honored in Colorado Springs as the founder of that city, where he is to be seen today larger than life in bronze astride his horse at the corner of Platte and Nevada.

Palmer formed a company known as the Denver and Rio Grande. His plan was to build a railroad from Denver south to the Rio Grande at El Paso, Texas, and on to Mexico City. By 1871 his line had reached Colorado Springs, and in that year Palmer sent for his wife and (if they would come) her six half brothers and sisters, who were young children, and her father. This exuberant group made the long trip across the plains by rail to Denver and traveled from there to Colorado Springs on the general's own railway.

Palmer's Denver and Rio Grande Railroad reached Pueblo in 1872; it never reached the Rio Grande, at least not the Rio Grande in Texas. The Atchison, Topeka and Santa Fe Railroad (generally known as the Santa Fe) was on the move in southern Colorado and in the Southwest. The two roads clashed, almost literally, and finally an agreement was hammered out by which the Santa Fe would focus on New Mexico and the Southwest and Palmer could have Colorado. Over the next couple of decades Palmer did reach the upper Rio Grande at Alamosa, Colorado, making good the railroad's name.

Palmer's specialty was the Baby Road, a small, almost toylike, train of narrow gauge (three feet) ideally suited for winding in and out of canyons and over passes that would make a mountain goat dizzy. The goal of Palmer's road was to reach the remote but rich mining towns. His tiny railroads meandered circuitously, with many sub-ends connecting remote spots as well as major points in every corner of the state. The narrow-gauge rails of the Denver and Rio Grande did much to develop mining, farming, and every other enterprise in mountainous western Colorado.

INDIANS

The story of Indian encounters with whites can be told basically in two parts. First, what happened on the plains, and second, what happened in the mountains. Indian trouble in Colorado started primarily with the discovery of gold. The plains Indians didn't mind a few white visitors, but when the great migration to Colorado began in 1858, it was clear to the Indians that their lands were being invaded, occupied, and despoiled. Buffalo (a means of livelihood for Indians) were being killed by the thousands. When railroads advanced across the prairie, it was plain that the white man had come to stay. Before the Colorado gold rush, the plains Indians had signed an agreement at Fort Laramie in 1851 consenting to the passage of Americans through their lands. But Indian representatives at Fort Laramie could not have imagined, and certainly had not agreed to, the mass migration into Colorado they saw in 1859. Their response was to attack the invader. The government invited the Cheyennes and Arapahoes to a parley in 1861 at Fort Wise (formerly Bent's Fort) and prevailed upon them to accept a reservation at Sand Creek.

Many young hawks of those tribes believed their leaders had taken leave of their senses. They defied their chieftains and raided migrating whites crossing the prairie. Governor Evans of Colorado worked valiantly to secure some sort of lasting agreement with the Indians. He was somewhat successful with the Utes of the mountains: at Conejos in 1863 he concluded an agreement with Chief Ouray under which they would move back to western Colorado. The previous year Chief Ouray had been invited to Washington to visit President Lincoln and had been put on the United States government payroll.

Plains Indians were tougher to deal with. There were clashes between Colorado troops and Cheyennes, which aroused the anger of whites and spurred their determination to end the Indian threat completely. The worst of these incidents was the massacre of the Hungate family thirty miles from Denver. Cheyennes murdered and scalped Mr. Hungate, his wife, and two children and mutilated their bodies. When the bodies were brought to Denver, a wave of panic engulfed the people of Colorado's towns and villages, who feared the Indians were ready to assault and murder them all. As if to confirm their fears, Indians attacked stations along the stage lines. Julesburg was attacked in July, the town burned, and many persons killed. Mail service could not continue, nor could freight be shipped. Scarcities developed, prices went up, famine threatened. Finally,

Ouray, Chief of the Southern Utes (center) and his sub-chiefs (c. 1870). His only son, kidnapped by Arapahoes, was located and returned by government agents, making Ouray a constant friend of the white man. He spoke Spanish fluently and English fairly well.

Governor Evans called upon the people to kill every hostile Indian they possibly could but to spare friendly Indians.

With winter approaching and the whites determined to fight back, the fighting spirit of the Indians momentarily declined and they tried to make peace. One such attempt was made at Fort Lyon (formerly Bent's Fort and Fort Wise) when a band of Arapahoes arrived and said they wanted peace. The band was directed by authorities to settle down at Sand Creek, about forty miles to the northeast of Fort Lyon in present-day Kiowa County. They were joined at Sand Creek by some Cheyennes. All told, there must have been six or seven hundred Indians — men, women, and children. Then one morning the encampment was attacked.

Agitated about the "red devils" who a few weeks earlier had practically cut Denver off from the Untied States, Colorado had raised an army called the Hundred Days Men. Knowledge of this may have played a part in convincing the Sand Creek Indians to be peaceful. Nevertheless, Colonel John M. Chivington, with these men and some other troops, decided to strike a blow to quash the Indian threat once and for all. They crept up on the unsuspecting camp on November 29, 1864, and killed many of them, old and young, men and women. Chivington's assault on the village can only be called a massacre. The event prompted a congressional investigation. The atrocity had the reverse of the effect planned by Colonel Chivington: instead of ending the Indian menace, it inflamed Indians all across the prairie and galvanized them, as nothing else could have, into a united all-out war against the white man. Again Denver was cut off from the nation as Indians cut traffic and supply lines. Governor Samuel Elbert of Colorado telegraphed Washington: "We must have five thousand troops to clean out these savages or the people of this Territory will be compelled to leave it." Blue coats came, the siege of Denver was lifted, and Indian hostilities faded, with only occasional clashes here and there.

One of the last and most famous Indian battles occurred in mid-September 1868 at Beecher Island on the Arikaree fork of the Republican River, about fifteen miles south of the present town of Wray in Yuma County. A team of about fifty scouts was jumped by Cheyenne Indians. The scouts (who had been looking for these Indians) retreated to an island in the river, where they were besieged by a thousand attackers. For nine days the scouts held out until rescued by a troop of cavalry from Fort Wallace, Kansas. The scene of the battle bears the name of Lieutenant Beecher, who was one of the first killed in the encounter.

The final battle with plains Indians in Colorado occurred on July 12, 1869, at Summit Springs, about fourteen miles southeast of the present city of Sterling. A band of Indians raiding in that general region was found encamped at Summit Springs by United States troops. Chief Tall Bull and fifty of his warriors were killed.

The Ute Indians in the mountains were, like their neighbors on the plains, continuously upset by the increasing habitation of the region by settlers. Although the Utes chose to sign treaties and were cooperative in the 1860s and 1870s, they were not totally peaceful; from the settlers' point of view they were a constant danger. Most of the treaties made with the Utes were gradually broken under the surge of colonization. Utes staged the last important uprising in Colorado partly because of actions by Nathan Meeker (one of the founders of Greeley), who was assigned as agent to the White River Utes in 1878. His dictatorial behavior produced a massacre of some settlers. Reprisal by federal troops followed, and in 1881 the Utes were prevailed upon to abandon all Colorado except a slice of land in the extreme southwestern corner, where they live today on the Colorado–New Mexico border near Mesa Verde National Park.

CATTLE

While miners were taking gold and silver from the mountains, ranchers on the plains were converting free grass to money through beef production. Colorado never had wide-open cow towns like Dodge City, Kansas, but it had cows. The great cattle drives from Texas to the north did not pass through Colorado until the 1860s, comparatively late in the history of that activity. Farmers (or sod busters, as the cattle drivers contemptuously called them) and their cursed barbed wire were gradually edging westward, forcing the cattle drives farther and farther west, until by the 1860s the northward trail went straight through Colorado close to the Front Range. By then, Colorado was rapidly being settled; the open range disappeared, and cattle drives through the region ended. The cattle business, however, stayed; the plains were cut into ranches, large and small. By the end of the 1870s, Colorado rangelands were crowded with "all the cows in Christendom" and with millions of sheep — and there was less talk about endless free grasslands.

Among the greatest early cattlemen was John Wesley Iliff. He left college and came to Colorado in the 1850s with $500. When he died in 1878 he had built a cattle kingdom that stretched along the South Platte River from Julesburg to Greeley. Another great figure in the story of Colorado cattle is John W. Prowers, after whom Prowers County is named. Exploiting the cheap grazing land in the 1860s, he amassed a fortune in land stretching more than forty miles along both sides of the Arkansas River. The cattle industry of Colorado helped balance the economy, which originally depended so heavily on mining.

COLONY TOWNS

Several of Colorado's towns were started by groups of people who set out from the East for the specific purpose of founding a settlement. As a cooperative team, the pioneers avoided many problems and difficulties that beset individuals operating alone. First was the advantage of mutual defense. Also, group travel was cheaper: railroads lowered their rates; land could be bought cheaper; community utilities such as irrigation ditches could be more easily installed by a group. By grouping together, settlers kept each other company, avoiding the isolation so demoralizing to individual ranchers.

Settlers pursued a new life in the West for various reasons. Some simply wanted to leave the crowded cities of the East. Others were unemployed because of economic depressions and sought new opportunities in the West. One of the first groups to arrive in Colorado was a colony of German immigrants who formed the German Colonization Society, in which labor, capital, and profits were pooled for five years. In 1870, they made their way to a point in the Wet Mountains about seven miles south of Silver Cliff, where they settled. They ran into all kinds of trouble, and the colony failed.

Nathan Meeker founded the Union Colony on the present site of Greeley, named in honor of Horace Greeley of the *New York Tribune,* Meeker's employer. The colony was a great success. Longmont was founded by the Chicago Colorado Company in 1871. Sterling was originally laid out in 1874 by a group from Tennessee and Mississippi. Some towns were set up by railroads and real estate speculators and advertised themselves as colony towns, capitalizing on the great success of Greeley. But these were not true colonies. Platteville, Fort Collins, Colorado Springs, and Pueblo were so advertised to attract settlers — the last two by the Denver and Rio Grande Railroad.

SILVER

Rich carbonates of lead and silver ore were discovered late in the 1870s near Leadville. This touched off a silver rush. In two years the population of Leadville jumped from 100 to 30,000. Horace W. Tabor was one of the new millionaires created by Leadville silver. He was a storekeeper who grubstaked two prospectors, August Rische and George Hook, to $64 worth of supplies. Rische and Hook found a spot that yielded silver ore worth $200 a ton. Within nine months Tabor had his holdings incorporated in a $20 million company. Later he became lieutenant governor of the state. The Denver and Rio Grande Railroad built a spur running up the Arkansas through the Royal Gorge (which Pike had called impassable) and into Leadville.

After the Ute Indians had moved from the mountains and been confined to a fifteen-mile strip in southwestern Colorado, silver mining boomed in western Colorado, spurred by excitement of the Leadville success. In 1880 Silver Cliff in the Wet Mountains was the third largest city in the state; today its population is fewer than 150. In 1879 silver discoveries were made in Aspen and Ashcroft; Rico, Telluride, and Redcliffe became centers for silver mining. The last of the great Colorado silver towns was Creede, where N. C. Creede discovered the Holy Moses mine.

In the 1890s a depression hit silver miners and farmers. The price of silver plunged, partly because the United States government quit minting silver coins and went over entirely to gold. The miners demanded the government start buying silver again. In this they found an alliance with farmers, who thought federal currency would be inflated if the government resumed buying silver, thus reducing the burden of their mortgages. Miners and farmers thus found common cause in the People's Party (or Populists). The national People's Party entered the presidential race of 1892 with General James B. Weaver of Iowa as candidate for president. Their program included a long list of proposed reforms, including freedom for silver. Weaver lost, but in Colorado the Populist candidate for governor, Davis H. Waite, was elected. In 1896 the Democratic party stole the platform of the Populists and nominated William Jennings Bryan after his "Cross of Gold" speech.

THE TWENTIETH CENTURY

And so we come to the twentieth century. Colorado has gone forward on so many diverse fronts that it is impossible in the scope of this chapter to describe its development. In population the state has grown from 540,000 in 1900 to about 3,300,000 in 1990. About 4 percent of Colorado's population is black, and about 12 percent is Hispanic. Other ethnic groups (chiefly northern Europeans) make up about 84 percent of the population. Population density is only about 29 persons per square mile, but almost 90 percent live in densely populated metropolitan areas along the eastern edge of the Rocky Mountains (the Front Range). More than half the people of Colorado live in Denver or its suburbs.

The state government spends about $4 billion a year. Government itself is the largest employer in the state, followed by wholesale and retail trade, services, and manufacturing. (The ski industry is now also one of the state's largest employers.) Government, trade, and manufacturing employ about 70 percent of all employed persons in the state, while mining today employs only 1.5 percent and agriculture only 5.4 percent. Mining today is a small part of the state's economy; gold and silver are among the least important minerals extracted from the ground of Colorado. More important are molybdenum, petroleum, coal, sand and gravel, uranium, vanadium, and natural gas. In agriculture, cattle are by far the most important product, followed at a great distance by wheat, hay, dairy and egg products, corn, sugar beets, sheep, hogs, and potatoes. The value of cattle exceeds the combined value of all the other above-listed agricultural products.

Colorado now has around eighteen thousand miles of surfaced roads and over thirty institutions of higher education. Things have changed very much since the turn of the century, even more so since Colorado's admission to the Union in 1876.

IS COLORADO A SOVEREIGN STATE?

The place of Colorado in the legal framework of the federal union was determined long before anyone dreamed there would be a Colorado. In most essentials the *legal* relationship of the states to one another and their *legal* relationship to the central government was decided more than two hundred years ago, in 1787, when the United States Constitution was adopted. That Constitution created a federal system in which all power is divided between the national government and the states, and each is legally sovereign over the work given it to do by the Constitution. Speech makers are fond of calling the states "sovereign": the sovereign state of New York, the sovereign state of Ohio, the sovereign state of Colorado. It rolls off the tongue so nicely. But what, really, is a sovereign state?

A *sovereign* is one who has no legal superior — a king, for example. "Here lies our sovereign lord the king, . . ." No one has the legal authority to make a sovereign king do anything, and that is why the sovereign is sovereign. True, we have no reigning monarchs in North America, no royalty. But we do have certain entities, or organisms, if you will, that are sovereign, that have no legal superior,

The cornerstone of the Colorado State Capitol was laid on July 4, 1890.

that cannot be made to do anything by any higher legal authority. Colorado is such an organism, an organism composed of the people of Colorado. They as a people are sovereign. It is not the government of Colorado that is sovereign. Rather, it is Colorado per se (in itself) that is sovereign — the people of Colorado as an entity, as a whole. At the same time, the United States of America as an entity was also made sovereign by the Constitution. And so we have two sovereigns, we have dual sovereignty, a sovereign nation of many sovereign states. This leads to trouble, as we shall see.

The Constitution created a *federal* system, a system that makes room for dual sovereignty. It created two co-equal entities — states on the one hand, a nation on the other — each sovereign. Each with its own power. Neither gets its power from the other.

Each state is sovereign and has no legal superior in those matters granted (or left) to the states by the Constitution. Likewise, the central government (which we generally call the federal government) is sovereign in those matters granted to it. This sounds like a clear-cut division of power. However, it is not. The history of American constitutional law is filled with cases of disagreement between the federal and state governments over exactly what is within state power and what is within federal power and over where the line between state and federal power lies. This distinction is made still more troublesome because some powers are given simultaneously to both the nation and the states — the power to tax, for example. Where there is an overlap, the legal authority of the central government is generally held to be supreme over that of the states in case of conflict.

DIVISION OF POWERS

The United States Constitution does not list the powers of the states. There is no list of state power, no possibility of easily seeing exactly what the powers of Colorado are as a sovereign state. Theoretically they are too vast to be counted or listed. But the constitution does list the powers of the central government. Almost everything *not* on that list belongs to the states. Almost, because there are certain things the states are expressly forbidden to do, such as coin money, and there are certain things that neither the federal government nor the states may do, such as deny freedom of speech. Except for those matters, the power of the states consists of power to do everything not given exclusively to the federal government. This scheme is nowhere better summarized than in the Constitution itself, which says, "The powers not delegated to the United States by the Constitution, nor prohibited by it to the states, are reserved to the states respectively, or to the people." (Tenth Amendment.) The power delegated to the federal government is called, as you might expect, *delegated power.* Power reserved to the states is called *reserved power.*

Let us add two more phrases: *express powers* and *implied powers.* Some of the powers delegated to the federal government are expressly stated, and some are merely implied therefrom. The Constitution is like a letter from home. One has to read between the lines. For example, consider this: the Constitution expressly gives the federal government power to levy taxes, but it does not say where the money shall be kept. Should the federal government hide its billions under mattresses? No, says the Supreme Court. The power to raise money implies the power to establish a bank to put the money in.

A great deal of what the federal government does is based upon such implications drawn from its delegated powers. Where does the federal government get constitutional power to pass a law making kidnaping a federal crime? Where is kidnaping mentioned in the Constitution? Nowhere. But the federal government does have express power to regulate commerce among the several states. And kidnaping is commerce isn't it? Commerce, of a sort? Yes, and so the Lindbergh Kidnap Law says that three days after a kidnaping occurs, it shall be assumed that the kidnaper has crossed a state line, making the whole escapade an unlawful form of interstate commerce. The federal victory garden of implied powers has grown and bloomed and ripened and produced a bumper crop of new powers across the board. It is among the greatest sources of federal power.

All this is significant for Colorado and for all its fellow states. Each advance of federal power is by necessity a retreat for state power. Take Colorado's power to tax banks, for example. We saw above that the federal government has power to establish a bank to keep its money in. But if the federal government has the implied power to run a bank, then by implication Colorado may not tax that bank, for states cannot tax the federal government or any of its instrumentalities, a bank being one. Nor may the federal government tax the states or any of the states' instrumentalities. This, by the way, is called *reciprocal immunity from taxation.*

The point is this: each addition of federal instrumentalities becomes a subtraction from what Colorado may tax.

The greatest curtailment of state power is not in the field of taxation. The erosion of state power to regulate commerce is greater. Remember, interstate commerce is chiefly regulated by the federal government. Colorado and the other states are permitted to make minor regulations that do not burden interstate commerce, such as requiring trucks to obey reasonable speed limits. But beyond that, states have to keep their hands off; they may not pass any laws affecting interstate commerce.

What, exactly, is interstate commerce? When you look up at a skyscraper and see a professional window washer at work on a platform fifty stories high, are you observing someone who is engaged in interstate commerce? Yes, if the windows belong to a company involved in interstate commerce. Is a radio station participating in interstate commerce simply because it sends electromagnetic waves into space? Yes, if the wave might reach another state, and all radio waves, no matter how faint, reach out beyond the galaxy. A multitude of such decisions adding new definitions and categories to interstate commerce have put a multitude of things beyond state power to regulate. The United States Supreme Court has the final say when any of these things are contested (and many have been) in court.

WHY HAS FEDERAL POWER GROWN?

The founders of the Republic expected that most of the work of government would be done by states. At that time so much was done by states that no attempt was made to precisely define the limits of state power in the Constitution. On the other hand, the work of the federal government was intended to be limited to such matters as national defense, foreign affairs, and coining money, which could be done more efficiently by a central government. No one wanted an overbearing central government. Its powers were inventoried one by one, were specifically listed. You can see them in Article I, Section 8, of the Constitution.

Since 1789 the federal government has taken on far more responsibility and power than the founders ever dreamed. Of course, state governments are also doing more today than ever before. All governments are doing more. And states retain, in theory, all the *legal* sovereignty they ever had. But in their relative influence over public affairs, the federal government has become the star player and the states have declined. In many activities, state government has evolved into a kind of aide-de-camp to federal administration.

The reason for this rise in federal power is clear. With each passing decade the problems with which governments deal have become more and more national in scope and less and less local. Consider commerce, for example. When the founders gave power to the federal government to regulate interstate commerce, they did not see this as power over the whole economy. After all, in 1789 very little commerce was interstate. Today, hardly a single business can be said to be wholly conducted within a single state without dependence to some degree on goods, services, or contracts outside the state. Even crime has become interstate in character, with criminals operating corporate-style out of New York, Chicago, or Los Angeles, controlling far-flung empires of crime and using interstate networks of transportation and communication. The major problems of the United States are national in scope. Depression or inflation cannot be solved in Colorado. They have to be solved nationally, if at all. Unemployment, race problems, and air pollution are matters largely beyond the capability of individual states to solve.

With each passing generation we are becoming more and more a nation and less and less a collection of individual states. We are sometimes told that the need for sovereign states is nil, that we can get along without them, that, in fact, they complicate things. Why have fifty different auto licenses, fifty different marriage and divorce laws, fifty different fishing laws, fifty of everything? The argument for states long ago in 1787 was clear: in each state almost all business and commerce was contained within its boundaries, and in fact, very little of it extended beyond city limits and county lines. People in different states rarely saw each other, rarely journeyed far. Travel was slow and hard. States were big enough to govern practically anything that needed governing. Most were about as big as a typical European nation. Moreover, most Americans thought of themselves as citizens of their state first and foremost, not as Americans. Many thought there was no need for a national government at all, that a national government would be too distant to control and would become remote and tyrannical like the crown in England had been.

But today the speed, efficiency, and ease of travel and communication have allegedly decreased the need for states. In 1787 there were no jet airplanes, no interstate highways, no railroads, no cars or trucks. It was harder to get to the county seat than it is for us to fly from Los Angeles to New York. A flight to the moon today takes little more time than it used to take most people to get to the state capitol!

The very principle of federalism is often challenged today. Some say we don't need dual sovereignty any more, maintaining that sovereign states do more harm than good — their sovereignty is said to get in the way of efficient government. States are no longer very effective checks upon latent despotism in the national government, we are told. The main check is not sovereign states but *social pluralism,* — the numerous organized pressure groups challenging government for power. The best defense against tyrannical national government is not federalism, but strong competitive political parties and interest groups, a tradition of civil liberties, an educated electorate, a fearless and independent court system.

But defenders of federalism insist that the very existence of states is healthy because it divides and diffuses power, helping to protect liberty by keeping power, at least some of it, out of the hands of a few at the top of the national hierarchy. Furthermore, diffusion of political power sets in motion many centers of energy and creativity. States are experimental laboratories testing out the strengths and weaknesses of new ideas for solving social problems. Also, states, as well as local governments, are the gymnasiums of democracy. They protect the institutions of democracy by giving people an opportunity to participate politically and to develop their democratic muscles, so to speak. Also, it is claimed that states have a closer understanding of the needs and customs of the people and are under fairly close public scrutiny.

No matter how the intellectual debate over federalism is decided, we know that federalism is gradually falling victim to the growing influence of the national government. It is not necessary to pass a constitutional amendment ending federalism: the same result is apparently developing in less overt ways not clearly visible to the public.

Almost since the first year of the Republic there has been a steady growth of federal power at the expense of states, caused in part by the Supreme Court taking a broad rather than a narrow view of federal powers as set forth in the Constitution. By chance, the persuasive John Marshall was chief justice of the Supreme Court during a critical and formative period early in the history of the Republic, 1801 to 1835. Dedicated to strengthening the authority of the national government, he and the court based decision after decision on broad interpretations of federal power.

The national government has effectively used its financial power to "bribe" states into doing things they might not otherwise do. Federal grants-in-aid have effectively expanded federal power. Perhaps 75 percent of the activities of the state of Colorado are influenced by the expectation of federal money. Nor has the federal government been content to acquire power over the states; it has gone straight to local governments, offering them money, too.

The growth of federal power over states has been broad based, touching so many sectors of state activity that it would be futile to try to list them. One sees federal involvement in state highway building, state welfare programs, state elections, state police training, higher education, sewer construction, urban renewal, and many other areas. However, Colorado is not about to disappear — it and all the states are collecting more taxes, spending more money, employing more people, doing more than ever before. But Colorado's autonomy, its freedom to act independently, has withered sharply away in some matters. Very often Colorado must say "Mother, may I?" to the federal government before it acts.

SOME MECHANICAL OPERATIONS OF FEDERALISM

The United States Constitution is like a wedding contract. The two governments, state and central, in effect vow to unite themselves until death do them part, and each party to the marriage promises the other certain things — each state promises certain things to the Union, and the Union promises certain things to each state.

OBLIGATIONS OF THE FEDERAL GOVERNMENT TO THE STATES

If the Constitution is a wedding contract, what are some of the things the federal government promises to the states?

Republican Form of Government. The United States Constitution says, "The United States shall guarantee to every state in this Union a republican form of government." (Art. IV, Sec. 4.) The precise meaning of the term *republican* is unclear, however, and the Supreme Court for almost two hundred years has tried to avoid defining the term, on grounds that the question, What is a republican form of government? is a political question, not a judicial one. "It rests with Congress," said the United States Supreme Court in *Luther* v. *Borden,* 7 How. 1 (1849), "to decide what government is the established one in a state . . . as well as its republican character." Law dictionaries define republican government as a government by representatives chosen by the people. The United States Supreme Court has declined to say whether direct legislation by the people through initiative and referendum procedures such as those used from time to time in Colorado is compatible with a republican form of government.

Territorial Integrity of the States. The Constitution plainly says,

"No new state shall be formed or erected within the jurisdiction of any other state; nor any state be formed by the junction of two or more states, or parts of states, without the consent of the legislatures of the states concerned as well as of the Congress." (Art. IV, Sec. 3.) Nevertheless, West Virginia was torn out of Virginia without the consent of a validly constituted Virginia legislature. Perhaps that incident can be excused, considering that it occurred in the midst of the Civil War. In all other cases the rules quoted above have been scrupulously followed. Vermont, Kentucky, Tennessee, and Maine were formed out of other states in line with constitutional law. Colorado was not detached from any other state at its birth. It had been a territory.

Protection and Assistance. One obligation of the national government, almost too obvious to be mentioned, is its duty to protect the nation and each state from external attack. The Constitution expressly gives the national government responsibility in the field of foreign affairs, war, and armed forces. States are forbidden to maintain armed forces without the consent of Congress. State national guards are closely supervised by the central government and may at any time be federalized. States from time to time ask the federal government for military assistance for various purposes, such as quelling disorders. The federal government may send assistance to a state whether requested or not.

Settling Disputes Between States and Between Citizens of Different States. If states sue each other, the Supreme Court of the United States decides the cases directly, and no other courts are involved. For example, in 1990 a water war erupted between Colorado and Kansas, one that will be settled by the United States Supreme Court. Kansas filed suit in the Supreme Court, alleging that Colorado steals water from the Arkansas River so that only a trickle flows over the border at Holly, Colorado, into Kansas. Some thirteen billion gallons of water are missing every year. Kansas alleges that Colorado has allowed hundreds of water wells to be sunk along the Arkansas in excess of what is permitted by a *compact* (something like a treaty) agreed to between Colorado and Kansas in 1949. The crux of the matter, says Kansas, is that Colorado has failed to regulate water well drilling and hundreds of unregulated wells have been drilled by Colorado farmers along the lower Arkansas and that even the Southeast Colorado Water Conservancy District is diverting unauthorized water supplies to the John Martin Reservoir and two smaller facilities east of Ordway. Kansas is asking the Supreme Court to shut down about fifteen hundred unauthorized Colorado wells and to make Colorado pay $100 million in punitive damages. The Supreme Court will decide whether a clear-cut case of theft is involved or whether this dispute is a nebulous clash of hydrological theories. Being busy with other things at the moment, the Supreme Court has appointed a helper, called a *special master,* in Pasadena, California, to hear the case and recommend a decision. Hydrology is pretty deep water for judges educated in law.

If a dispute is between citizens of different states, as when a citizen of Colorado sues a citizen of, say, Kansas, the case may be filed in federal court if it involves more than a certain amount of money. Although the Supreme Court does not take such cases on original jurisdiction, as it does in the case of disputes between states themselves, still, the federal court system offers a neutral forum for plaintiffs who do not want to be at the mercy of state courts in the defendant's home state.

OBLIGATIONS OF THE STATES TO THE NATION

Election of Federal Officials. One of the curiosities of American government is that the national government does not hold any elections at all, except, of course, in Washington, D.C. All elections for federal office — Congress, president, and vice president — are held through the mechanism of state elections, paid for and administered by each state.

Consideration of Amendments. After Congress passes constitutional amendments, they are submitted to the separate states. The states are obligated to consider them but are not obliged to pass them. If three-fourths of the states pass a proposed amendment, it becomes part of the Constitution.

OBLIGATIONS OF THE STATES TO ONE ANOTHER

Full Faith and Credit. Although states of the Union are supposed to be sovereign, they are not supposed to be so sovereign that they disregard one another's official acts. The Constitution commands each state to give "full faith and credit" to the public acts, records, and judicial proceedings of every other state. (Art. IV, Sec. 1.) The term *act* has been interpreted by the United States Supreme

Court to mean only the civil laws of the state in this context. It excludes criminal laws of another state. An example of a civil law would be one that spells out requirements for a legal and binding contract. If a contract is made in Georgia and is legal in Georgia, it will be enforced in New York or Colorado. A *record* is a deed, a mortgage, a lease, a birth certificate, a contract, and so on. A *judicial proceeding* is a court order in some matter over which the court has jurisdiction. For example, a divorce granted by a court in Colorado will be recognized in Alabama, so long as the Colorado court was legally authorized to grant the divorce. A state may question the legality of a divorce granted to someone who moved to another state temporarily for the sole purpose of getting a divorce.

Extradition. Extradition occurs when one state delivers a person charged with a crime back to the state whence he has fled. The Constitution puts an obligation on the governor of each state to see to it that such people are returned: "A person charged in any state with treason, felony, or other crime who shall flee from justice, and be found in another state, shall on demand of the executive authority of the state from which he fled, be delivered up, to be removed to the state having jurisdiction of the crime." (Art. IV, Sec. 2, Cl. 2.) By judicial interpretation "shall" be delivered has been changed to "may."

In Colorado there are about eight hundred cases of extradition each year, including persons delivered from, and to, the state. The governor has to approve (or disapprove) each case, a task so great that the assistance of attorneys in the Department of Law is required to evaluate and process extradition cases. It is rare for the governor of any state to refuse a request for extradition, although requests for extradition of persons wanted for misdemeanors are scrutinized and the merits of the request investigated more carefully than requests for extradition of persons wanted for more serious crimes. In 1978 Governor Richard Lamm refused to extradite a woman who allegedly took her son illegally out of the state of Florida and away from the boy's father and grandparents. Sometimes a governor who doubts the wisdom of an extradition will initiate conversations with the requesting state. Comity (courtesy) prevails among the states in extradition matters: a state that does not cooperate with other states will not receive cooperation in return.

Privileges and Immunities. The Constitution is nowhere more

confusing than where it says, "Citizens of each state shall be entitled
to all the privileges and immunities of citizens of the several states."
(Art. IV, Sec. 2.) It is not at all clear what privileges and immunities
we have as citizens of the Union. That confusion did not prevent the
authors of the Fourteenth Amendment, almost a hundred years
after the founding of the Republic, from saying the same thing over
again: "No state shall make or enforce any law which shall abridge
the privileges or immunities of citizens of the United States." From
time to time the courts attempt to define these privileges and
immunities, as did a court in 1823, which made this list: "Protection
by the government; the enjoyment of life and liberty, with the right
to acquire and possess property of every kind, and to pursue and
obtain happiness and safety — subject, nevertheless, to such re-
straints as the government may justly prescribe for the general good
of the whole. The right of a citizen of one state to pass through, or
to reside in any other state for purposes of trade, agriculture,
professional pursuits, or otherwise; to claim the benefit of the writ
of habeas corpus; to institute and maintain actions of any kind in
the courts of the state; to take, hold, and dispose of property, either
real or personal; and an exemption from higher taxes or impositions
than are paid by the other citizens of the state." (*Corfield* v. *Coryell,*
6 Fed. Cas. 546.)

Nevertheless, states like Colorado do seem to be able to get away
with such seemingly discriminatory laws as those that restrict the
practice of professions such as law and medicine to persons licensed
within the state and laws restricting the right to hunt and fish, to
attend state universities, and so on.

THE IMPORTANCE OF LOCAL GOVERNMENT

For most of us, local government is the government we are most likely to deal with and that is most likely to deal with us daily. The cop on the corner, the street in front of our home, the indispensable sewer, the electricity at our command, the water we drink, the school we or our children attend, the park down the street — much that is intimate, crucial, and commonplace in our lives is the work of local government. Why local government should bore people is a mystery. Perhaps (as the army officers' manual says) familiarity breeds contempt. Yet, most people don't know half as much about their familiar local government as they think they know.

Local governments are important partly because, like insects, they are everywhere. An insect may not be a very flattering object of comparison, but there are times when we want to reach for a flyswatter when confronted by the swarm. In the United States there are about seventy-five thousand local governments. Colorado, one of the lesser populated states of the Union, has over fourteen hundred local governments. By local governments we mean counties, cities, towns, school districts, and special districts.

The number of local governments in the United States, and in Colorado, has sharply declined in recent decades. In fact, since 1942 approximately half have disappeared, and a similar decrease occurred in Colorado. This precipitous decline is due almost entirely to reduction in the number of school districts. Thousands of school districts across the nation have consolidated with other school districts. In Colorado the number of school districts decreased from 319 in 1962 to about 177 today. Other forms of local government have not experienced a similar decrease. The number of counties in the nation has hardly changed since 1942; the number of municipalities has increased, and the number of special districts has gone up substantially, a disturbing trend in the eyes of some critics.

ITS CRITICS AND DEFENDERS

Some people think we have too many local governments; others think we don't have enough. As with most political questions, strong arguments on both sides can be made. Defenders of local government say government should be close to the people — as little governing as possible should be done from state or federal capitals. Schools, for example, should be managed locally, textbooks locally selected, teachers locally hired and fired. Defenders of local government want ordinary people to feel free to walk into city hall, put their feet on the mayor's desk, and have an eyeball-to-eyeball chat about what's going on. Many people cannot get to the state capital without major effort and aren't likely to see the governor when they do; they end up in the office of a bureaucrat who doesn't know them and doesn't understand them. When power goes to Washington it goes clear out of reach: the bureaucratic status symbols are even more overpowering, the distance even greater — too great for bureaucrat, too great for citizen. The classic way of expressing all this is that local government knows best "where the shoe pinches." Advocates also believe local government is where a democratic people learns the art and practice of self-government — the more local government diminishes, the more democracy diminishes.

On the other side, critics of local government point to the inefficiencies of the multitude of local governments. They deny being hostile to local government as an institution of American government but claim they want to make local governments more efficient by combining, consolidating, improving them. Why should there be a county, a city, a school district, and four or five special districts operating on the same terrain? Why not combine them? If there are small counties side by side, why not combine them? If there are small school districts side by side, why not consolidate them? There are economies to be gained from bigness: advantages in purchasing, in utilization of equipment and people, advantages, for example, in one big well-staffed and well-equipped police department over several small and poor departments. Democracy works better, they say, where citizens can focus their attention on one consolidated government instead of trying to keep track of six or seven. Local government already suffers from low visibility, and there seems to be public apathy, even boredom, toward its important work. Given such a condition, everything should be done, argue the reformers, to consolidate local government into something less confusing. The public might be less bored if less confused. Democracy is a good thing, but there is a glut of democracy at the local level; people are dazed and sated with it. The democratic process would work better by reducing the number of local governments and elected officials, by reducing the democratic sweets and bringing the public out of its diabetic coma. So argue the critics of local government. That is not their whole case, but it is the essence of their case.

APATHY AND REFORM

It is an oddity of political science that while local government is the government about which we have the most firsthand knowledge, it is the government people know least about. The boredom of most people with local government contrasts with the interest they take, avid by comparison, in the affairs of the federal government, which is remote from ordinary people. No matter how distant the federal government may be, it comes into every living room through the medium of television. It is often more interesting to watch a president than to watch a mayor. The affairs of the national government are reported by the highest-paid commentators; the affairs of local government are reported (if at all) by the least prominent broadcasters, and the news itself is ferreted out at the local level by inadequate and poorly paid staff. In most towns there is no television news coverage at all to compete with news from Denver and Washington. In Denver, television coverage of local affairs naturally focuses on Denver itself and not on the legion of suburbs. Most local governments get their only coverage in the newspaper press. Newspaper coverage is fine, but unfortunately, as teachers know, most people do not care to read and aren't very good at making sense out of what they do read. The written word is no match, in the short run, for the spoken word, and even less a match for pictures. It is worth noting here that the media generally represents those who own the media as well as those who offer support through advertising, which is to say, the groups in society who have "made it" and who tend to be contented with things fundamentally as they are. This is one of many reasons why it has been difficult to reform local government.

Another reason for slow reform is that local officeholders are reluctant to upset the apple cart, that is, the system under which they hold office and exercise power and influence. Consolidation of local governments has thus been difficult. Of course, this reluctance to reform afflicts (or blesses) other levels of government. And we should not assume that all reform proposals are worthy. Compulsive reformers are always reluctant to recognize that existing institutional and social arrangements usually have merit, considerable genius, and good sense. After all, without merit, those institutions might never have come to prevail in the first place. Yet, it is also true that yesterday's good institution may no longer be as good in the light of today's circumstances.

LEGAL STATUS OF LOCAL GOVERNMENTS

The United States Constitution makes no mention of cities, no mention of counties, no mention of schools or school districts, nor of any local government at all except the seat of the government of the United States. If a copy of the Constitution were placed on board a spaceship for the benefit of people on another planet, they would have no idea from reading our basic law that local government exists in America. Yet, local government is everywhere around us.

The Constitution recognizes only two levels of government: (1) national and (2) state. The Constitution divides all power between national and state government. It gives no power to local government at all, nor, to repeat, hardly mentions such a phenomenon. Local governments are creatures of the state, deriving all their powers from the state. Each local government, whether city, county, school district, or special district, is created by the state and is considered an extension or arm of the state. Thus, when the Fourteenth Amendment declares that no state shall deny to any of its citizens life, liberty, or property without due process of law, it also means that no local government, nor any other agency or instrumentality of the state, may do so either. To put it differently, what Colorado is forbidden to do by the Constitution, all local governments in Colorado are forbidden to do. Thus the guarantees of the Bill of Rights — freedom of speech, press, religion, assembly, and so forth — are all guaranteed against abuse by local governments such as Vail or El Paso County or School District 11 no less than abuse by the state itself. These guarantees are read into the Fourteenth Amendment and are applied to states, and through states to local governments.

In general, the legislature of each state of the Union has power to create, change, or abolish any local government within the state, except to the extent that power is limited by the state's own constitution. The Colorado Constitution does limit the legislature's authority and does channel that authority somewhat. Those limitations are extensive concerning counties. The Colorado Constitution has a lot to say about the organization of counties and the duties of their officers. It also has something to say about cities, but it does not have much to say specifically about the organization and officers of cities. The Colorado Constitution also says something about school districts, confining itself mainly to school financing. It says little about special districts (but does refer to regions). Where the Colorado Constitution leaves off, the state legislature begins. Most state law concerning local government is not constitutional law but statutory law enacted by the legislature.

Legislation giving power to local governments is strictly construed by the courts. If there is any doubt about what power the legislature intended to give a local government by the terms of a law, the courts will take the narrowest possible view. This follows Dillon's

Rule, which, as John F. Dillon stated in his *Commentaries on the Law of Municipal Corporations* (5th ed., Boston: Little, Brown & Co., 1911, Volume I, Sec. 237), a municipal corporation may possess only powers "granted in express words," those powers "necessarily or fairly implied in or incident to the powers expressly granted," and those powers "essential to the accomplishment of the declared objects and purposes of the corporation — not simply convenient, but indispensable." Dillon also says in his *Commentaries* that "any fair, reasonable, substantial doubt concerning the existence of power is resolved by the courts against the corporation, and the power is denied."

CITIES

URBANIZATION IN COLORADO

Most people do not think of Colorado as an urban state. On the contrary, they think of mountains, trees, wide open spaces. Even the people of Colorado hold an outdoorsy view of their state, which obscures an important truth about us: we are a highly urbanized state. It is not necessary to look to New York or New Jersey to find the masses huddled in cities: they are huddled in Colorado cities, too. There aren't as many of us: the state's population in 1991 is between three and four million. Over 80 percent of Colorado's people live in what the Census Bureau calls standard metropolitan statistical areas (SMSAs), of which there are five in Colorado: Colorado Springs, Denver-Boulder, Fort Collins, Greeley, and Pueblo. In recent years, the fastest growing large population areas have been along the Front Range — the Colorado Springs–Denver–Fort Collins areas. And some smaller places far from the great metropolitan centers have also boomed, many of them associated with the ski industry, such as Aspen, Breckenridge, Vail, and Steamboat Springs.

REASONS FOR URBAN GROWTH

Urbanization has greatly increased during the past century, while rural population has decreased in proportion. The Colorado picture has also been the national picture. Although the process has slowed in recent years, it still continues. Why urbanization?

Mechanization on the farm has made it possible for few to do the work of many. Other forms of scientific agriculture, such as the development of high-yield corn, make farmers more efficient. Also, a rising standard of living with growth of manufacturing has attracted millions to the cities, where jobs can be found and money earned can be spent. People who once lived in rural poverty or semipoverty can find jobs in the city — cleaner, better-paying jobs. They live in cleaner and better houses, wear cleaner and better clothes.

The population of the United States is at the same time increasing. Cities grow because there are more people, and those people are not needed on farms. There are other reasons for urban growth that we will not analyze here. It is sufficient to say that in Colorado, and in the nation, cities are important because that is where most of us live. And the problems of cities (crime, delinquency, transportation, education, planning, urban renewal, and so forth) are important because they are the concerns of most Americans and Coloradoans. As political scientists, we are interested in the governmental mechanisms through which urban areas solve their problems. These mechanisms include all forms of local government and the institutions that coordinate the relationships of those governments — with each other, as well as with the state and with the national government.

MUNICIPAL CORPORATIONS

In the mind of a lawyer, a city is not a city, but a *municipal corporation*. To fully understand that piece of legal jargon, it is useful to consider first what a corporation is, legally speaking. It is commonly defined by lawyers as an *artificial person,* created by a government and consisting of a number of natural persons under a common name. The artificial person continues notwithstanding the change of individuals who constitute it. For certain purposes, such as owning property, making contracts, and using the courts, a corporation is considered a natural person.

Lawyers classify corporations as either public or private. A private corporation is composed of private individuals and serves private purposes. A public corporation serves public purposes and has governmental powers and functions. A municipal corporation is a public corporation. It is an artificial person, can sue and be sued, own property, and do many other things of a governmental nature. A municipal corporation is not entirely voluntary. Everyone who lives within a certain geographic boundary is a member of it. This differs from a private corporation, which is entirely voluntary and has no geographic boundaries. Corporations are created by the state, whether private or public. Although the procedure for incorporating a laundry and incorporating a city are somewhat different, the object is the same: to create a corporation.

A county in Colorado and in most other states is not a corporation, either public or private. A county is not (in theory) created for the particular advantage of its inhabitants but is created by the state to serve the purposes of the state. On the other hand, a municipal corporation is created at the behest of the inhabitants of a certain area to serve their peculiar public needs. Of course, a municipal corporation may, like a county, also serve the interests of the state, in addition to its other purposes.

In Colorado, if you want to incorporate a town or a city, the procedure will depend somewhat on the size of the population to be incorporated. Basically, the procedure is this: first, circulate a petition within the area to be incorporated calling for incorporation. If the required number of people sign, the petition goes to a district court asking that an election be held in the area. If the court finds that the area is, in fact, urban in character and meets certain other requirements, it will order an election; if a majority of the qualified voters of the proposed town or city vote for incorporation, then incorporation takes place. (The new municipality must then pay all the costs of the election.)

The procedure for discontinuing a municipal corporation is somewhat similar. A petition to discontinue is circulated among residents of the municipality. If 25 percent of the qualified electors sign the petition, then the district court submits the question to a vote. If two-thirds of the voters vote to discontinue, the incorporation is considered to be ended — after the municipality has paid its debts. If there is no money to pay debts, the municipality is kept alive solely to levy and collect sufficient taxes to pay the bills. If that happens, the board of county commissioners and the county officers act as the governing body and officers of the municipality in its final debt paying stage.

Sometimes towns are simply abandoned — Colorado has more

than one ghost town. When any town has failed for five years or longer to hold any election for officers, anybody left in town (or the county attorney) may apply to the secretary of state to determine that the town is abandoned. For that purpose the secretary of state holds a public hearing. If he or she decides that the town really has been abandoned, the town is thereby dissolved. City property (streets, fire stations, typewriters, et cetera) becomes county property. If there are any unpaid debts, payment is accomplished as described above for discontinued municipalities with unpaid bills.

STATUTORY CITIES AND TOWNS IN COLORADO

In Colorado, if the people of a certain geographic area wish to set up a municipal corporation, they must incorporate as a town if their population is under 2,000 or as a city if more than 2,000. Both cities and towns have the choice of incorporating under the home rule provision of Article XX of the Colorado Constitution (those that do are said to be *home-rule cities*) or incorporating under laws passed by the legislature (*statutory cities or towns*).

Towns. Colorado's nearly two hundred statutory towns must, under the statutes, have a governing board consisting of six trustees and a mayor elected at large. The mayor is considered a member of the board and presides over it. But if the board wishes to confine the mayor's voting power to merely breaking ties, they may do so. However, if they do, the mayor automatically (by state law) acquires new power to veto appropriations and contracts made by the board, and his or her veto can be overruled only by a two-thirds vote of the board. The board appoints other municipal officers such as clerk, treasurer, town attorney, marshal. Presumably, the board may appoint a manager and put him or her in charge of other town officers and employees, although the statutes do not provide for a city manager form for towns.

If you violate a town ordinance, do not make the mistake of thinking the town marshal's authority ends at the town boundary. He has the same power that sheriffs have by law, coextensive with the county in cases of violation of town ordinances. All elected officials serve two-year terms, unless the board of trustees provides four-year terms by ordinance. (Home-rule towns may organize themselves in almost any way they like.)

Cities. Only a handful of Colorado's nearly three hundred

municipalities are statutory cities. This is partly because most towns that must reorganize, having exceeded a population of 2,000, choose to become home-rule cities rather than statutory cities. Secondly, most cities simply find home rule a more flexible mode than the statutory-city mode. (Towns, on the other hand, seem content with remaining statutory towns.) If a city chooses to be a statutory city rather than home-rule, it must organize its government according to the designs set forth in the statutes, and the powers of the city are limited as provided by statutes. Home-rule cities, by contrast, have greater latitude in both their organization and their powers, although a statutory city does have the choice of organizing itself either as a mayor-council form of government or as a council-manager form.

Mayor-Council Form of City Government. In the mayor-council form of statutory-city government there is a mayor elected at-large and several council members elected from wards. The council members and the mayor together constitute the city council. Also elected at-large are a clerk and a treasurer, although the council may provide by ordinance for their appointment by the council. All other city officers are appointed by the council. These may include a city attorney, health commissioner, city engineer, supervisor of streets, superintendent of water, superintendent of sewers, chief of police, municipal judge, and other officers as needed. All elected officials serve two-year terms. The mayor is the administrative head and ceremonial head of the city and may be conferred other powers by the council. His formal powers are usually not as great as his prestige. His duties and powers depend largely on what the council gives him, and this varies from city to city.

In Colorado, the mayor of a statutory city is considered a member of the city council, with full voting power, and presides over it. But if the council wishes to confine the mayor's voting power to merely breaking ties, they may do so. However, like statutory towns, if the council does so limit the voting power of the mayor, he or she automatically (by state law) gets new power to veto appropriations and contracts made by the council, and the veto may not be overruled except by two-thirds vote of the council.

Some mayors are weak; some are strong. When a mayor is given authority over hiring and firing and how and when money is to be spent, he is considered strong. If, on the other hand, he isn't allowed to do much besides call himself mayor, and if the council itself does the hiring and firing and spending, then the mayor is weak. A mayor who is elected at-large has a natural advantage over a council whose members are representatives of wards. Some mayors are therefore stronger politically than the individual council members. Also, the mayors of some towns are stronger than the mayors of other towns in a political sense simply because they are effective and popular politicians. It may even be that a mayor who is technically weak in appointive and fiscal powers becomes strong in those same matters through political influence over the council.

Council members, to repeat, are elected from wards. The ward system has its pros and cons. Some say it is better to elect council members at-large, that is, to permit all the voters in the city to elect all the council members. When you divide a city into wards, say at-large advocates, the result is that each council member elected from a ward tends to put the interests of the ward above those of the city in order to get reelected to the council. What is good for the ward, however, may not be good for the city as a whole, and under the ward system the selfish interests of the ward are often put in conflict with the general interest of the city. What, for example, would a council member do if there were two possible locations for a new fire station, and the best place for it, from the point of view of the city, were outside his ward, though the best possible place for it from the point of view of his ward were inside his ward? Those who favor at-large election of council members say a member elected by all voters of the city would not have to please the narrow interest of one section or ward of the city. On the other hand, ward advocates argue that the ward system assures all sectors of the city fair representation and equal treatment and assures that certain neighborhoods of favored classes will not be given undue advantage in the actions of the council.

As with many political science questions, the ward-versus-at-large question has several sides; virtue is not concentrated entirely on either. Some home-rule cities, with power to arrange things as they like, have struck a compromise by electing some council members by wards and others at-large. Colorado Springs, for example, has done so.

Council-Manager Form of City Government. If a Colorado city decides to organize itself as a statutory council-manager city, it will

not elect its mayor at-large. The council chooses one of its own
members as mayor. The council is made up of two members elected
from each ward of the city and one from the city at-large. The mayor
presides over the council, is head of the city for all ceremonial
purposes, and may be conferred other duties and powers by the
council. The council appoints a city attorney, a municipal judge, and
a city manager. The manager serves an indefinite term and is
removable at the pleasure of the council, for cause. The manager has
power to appoint and remove all officers and employees of the city,
except the city attorney and the municipal judge. The manager is
chief conservator of peace within the city, supervises the city administration, enforces ordinances, makes recommendations to the council, advises the council of the financial condition of the city, prepares
an annual budget, and makes reports to the council. The manager
is not the boss or dictator of the city. He is, to repeat, an employee
of the council, a very special employee. He can spend no money
unauthorized by the council, and he cannot levy taxes. Nor can he
enact ordinances; only the council has that power. However, the
manager is sometimes authorized by the council to make rules
pursuant to ordinances, and these rules have the force of law. In
short, the manager works within the circle of power granted to him
by the council; he or she is hired by the council, reports to the council,
and may be fired by the council at any hour of the day or night.

However, many city managers do influence their council. A
full-time professional manager becomes expert on all sorts of problems faced by the council. The council is usually composed of part-
time amateurs uninformed about technicalities important in
decision making. Consider the question whether to use concrete or
asphalt or some other form of paving on a certain street. The city
manager is apt to be in a good position to advise on the merits and
costs of alternative paving materials. If he is a good manager, he will
know how to get information needed by the council and how to
report it to the council without making them feel ignorant. A good
manager needs to be a good politician, not so much in a partisan
sense as in a bureaucratic sense. A manager must always keep a
majority of the council on his side; the instant he loses his majority
he had better start looking for a new employer. So long as he or she
retains the confidence of the council and can supply them with

MAYOR-COUNCIL FORM OF CITY GOVERNMENT

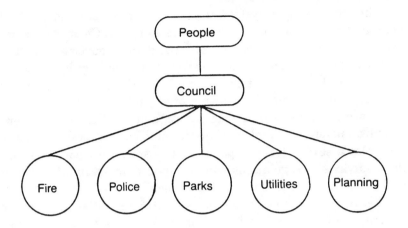

COUNCIL-MANAGER FORM OF CITY GOVERNMENT

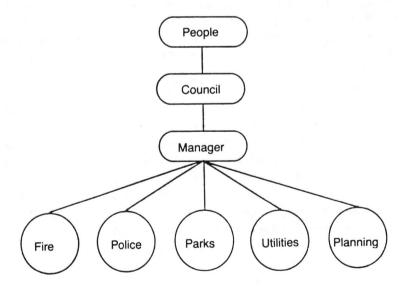

sound professional advice in a politic way, he or she can become a great force in civic affairs.

The city manager system of government is being adopted by more and more cities in the United States and in Colorado. As life becomes more technological, so does the work of government. It is increasingly important to run governments (whether city, state, or national) with the help of professionals — the day of the amateur and political hack may be drawing to an end. Governments at all levels are doing more than ever before, and what they do is more complicated and technological. Amateurs cannot build a power plant, lay a sewer, design a pollution-free sewage disposal system, draw subdivision regulations, conduct up-to-date fire fighting, equip and train a professional police department.

Because amateurs cannot do such things, cities (and other governments) turn to professionals, to people who have formal education in the specifics of their profession. Cities now more commonly than before recruit a police chief with a degree in police science, police officers with baccalaureate degrees, treasurers with degrees in accounting; they look for utilities directors with degrees in engineering or business administration and city planners with degrees in city planning. It is commonplace for cities to select managers with degrees in public administration and to ask them to hire professional department heads who in turn will staff their departments with professionals. It is the duty of the manager to be the presiding officer and coordinator of a bureaucratic team staffed, not on the basis of political activity but on the basis of merit. That is how the council-manager system is supposed to work. It does not always work as idealized by advocates of city manager government, but it seems to work better than other systems in many cities.

The council-manager system is not without its shortcomings. Small towns often cannot afford a full-time professional manager, cannot keep one busy. On the other hand, large cities such as Los Angeles or Denver, which can easily afford good managers, often prefer to put strong, popularly elected mayors in charge of city administration. A city manager in Denver might lack political strength necessary to mobilize the municipal bureaucracy behind important civic projects or goals. The larger the city, the stronger must be the hand that directs it. Council-manager systems work best in cities with populations from 5,000 to 100,000. Where a council-manager system is used, its success depends on having a competent, sensible manager and a competent, sensible council. A good council will not unreasonably intrude on the work of a manager; having hired him, a council should let him do his job.

HOME-RULE CITIES

Home rule is for municipalities that want more freedom than the legislature has allowed statutory cities to design their government and its powers. Colorado has *constitutional home rule,* not *statutory home rule.* Constitutional home rule is given directly by the state constitution (in Colorado, Article XX of the Constitution). Statutory home rule, on the other hand, is nothing more than a statement by the legislature that municipalities have home-rule freedom — a statement subject to change at any time by the legislature. Statutory home rule is not even considered worthy of the name by home-rule advocates. Constitutional home rule, on the other hand, is a grant of freedom straight from the constitution and stands above the reach of legislative interference.

To become a home-rule city in Colorado, a city council calls an election for twenty-one members of a charter convention. The charter convention drafts a charter stating the proposed organization and power of the city and has sixty days to do this. The proposed charter is given to the city clerk, who publishes the document in the official newspaper of the city three times, one week apart. In the first publication, the clerk calls a special election in which the voters may express their approval or rejection of the charter. If adopted, the charter is delivered to the secretary of state and becomes the supreme state law of the city. This means that no law in the state, not even the state constitution, is superior to the charter in municipal affairs. The constitution of the state of Colorado provides that such charters (and the ordinances made pursuant to them) supersede within the territorial limits of the city any law of the state in conflict therewith.

Now, in all this discussion of home rule, there is one weasel phrase: "municipal affairs." The home-rule autonomy seemingly granted by the constitution actually stands on a shaky foundation. The problem with being granted home-rule freedom within the sphere of municipal affairs is that nobody really knows what a municipal affair is. The state retains its full authority to legislate on statewide matters, and such legislation is binding on the whole state, including home-rule cities. What is "municipal" and what is "statewide"? There is no adequate definition of either term, yet the edifice of home rule rests on this indefinable distinction. Whenever the state wants to take an action, it calls that action "statewide." Whenever a home-rule city wants to do something, it calls the action "municipal." When there is a battle between the city and the state, the issue can be decided only by the courts. In the case of *Cañon City v. Merris,* 137 Colorado 169 (1958), and in a series of subsequent cases, the Colorado Supreme Court has wrestled with the question of what is and what is not a matter of statewide concern outside the legislative authority of home-rule cities.

There are about sixty home-rule cities in Colorado, including Alamosa, Boulder, Golden, Greeley, Gunnison, Colorado Springs, Denver, Fort Collins, La Junta, Manitou Springs, and Pueblo.

COLORADO SPRINGS

Colorado Springs is an example of a home-rule city with a council-manager form of government. In 1990 the Colorado Springs Standard Metropolitan Statistical Area (consisting of El Paso County) had 394,000 people — about 60 percent of them in the city and 40 percent in suburbs and unincorporated areas. Colorado Springs has been a home-rule city since 1909 and has used the council-manager system since 1920. The city council consists of nine members elected on a nonpartisan basis; five are elected at-large, four from wards. Council members serve four-year terms; terms are staggered so that every two years about half the council seats are filled by election. Candidates for council must be at least twenty-five years old and must have been citizens of the city for five years, although the five-year provision is of questionable constitutionality. Council members are nonsalaried.

The mayor is popularly elected, and presides at council meetings. The council appoints an attorney, an auditor, a clerk-treasurer, municipal judges, and a city manager. The terms of office, salaries, and duties of these officials are prescribed by city ordinance, that is, by the council. About twenty nonsalaried authorities, boards, and commissions assist in overseeing various city functions; the members of these agencies are appointed by the council and/or mayor.

The executive head of the city is the city manager appointed by the city council, which may remove him at any time by two-thirds vote. He or she is responsible for enforcing laws and ordinances of the city, appointing heads of departments, hiring city personnel, purchasing materials and supplies, and preparing an annual budget for consideration by the council.

DENVER

Denver has the unique distinction in Colorado of being both a city and a county: one government has served in both capacities since 1902. Denver is a home-rule city and county. As a matter of fact, the home-rule article of the Colorado Constitution (Art. XX) was first put into the constitution around the turn of the century as a result of Denver's struggle to escape the clutches of the state legislature, which was in the habit of trying to run Denver.

Although Denver is a city-county, it has more of the trappings of a city than of a county. For example, it has a mayor, which counties obviously do not have. It has a city council rather than a board of county commissioners. It has no independently elected sheriff, clerk, coroner, assessor, treasurer, or surveyor such as one finds in almost all counties. Rather, these functions are assumed by officials of various titles appointed by the mayor. Denver has no partisan elections. Like all Colorado cities its elections are nonpartisan (county elections are partisan).

In its governmental organization, Denver has a mayor-council system and gives great power to its mayor, who is directly elected at-large to a four-year term. The mayor is strong in the sense that he has power to appoint the heads of the seven departments of government (who make up his cabinet), plus the city attorney and the city clerk and recorder. He is also permitted by the city-county charter to designate fifty other positions, which he may fill. The mayor, of course, chooses to appoint the managers of most major city offices (he usually includes among the fifty his own personal staff) and a collection of other intriguing positions throughout the city. Most other jobs in Denver's government are filled through some form of merit system. The mayor also appoints many of the members of independent agencies, boards, and commissions, although these are effectively removed from the mayor's control because he rarely has power to remove them, except for *cause* (proven failure to perform duties). Members of such independent agencies, boards, and commissions usually serve for fixed overlapping terms, and very few mayors ever get a chance to appoint all the members. For example, the Board of Water Commissioners has five members appointed by the mayor to serve six-year staggered terms, but the mayor may not remove any member except for cause. The Denver Water Department is an independent, publicly owned, nonprofit agency operated under the city-county charter by the Board of Water Commissioners. The department runs Denver's water system and supplies water to areas outside Denver as well.

Denver also elects an auditor, who serves a four-year term. The auditor is the general accountant for the city. He or she is mainly concerned with assuring the legality of expenditures. The auditor's array of powers over financial administration of Denver is quite remarkable, and he is in a good position to be obstructive if he chooses to be.

The Denver Board of Councilmembers (popularly known as the city council) has thirteen members, all but two elected from councilmanic districts to four-year terms. The two are elected at-large by all the voters of Denver and also have four-year terms. All members of the council are elected at the same time. Ordinances passed by the council may be vetoed by the mayor, but the veto may be overridden by a vote of nine members.

Denver also elects two members of the three-member Election Commission, who serve four-year terms. The nonelected member is the Clerk and Recorder of the City and County of Denver, who serves by virtue of his or her office (ex officio). The Election Commission runs Denver elections: it controls registration of voters and the holding of elections, it canvasses election returns (counts the votes), and it issues certificates of election.

The electorate of Denver has the power of referendum to force a popular vote on an ordinance passed by the Board of Councilmembers. Voters also have the power to initiate ordinances, which go on the ballot if the council does not pass them. Denver also has a system for recalling from office any elected official.

COUNTIES

SIZE AND NUMBER

Colorado has sixty-three counties including the City and County of Denver. (See p. 63 for discussion of Denver's government.) Denver County has the distinction of being the smallest county in land area while at the same time having the largest population, close to half a million. The least populated county is Hinsdale, with only about 500 people, although it has over a thousand square miles of land area. Hinsdale County is not the only county with fewer than 1,000 people. Its neighbor, Mineral County, likewise has only about 500, as does San Juan County, with about 800. Four other counties have fewer than 2,000 people: Custer, Dolores, Jackson, and Kiowa. All told, in 1990 fifteen Colorado counties had fewer than 4,000 inhabitants — approximately one-fourth of Colorado's counties. On the other hand, nine counties have over 100,000 people each: Adams, Arapahoe, Boulder, Denver, El Paso, Jefferson, Larimer, Pueblo, and Weld, while one other, Mesa, was in 1990 fast approaching 100,000. Most Colorado counties have between 4,000 and 20,000 inhabitants (see Table 3–1).

Table 3–1: Population of Colorado Counties in 1990: Preliminary Census Bureau Count (August 1990)

County	1990 Count	% Change Since 1980
Adams	263,599	+7
Alamosa	13,579	+15
Arapahoe	389,739	+33
Archuleta	5,327	+46
Baca	4,553	-15
Bent	5,041	-15
Boulder	227,544	+20
Chaffee	12,633	-5
Cheyenne	2,394	+11
Clear Creek	7,488	+2
Conejos	7,450	-4
Costilla	3,176	+3
Crowley	3,939	+32
Custer	1,922	+22
Delta	20,920	-1

County	1990 Count	% Change Since 1980
Denver	420,414	-6
Dolores	1,504	-9
Douglas	59,513	+137
Eagle	21,887	+64
El paso	394,106	+27
Elbert	9,629	+40
Fremont	32,187	+12
Garfield	29,910	+33
Gilpin	3,070	+26
Grand	7,923	+6
Gunnison	10,225	-4
Hinsdale	467	+15
Huerfano	5,991	-7
Jackson	1,592	-15
Jefferson	435,642	+17
Kiowa	1,681	-13
Kit Carson	7,132	-6
La Plata	32,168	+17
Lake	5,975	-32
Larimer	181,430	+22
Las Animas	13,688	-8
Lincoln	4,523	-3
Logan	17,596	-11
Mesa	92,832	+14
Mineral	556	-31
Moffat	11,318	-13
Montezuma	18,569	+12
Montrose	24,323	-0.1
Morgan	21,882	-3
Otero	20,095	-11
Ouray	2,292	+19
Park	7,115	+33
Phillips	4,127	-9
Pitkin	12,534	+21
Prowers	13,527	+1
Pueblo	122,312	-3
Rio Blanco	5,938	-5
Rio Grande	10,739	+2

County	1990 Count	% Change Since 1980
Routt	14,087	+5
Saguache	4,602	+17
San Juan	743	-11
San Miguel	3,638	+14
Sedgwick	2,690	-18
Summit	12,715	+44
Teller	12,454	+55
Washington	4,812	-9
Weld	131,480	+7
Yuma	8,943	-8

Source: U.S. Bureau of the Census

Ought Colorado to abolish the high population counties and turn them into cities, as has been partially done in the case of Denver, and abolish most of the small counties by combining them into larger counties? There is much to say, pro and con, about these seemingly fanciful ideas.

However, rearranging counties is difficult. The territorial integrity of Colorado counties is guaranteed by the state constitution, which provides that no part of the territory of a county may be stricken off and added to an adjoining county without the consent of a majority of all the qualified voters of the county whose territory is to be stricken off (Art. XIV, Sec. 3).

WHAT IS A COUNTY?

In legal theory a county differs from a city in that while a city is established to serve the special needs of its inhabitants, a county is set up to serve the needs of the state at large. Counties are political subdivisions of the state created to aid in the administration of state law and also to provide local self-government. Insofar as one purpose of a county is to provide local self-government, this brings it very close to being a municipal corporation, and in fact several states do regard counties as involuntary municipal corporations, not voluntary creations of the members thereof, but still, corporations.

The word *county* comes to us, along with so much else, from early

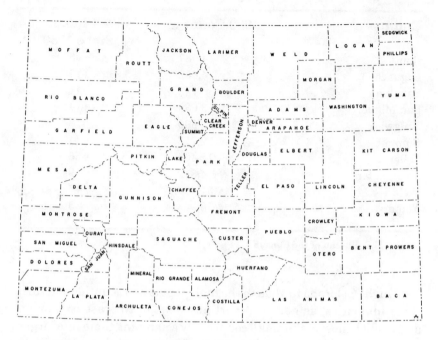

Colorado Counties.

English terminology. In England, counties were the major subdivisions into which the kingdom was divided. Each county was under the immediate charge of a count. The English had two words for this political subdivision, one of French origin, *county,* the other of German origin, *shire.* We get the word *sheriff* from *shirereeve,* the principal administrative officer of a shire (or county) working directly under the count himself.

All Colorado counties do similar work — overseeing such things as public safety, zoning, building regulation, welfare, health, hospitals, parks, recreation, highways, justice, assessment, and record keeping. Because the circumstances of each county are unique, the amount of money spent on each activity varies from county to county. Hinsdale County, with fewer than 1,000 people, spends less on welfare than it does on highways. This is because Hinsdale has to maintain approximately one mile of road for each of its inhabitants. El Paso County, in contrast, spends much more on welfare than highways. Roughly speaking, a county has to have 15,000 to 20,000 inhabitants before its welfare costs exceed its highway costs.

The importance of county government to the average citizen depends in large part on whether he or she lives in a city. If so, the city provides many services for which rural people look to the county. This, incidentally, is why the per capita expenditures of rural counties tend to be higher than the per capita expenditures of urban counties.

COUNTY COMMISSIONERS

Although their role is described in the constitution and laws of the state, one might visualize county commissioners as a collective chief executive of the county government. The board of commissioners is primarily in charge of those county activities not specifically given by law to other elected county officers, such as the clerk, treasurer, sheriff, coroner, assessor, and surveyor. These other elected officials have administrative powers separate and largely independent of the board. County government as it exists in nearly all of Colorado's counties today is a multiheaded creature — a political monstrosity disturbingly awkward, oafish, and ponderous. Although the board of commissioners is generally considered the kingpin of this multiheaded enterprise, and although the board is in charge of paying the county's bills and levying taxes, it has great difficulty controlling the work of county agencies carrying out state-mandated functions and headed by popularly elected officials.

Commissioners have very little power to set the salaries of the elected county officials, or their own salaries — this is done by the state. Colorado's constitution requires the legislature to fix salaries of all elected county officers in nonhome-rule counties. In so doing, the legislature is supposed to give consideration to population, assessed valuation, motor vehicle registrations, building permits, and other things that affect the workloads of county officers. For purposes of setting the salaries of commissioners, sheriffs, treasurers, assessors, and clerks, the legislature has established five categories of counties and set forth the base salaries of elected officers in each category. (County surveyors and coroners are paid by fees and thus are not included in this scheme.) In 1991 Class I counties are mandated to pay their county commissioners $50,000 a year, their sheriffs $56,000, their treasurers, assessors, and county clerks $50,000 each. Class I counties include Adams, Arapahoe, Boulder, El Paso, Jefferson, Larimer, Pueblo, and Weld. At the other end of the scale, Class V counties are mandated to pay their commissioners $18,000, their sheriffs $28,000, their treasurers, assessors, and county clerks $25,000 (*Colorado Revised Statues,* hereafter cited as *C.R.S.,* 30–1–101). Some critics of the present system believe salaries of all elected county officials (including the commissioners' own salaries) should be set by the commissioners in each county. This idea is, of course, opposed by those who believe in the continued autonomy of elected county department heads.

County commissioners have always had the power to set the salaries of department heads who are not elected. They also have power to make the general county operating budget and thus to determine the operating budget of all departments of county government, including those headed by elected officials. But even in so doing, the commissioners' power is severely limited because almost everything done by the elected officials is mandated by the state — they must do those things — and the commissioners must finance them.

In addition to its power to tax and pay county bills, the board does such other things as establish precincts; lay out, alter, and discontinue roads; license various activities; establish airports and dumps; buy, sell, rent, and make rules for use of county property. An important additional part of the board's work is to make regulations pertaining to building and to plan and zone the physical development of unincorporated areas. To help it with these duties, the board is authorized to appoint a five-member county planning commission and may also participate in establishment of regional planning commissions.

Unless a county has a population exceeding 70,000 or is a home-rule county, its board of commissioners must consist of three members. If more than 70,000, the county may, if it wishes, have a board of five members, and home-rule counties, such as Weld and Pitkin, may have any number of commissioners they wish. There are a number of counties with more than 70,000 inhabitants, including Adams, Arapahoe, Boulder, Denver, El Paso, Jefferson, Larimer, Mesa, Pueblo, and Weld. All have three-member boards except Denver, El Paso, and Weld. Members of the board are elected for a term of four years on a party ballot. Terms are staggered.

OTHER COUNTY OFFICERS

Besides county commissioners, the constitution provides that each county shall elect a county clerk, a sheriff, a coroner, a treasurer, a superintendent of schools (optional), a surveyor, an assessor, and an attorney (the attorney may be appointed). These elected officers serve four-year terms.

CLERK

The clerk is the county's record keeper. You go to the clerk's office to find the books, papers, and records of the county, including mortgages, plats, marriage certificates, divorce decrees, birth certificates, and adoption papers. The clerk is also the clerk or general secretary of the board of commissioners. As chief election official of the county, the clerk performs many election functions — registration of voters, preparation of ballots, establishment of election precincts, and so on. As an agent of the state Department of Revenue he or she administers motor vehicle licensing.

SHERIFF

The office of sheriff is the most ancient of all county offices, stemming from the earliest period of English history. In Colorado, the sheriff is the chief law enforcement officer of the county. He does not enforce the ordinances of incorporated cities (except occasionally by contract); on the contrary, the law he enforces is state law, and his enforcement duties are chiefly in the unincorporated areas of the county. In urbanized counties, the work of sheriffs has tended to become less significant, because most crime is in cities and therefore outside the sheriff's jurisdiction. Enforcement by state police has also tended to diminish the work of county sheriffs. The sheriff ordinarily runs the county jail and assists the courts, both outside and inside incorporated areas.

CORONER

The office of coroner is another ancient office whose title and functions continue in modern English and American local government. He is primarily a judicial officer, his duty being to inquire into the causes and circumstances of any death in the county through violence, or suddenly, or with cause for suspicion. The examination made by the coroner is a *coroner's inquest* and is held with a jury. The office of coroner ideally is filled by a lawyer who is also trained as a physician. Coroners are not paid a salary in the usual sense but are paid a set fee each day actually and necessarily employed in the performance of their duties.

TREASURER

The treasurer not only receives, holds, and disburses county funds; he is also the tax collector for the county and for other units of government within the county. He is often comptroller of the county budget, responsible for keeping expenditures within the budget. He may issue periodic reports to the commissioners and publish periodic reports in the newspapers. The treasurer cannot spend the money in his custody; he or she simply honors warrants for expenditures signed by the board of commissioners.

SUPERINTENDENT OF SCHOOLS

This office sounds more authoritative than it is. Actually, the superintendent prepares reports for the state Board of Education, and as that is his or her primary duty, there is little excuse for a superintendent at all because school districts are quite competent to do most of the necessary reporting. Almost all counties have done away with the position.

SURVEYOR

The surveyor represents the county in boundary disputes, establishes boundaries of county property including road rights-of-way, keeps a record of all survey monuments in the county, examines all maps and plots before they are recorded, and files in his or her office all surveys pertaining to work authorized by the county board. County surveyors are not paid a salary in the usual sense but are paid a set fee for each act related to their official duties.

ASSESSOR

Much of the tax revenue of counties and other local governments is raised by property taxes, that is, by taxes on the value of real estate. It is the duty of the assessor to determine the value of each piece of taxable real estate in the county. If you have a dispute with the county assessor over the value of your property, you can appeal the assessment to the county board of equalization. In each county (except Denver) the board of county commissioners serves also as the county board of equalization. The board may raise, lower, or adjust any assessed valuation so that all valuations are just and equalized within the county. Beginning about the middle of July every year, the board meets to hear appeals in cases where a protest against the assessor's assessment has been rejected by the assessor. If, then, the board also denies the appeal, the property owner may carry his appeal to the state Board of Assessment Appeals, and thence to a district court. The state Board of Assessment Appeals is an agency within the Department of Local Affairs.

Equalization of property tax assessments means assessing everybody's property according to the same standard. Whatever percentage of actual value may be mandated by the constitution or by the legislature, some county assessors habitually assess property short of the mark, a politically popular thing for elected assessors to do, and county boards of equalization tend to acquiesce in it. The state, however, does not acquiesce so easily. It has an interest in seeing to it that all counties assess at the same percent of market value, and a state Board of Equalization exists to achieve that goal. The state Board of Equalization has power to raise or lower the aggregate assessments of any county and may compel compliance with its orders by mandamus or injunction proceedings in court.

When a county assessor underassesses property in a county, it becomes necessary for all units of government in the county (which rely on the county's assessment) to apply a higher millage rate to realize the same revenue that a lower millage rate on higher assessments would yield. (The amount of revenue yielded by a property tax is calculated by simply multiplying the assessed value of property times the millage rate.) From the point of view of the county and of all units of government within the county using the county's assessment, it makes little difference whether the assessment is high and the millage rate low, or the assessment low and the millage rate high.

Members of the state Board of Equalization are the governor or his designee, the speaker of the House of Representatives or his designee, the president of the Senate or his designee, and two members appointed by the governor with the consent of the Senate, each of whom is supposed to be knowledgeable and experienced in the field of property taxation.

ATTORNEY

As the Colorado Constitution gives a choice between electing or appointing county attorneys, the legislature has enacted a law requiring that they be appointed. The attorney's job is to serve as lawyer for the county.

SUGGESTED IMPROVEMENTS IN COUNTY GOVERNMENT

A commonly heard suggestion for improvement of counties is that they take advantage of a provision of the Colorado Constitution permitting counties to adopt home-rule charters. The internal administrative structure of counties in Colorado has not changed much for a century; furthermore, the state constitution imposes an identical structure on all counties except home-rule counties. That structure is not necessarily bad, but, on the other hand, it is not necessarily good for all counties. Counties are not identical in size or in the complexity of their administrative apparatus, nor are they identical in how they want to run their affairs. Constitutional home rule is offered to accommodate this variety of conditions.

Home rule for a county does not mean it is free to alter its functions, services, and facilities. All counties must, whether home rule or not, provide every function, service, and facility and exercise every power required of counties by law. After all, a county is first and foremost an agency through which the state works in the process of governance. But home rule does enable a county to design its internal governmental organization in whatever way best suits it and frees it from the organizational structure imposed on non-home-rule counties by the constitution and laws of the state.

At present, only Weld and Pitkin are home-rule counties. (Denver, of course, is not a county but a city-county. It, too, has home rule.) El Paso County voters defeated a proposal in 1976 to establish a home-rule charter commission. Counties may, at their option, adopt home rule by a procedure that starts with a petition signed by not less than 5 percent of the registered voters of the county. Proponents of home rule in a particular county get the ball rolling by circulating this petition, which calls for putting a question on the ballot asking voters of the county whether they wish to form a *charter commission*. If enough people sign the petition, the question goes on the ballot. In the same election, voters are asked to vote upon various candidates who have offered themselves for service on the commission. If voters vote to have a charter commission, then a commission composed of successful candidates for commission duty comes into existence. However, mere election of a charter commission does not in any way commit the county to home rule, though it may be a test of feeling. The commission goes to work drafting a home-rule charter. Finally, the product of their genius is put to the voters. If voters turn down the proposed charter, the whole procedure comes to an end, and the county remains as it was. If voters accept the charter, the county becomes a home-rule county under the charter just adopted and organizes according to its provisions.

Many advocates of county home rule wish to see home-rule charters adopted that set up *modern administrative practices*. Basically this boils down to something similar to the city manager system. The board of county commissioners would be the only elected officials in the county. They would appoint a county manager who in turn would appoint all department heads: the clerk, the sheriff, the coroner, the treasurer, the surveyor, the assessor. The administration of the county would be a hierarchy running from the commissioners, through the manager, to the lowest worker. Usually this system is accompanied by a plan for appointing, rewarding, disciplining, removing, and retiring most county employees under rules of a civil service merit system.

Advocates of the county manager system are appalled by the chaos they see in the old system of administration prevailing in most Colorado counties. The old system is not one government, but six or seven minigovernments, none of which can be controlled by the county board of commissioners. The sheriff, as an elected official, is not subservient to the commissioners; he runs his department the way he wants, hires whom he wants (often political supporters), promotes, disciplines, and fires anybody he wants for almost any reason he or she wants. The other elected officials do likewise. Each county thus organized is a disjointed collection of tsardoms. There can be no county-wide personnel system because each elected official runs his own personnel system. Reformers claim that these poor administrative practices would be ended if an efficient county manager system and a modern personnel system were introduced.

Defenders of the old order say the old way is more efficient and more democratic than the reforms would be. The old way is more democratic because under it there are more elected officials, making the government more responsive to the public. The old way is also more efficient because when an elected official such as a county clerk has absolute power to hire and fire and uses that power to hire political friends, the efficiency of the office is very high — each worker has a vested interest in seeing to it that his or her boss is reelected, a vested interest in seeing to it that the office is well run and responsive to the public. Furthermore, it is efficient because workers hired in that manner (that is, by the spoils system) are well disposed toward their employer and in no mood to join unions. So say the defenders of the old system.

Amendments to Colorado's constitution have opened the door, legally, to great reforms in local government: home rule for cities, home rule for counties, regional service authorities. But an open door legally is not necessarily an open door politically. There has been no rush to establish home-rule charters for counties nor to establish regional service authorities. There is reason for foot-dragging in these matters; the dominant political powers under the present system of county government have little wish to change the status quo. The same general principle applies to regional service authorities: why should those who hold power in the counties and cities wish to surrender any part of it to a regional service authority? Unless the power structure of a given region sees an advantage for itself by creating a regional service authority, proposals to establish such an authority in the region will have a very tough fight. Furthermore, although county home rule may have organizational flexibility, it cannot give equal flexibility in financial matters because counties must do the various things they are told to do by the state.

School Districts, Special Districts, and Metropolitan Areas

SCHOOL DISTRICTS

A school district is a government. It is quite a bit like a city or a county, except that it is a one-function government. That function is to provide elementary and secondary schools. It has an elected governing board (the school board); it has a chief executive (the superintendent of schools); it has the power to tax residents within the boundaries of the school district; it has the power to borrow money, spend money, and do all the things governments usually do, but, to repeat, everything relates to providing schools.

Why don't city or county governments run the schools? Why have separate governments do it? The answer is that schools were, and perhaps still are, believed to need protection against and isolation from the machinations of ordinary city and county politics. The school district is a monument to man's effort to keep ordinary politics out of schools. Local politics was once considered more unsavory, more corrupt, than perhaps it is considered today. There was a common wish to spare the school system those misfortunes. American public schools have been comparatively free from such vices as theft of funds or appointment of teachers by political favoritism.

PUBLIC SCHOOL FINANCE

In many Colorado counties more property taxes are collected to support schools than to support the entire county government itself. The biggest single property tax user in the state of Colorado is the public school system.

State Support. Not all money spent by school districts comes from local property taxes. The state of Colorado massively supports education. Over a half million children are enrolled in elementary and secondary education in Colorado and more than one hundred thousand in public higher education. Education, all levels, is the biggest expense the state bears. About 65 percent of the Colorado general fund has been spent in recent years on education — 21 percent on higher education and 44 percent on other education — in addition to revenue raised by local school districts. Clearly, taxpayers and legislators of Colorado have a right to be interested in how efficiently this great venture called public education — so monumentally supported by state and local governments — is carried forth.

Use of the real property tax to support schools has come under attack because some school districts are richer than others. Is it fair, ask critics of the property tax, that some children should have a poor education because they happen to live in a poor district that cannot raise as much revenue for its schools as other districts? Of course, the same question could be raised about financing anything — roads, hospitals, police, fire. The property tax system of financing public education is alleged by some to be unconstitutional in that it denies equality in the distribution of a public service. Although the United States Supreme Court upheld the system in 1973 (*San Antonio Independent School District* v. *Rodriguez*), the California Supreme Court went right ahead in 1976 and declared the property tax system of financing public schools to be a violation of California's state constitution (*Serrano* v. *Priest*). An attempt was made in Colorado to do the same thing. In 1977, Josie Lujan of Del Norte and a group of other parents from sixteen low wealth and mostly rural school districts from all parts of Colorado sued the state Board of Education on grounds that their children were not receiving an education equal to that of high wealth school districts. In 1979 a state district court ruled that the Colorado school-financing system did indeed violate the Colorado Constitution, which requires the legislature to establish a "thorough and uniform system" of education (Art. IX, Sec. 2). In 1982, however, the Colorado Supreme Court reversed the lower court and upheld the property tax system of financing schools on essentially the same grounds used earlier by the United States Supreme Court in the San Antonio case. The Colorado court said that although education is an important public service, it is not a fundamental constitutional right guaranteed by the state or federal constitution. Also, the existing system, said the state supreme court, rationally serves a legitimate state purpose, namely, local control of public schools (*Lujan* v. *State Board of Education,* 649 P. 2nd 1005).

The issue continued to ferment. Many people couldn't get it out of their heads that school equality was somehow related to equality of opportunity — a cornerstone of our way of life in America. People questioned whether or not school equality was more fundamental than fire department equality, or sewer system equality, or street department equality. By 1990 at least a dozen state supreme courts had declared state school funding systems that rest heavily upon a property tax unconstitutional under state constitutions. And yet in about a dozen other states the courts have dismissed such suits.

Whether one wins or loses a lawsuit of this nature, the process of making a court case out of the issue serves to put the question on a front burner for public discussion. Many legislatures (such as Colorado's) have not waited to have their state system of funding public education declared unconstitutional but have seen a need for change and responded to it. Many states, including Colorado, have taken steps in recent years to improve their equalization efforts in public school funding. In 1988 the Colorado General Assembly (and one of its interim committees) made a great effort to reform state aid to public schools. Their purpose was to fine-tune that aid to help equalize the inequalities of school districts. The Public School Finance Act of 1988 resulted from that effort. (See page 310 for the details of this law.)

Local Financing and Control. With regard to schools, taxpayers are in the grips of a conflict. On one hand, most taxpayers seem to want local control of schools. This is almost an article of religious faith in America and in Colorado. Yet taxpayers do not want local governments to bear the complete cost of schools; they want as much state and federal aid as possible. And therein lies the contradiction: he who pays for schools will control schools. To demand local control and also to demand state and federal financing is to demand opposite and hostile conditions. Federal and state officials may solemnly swear not to interfere with local control of schools, but ultimately it is as certain and fixed as the laws of nature that they will interfere, because money is power.

EFFICIENCY OF SCHOOL DISTRICTS

How efficiently run is this vast enterprise of public education upon which so many hundreds of millions of dollars are lavished by taxpayers? Unfortunately, it is hard to measure the efficiency of a public service. You cannot measure it on a profit or loss basis as you might measure the efficiency of a filling station. Very few of the services of government are run on a profit and loss basis — certainly public education is not. Educators even disagree on what the goal of education is, and if we don't know what the goal is, there is no way of measuring how well we are reaching it.

The standard criticisms aimed at local governments generally are aimed at some school districts that are said to be too small in population to be efficient. It is stressed that school districts and schools should, where possible, consolidate. Rather than have small school districts running poorly staffed and poorly equipped schools, we should have (according to some critics) fewer districts that are more populous, that run fewer, but bigger and better, schools.

In Colorado, hundreds of school districts in the past thirty years have been consolidated with other districts. Today, about 176 districts in the state operate more than twelve hundred schools with over thirty thousand certified personnel. Few, if any, one-room schools remain, and most schools are of adequate (if not admirable) size and quality. There would be resistance to further consolidations of schools and school districts that would result in the need to bus children long distances. Parents want schools near home and often claim it is better to have neighborhood schools close to the children and close to the supervisory eye of parents than to have distant, but better, schools. The urge for neighborhood schools is powerful in

Colorado and in America, and it may be more powerful than the urge for better schools.

STATE BOARD OF EDUCATION

The general supervision of the public schools of the state of Colorado is vested in a state Board of Education, whose powers and duties are prescribed by law. The board now has seven members, one elected from each Colorado congressional district and one elected at-large. The board appoints a commissioner of education, a position not included in the classified civil service of the state. Besides its general supervisory duties, the board makes recommendations to the state legislature concerning school policies and financing.

SPECIAL DISTRICTS

A special district is a government set up to do (ordinarily) only one thing. A special district is very much like a school district. In fact, a school district is a special district, although not commonly called such. There are all sorts of special districts, some in rural areas to provide urban-type services, and some in urban areas to provide certain special services not furnished by a city or county government in the area. There are cemetery districts, drainage districts, fire protection districts, irrigation districts, soil conservation districts, water supply and sanitation districts, and so on. Most special districts are one-purpose governments, although from time to time they have more than one function and act as a halfway house on the way to the incorporation of a town or city. In Colorado law, these multipurpose districts are called *metropolitan districts* if they provide two or more urban-type services. No special district may be set up wholly within the boundaries of a municipality without the consent of that municipality's governing body. Like other governments, special districts are empowered to tax, spend, sue, be sued, make contracts, buy and sell property, and so forth. Each special district has a name and a governing board.

A special district is governed by a five-member board of directors. Some special districts (such as cemetery districts) may be set up by the board of county commissioners upon receipt of a petition signed by a majority of the property tax–paying electors in the area of the proposed district. In such districts, county commissioners also appoint the district board of directors. In contrast, many districts have elective boards and are set up by a method vaguely similar to the procedure used for incorporating a new town. Commonly, however, special districts with elective boards hold no elections. This is because state law allows special districts to avoid the cost of holding elections if the number of candidates does not exceed the number of board vacancies.

Special districts suffer one disadvantage more acutely than any other variety of local government: few people know or care much about them. Most of us are taxed by special districts and don't know it. On election day when candidates are running for special district offices, there is monumental apathy and indifference by voters. The situation is made worse by the overlapping of special districts, which in turn overlap cities, towns, counties, and school districts. This swarm of local governments, this complexity of government, is far beyond the ability of the average voter to comprehend. It is a glut of democracy. There are more special districts in Colorado (over a thousand of them) than there are cities, towns, counties, and school districts put together; they represent the most common form of local government in the state. Arapahoe County has about seventy of them. El Paso and Weld counties each have about forty. Pueblo County has about twenty-four. Even Hinsdale County has a couple.

It is sometimes said that special districts are useful because they usually do only one job and do it well. This claim is hard to prove, for data are scarce on whether a special district does its one job better than cities or counties ordinarily do the same kind of job. Perhaps a more valid argument for special districts is that they tend to do jobs and provide services that no other local government is providing at the time they are set up. Regional service authorities, which are now authorized to be set up, are not envisaged as single-purpose, but as multipurpose, special districts.

Besides special districts, there are *authorities,* which sometimes seem to be special districts. An authority is a taxing unit created by some unit of government, such as a county, to provide a particular additional service. The authority does not itself provide the service but only taxes the inhabitants within it to support the service. The government that creates the authority actually performs the service, and the governing board of that unit of government also serves as the governing board of the authority. An authority may not be set up without the prior consent of voters within its proposed boundaries. State law authorizes creation of authorities for such purposes as downtown development, post-secondary educational facilities, health facilities, housing finance, law enforcement, public airports, regional service, river basin development, and water resources.

METROPOLITAN GOVERNMENT

There are many local governments in Colorado: governments within governments within governments. They overlap each other geographically and sometimes offer duplicate services. They are very expensive. Many observers conclude that we need to put a stop to this overlapping and duplication and tighten up government at the local level to make it more efficient, more effective, more economical, more visible, and more understandable to voters. This need is particularly acute in metropolitan areas, where so many Coloradoans live and where so many problems exhibit themselves in rawest form.

Changes in governmental structure have not kept up with changes in how and where people live. Immigrations of people into the cities have not been met by adequate governmental change to accommodate the needs and problems of those vast numbers. Cities, suburbs, school districts, counties, special districts thrive next to, and within, one another. What is needed, according to many observers, is many fewer local governments in metropolitan areas. Perhaps all that is needed is one government with one governing board and one chief executive: one governmental apparatus with sweeping geographical boundaries encompassing the entire metropolitan area — the central city and all its suburbs — extending outward to include the immediate countryside in all directions, a flexible boundary line that can be extended to bring in new areas as they are settled on the outskirts. Several solutions, each suffering various degrees of imperfection, have been suggested to achieve this goal of metropolitanwide government.

CITY-COUNTY CONSOLIDATION

Denver, as we have seen, is an example of city-county consolidation. Since 1902 Denver has been both a city and a county, exercising the powers and functions of both. It is the only city-county in the state of Colorado, although there are several others in the nation, including the City and County of San Francisco and the City and County of Honolulu (which includes the entire island of Oahu). The purpose of city-county consolidation is to dispense with one whole governmental layer in counties dominated by a large city.

If a city and a county want to consolidate, all sorts of political headaches are raised. First, consolidation condemns all the other cities and towns in the county. They may not want to give up their independence. Second, the state legislature has to enact a bill abolishing a county, because when you combine a city and a county, you no longer have a county, but a city-county. Some people in Aspen want Pitkin County and Aspen to consolidate, but the idea has fallen into a morass of these problems.

CITY-STATE

The city-state idea proposes to simplify government still further by combining the city, the county, the state, and all special districts within the boundaries of a metropolitan area into one government. One might think this idea suitable for a tiny state like Rhode Island dominated by one great city like Providence. No doubt there would be an outcry here if Colorado were converted to the state of Denver, though over half the people of Colorado live in the Denver metropolitan area. But suppose Denver and its metropolitan area were separated from Colorado and made a new state? This is not such an outrageous proposal when you consider that the City and County of Denver is treated almost like a state by the constitution of Colorado, which reads like a constitution for Denver almost as much as for the state. That is a slight exaggeration, but, still, the state constitution is really a constitution for (1) Denver and (2) the rest of the state, though not necessarily in that order of importance.

Before 1902 Denver was run by state politicians; a rebellion against this condition led the inhabitants of Denver to secure a constitutional amendment making it a home-rule city and county. Instead of the state running Denver, Denver turned the tables and, after 1902, commenced running not only its own municipal affairs but, by consolidation with the county, took over many state functions within its boundaries (the major function of a county being to carry out state functions at the local level).

The city-state idea is somewhat fanciful as a solution to metropolitan problems. No state legislature is likely to give its approval to any proposal to carve away its great cities, and the United States Constitution forbids removal of any part of any state without prior approval of the state from whose territory the subtraction is being made. Impractical though it may be, the idea has merit (as many impractical ideas do) in theory: not only would a city-state consolidate levels of government, it would free the metropolitan area from foot-dragging by adjacent rural areas in the solution of metropolitan problems if the new state were to include open space on its borders.

METROPOLITAN SPECIAL DISTRICT

A metropolitan special district, as we use the term here (not to be confused with our previous use of a similar term on p. 81) spreads across the whole metropolitan area without obliterating existing governments but perhaps taking over one or more of the functions of such governments. For example, it may take over police. Now this could grieve the police departments — to be gobbled up — and would alert all other governmental agencies to the danger of a similar fate. To avoid the united opposition of all endangered departments, the best strategy may be to take them one at a time into a metropolitan government, rather than all at once, and to do so over a period of years. Yet, it is fear of just such a strategy that often generates powerful hostility from all quarters of the bureaucracy to any attempt, no matter how modest, to set up metropolitan special districts.

One way to grease the skids would be to absorb most of the functions of a department without erasing the department altogether. Leave the city police chief, leave the city itself, but transfer substantial functions so that what remains is like the skin of a snake after the snake has crawled out. Even if the snake has crawled out, a police chief or a mayor or a city council member can still look himself or herself in the mirror and say, "I am the chief of police," or "I am the mayor," or "I am a member of the city council." This strategy softens the political problem of consolidating governments.

FEDERATION

Federation is another approach that spares the sensibilities of participants. Again, it involves setting up a new layer of government, but here a layer run by local governments within its boundaries. The federation would have a governing board made up of representatives of each member government and would take over certain functions done better on a metropolitan basis.

INTERGOVERNMENTAL COOPERATION

Intergovernmental cooperation does the least damage to established institutional patterns. The Pikes Peak Area Council of Governments (PPACG) is an example of an agency designed to foster intergovernmental cooperation. The PPACG is not a government. It lacks power to do anything but give advice and information. Created in 1967, the PPACG is a voluntary advisory board of local elected officials seeking to identify regional issues and opportunities and to pursue cooperative solutions to areawide problems. The board is composed of representatives from El Paso, Teller, and Park counties and about a dozen municipalities. Each member government has one representative on the board, except El Paso County and the city of Colorado Springs, which have three each.

ANNEXATION

One way to work toward metropolitanwide government is to make it easy for central cities to annex neighboring towns and territory. The obstacle here is that neighboring territories and towns are often wildly opposed to being annexed to big cities. They are against it for various reasons: they don't want to be swallowed up by a giant; they don't want to be involved with the social problems of big cities; they don't want to be taxed by the city to help pay for the armies of police and social workers required to deal with those problems; they don't want their children bused.

Denver's Annexation Problems. A recent amendment to the Colorado Constitution makes it harder, not easier, for Denver to annex neighboring territories. This Poundstone amendment gave Denver exactly the same status as any other county of the state when it comes to annexing pieces of other counties. Before the amendment, the City and County of Denver was treated more like a city than a county for purposes of annexation. In Colorado it is easier for a city than for a county to annex neighboring unincorporated territory. When a city annexes territory, it generally needs the permission of a majority of the people who inhabit the area being annexed. When a county annexes neighboring territory, it is striking off a piece of another county, and the Colorado Constitution gives territorial integrity to counties by saying, "No part of the territory of any county shall be stricken off and added to an adjoining county, without first submitting the question to the qualified voters of the county from which the territory is proposed to be stricken off; nor unless a majority of all the qualified voters of said county voting on the question shall vote therefore." (Art. XIV, Sec. 3.) Because Denver, under the recent amendment, is now treated as a county rather than a city for purposes of annexation, all the voters of the entire county whose territory is being taken — not only the voters within the territory being annexed — would have the right to go to the polls and approve or disapprove by majority vote. Counties tend to have some pride: they are not likely to vote in favor of surrendering territory, although Adams County voters in 1989 did cede land to Denver for an airport. Before the Poundstone amendment, Denver was the only county in the state that could strike off pieces of other counties without the consent of the county being cannibalized.

When the City and County of Denver annexes territory, the school district boundaries (there is only one district in Denver) move with city-county boundaries: the two boundaries are made coterminous by the Colorado Constitution. School District Number One of Denver was recently the target of a court order requiring significant racial busing. The United States Supreme Court has held that the state constitution permits busing within, but not across, certain political boundaries, if necessary to achieve racial balance. Every new piece of territory annexed by the City and County of Denver falls into Denver's school district and becomes immediately subject to busing, which could take children far, wide, and deep into Denver. Many suburban people have fled Denver precisely to avoid busing and to avoid the many troublesome and expensive problems of Denver. The Poundstone amendment was put on the ballot at the behest of suburbanites surrounding Denver as a measure for self-protection against Denver and its school district. It slows Denver's expansion and spurs the drive for other forms of metropolitanwide government in the Denver area.

Annexation by Colorado Cities. Colorado's annexation laws do not make annexation especially easy for cities. Basically, these laws, like those of most states, require the prior consent of the people in the annexed territory. Thus, all the forces of suburban separatism are encouraged.

To be specific, the procedure by which a Colorado city or town annexes neighboring unincorporated territory is as follows: first, the territory must have a common boundary with the city; in fact, one-sixth of the boundaries of the territory to be annexed must abut the city. A petition is circulated among property owners in the territory to be annexed; if more than 50 percent sign it and if those who sign own more than 50 percent of the land, the city council may annex without an election, by passing an ordinance of annexation.

Annexation may also be accomplished by election. If the city council receives a petition signed by 10 percent of the qualified electors in the area to be annexed, or 75 such electors (40 in counties with a population under 25,000), the council may annex the area after an election in which a majority of qualified electors and landowners (who may vote even if they are not qualified electors) approve the annexation.

One point in Colorado law favors the right of cities to annex despite the wishes of people in the area to be annexed: a provision that permits cities to annex by simple ordinance any area completely surrounded by a city, providing the area has been surrounded for three years. None of these procedures apply to Denver, which, being a city-county, must annex like a county.

EXTRATERRITORIAL JURISDICTION

A partial solution to the need for metropolitanwide government is to give the central city power over some matters beyond its borders. For example, a city might be empowered to control contagious diseases within, say, three miles of its territorial limits. Or cities might be given jurisdiction over water courses for, say, ten miles beyond their limits, control over industries, garbage nuisances, cemeteries, vice, and immorality, and the power to quarantine within so many miles beyond their boundaries. Recent proposals to give Colorado cities extraterritorial jurisdiction have failed in the legislature and have been opposed by lobbyists for counties. Naturally, any extraterritoriality by cities would be at the expense of county power. Colorado cities such as Colorado Springs do have power to extend certain services beyond the city limits, resulting in a certain extraterritorial influence. The idea of giving cities extraterritorial power is criticized for being undemocratic: it gives a municipality power to control the affairs of people beyond its borders without their consent. Also, extraterritoriality is a rather piecemeal approach to the problem of metropolitan government.

REGIONAL SERVICE AUTHORITIES

The greatest obstacle to establishing metropolitan government is the hostility of persons and interests who would lose power, prestige, and identity. Take identity: people who have pride in Colorado Springs might object to merging the city with some larger unit of government because it would cease to be Colorado Springs. If the name *Colorado Springs* were retained to identify the new, larger unit of government, people who live in the suburbs would object to losing their identity.

Stronger, perhaps, than the political opposition of those who fear loss of identity would be the opposition of bureaucrats, elected officials, and numerous vested or special interests who fear loss of jobs and power. A city-county consolidation would mean, for example, that either the chief of city police or the county sheriff would be dispensed with, and maybe both of them would have to go. If there is consolidation of a collection of cities and towns with the county, many police chiefs would see their jobs vanish; not only the chiefs but the chiefs' lieutenants and whole police departments could lose their jobs. They might be merged into the new metropolitan police department, but who knows how that restructuring would affect status and career. Fear of the unknown would play its role. The fears of police chiefs and police officers would be mirrored in every department of every government about to be swept into the web of a new supergovernment. Not only bureaucrats, but elected office-holders look with sidelong glances at proposals that would put them out of office. And why should a vested interest, say the building industry, that possibly holds the sympathetic support of a majority on the city council wish to see that council shorn of power over planning, zoning, and building inspection?

Colorado voters added a provision to their state constitution in 1970 to help the process of consolidation and centralization of county services. (Art. XIV, Sec. 17.) The amendment allows formation of regional service authorities, which may provide almost any function, service, or facility authorized by statute. Such a service authority may be set up to cover several counties and numerous towns, providing them with one or more services that each would otherwise have to provide for itself. A service authority is really a multipurpose special district. No such authority may be set up unless a majority of the voters within the territory to be included approves the proposal. Service authorities may not overlap. A service authority may, however, include as much or as little territory as its founders wish: it may include a part of a county, a whole county, several counties, or parts of several counties, although the state constitution, true to its peculiar style, has something special to say about the Denver metropolitan area. Here it provides that any regional service authority formed in the Denver metropolitan area must include all Denver and all, or portions of, Adams, Arapahoe, and Jefferson counties as well. But a service authority may not include only parts of municipalities. The General Assembly determines by statute the functions, services, and facilities that may be provided by a service authority and the manner in which the members of the governing body are to be elected. Although a service authority may provide any function, service, or facility permitted by statute, each provision must be approved by the electors of the district.

METROPOLITAN GOVERNMENT IN THE DENVER AREA

The City and County of Denver is surrounded and overlain by a multitude of other local governments, some of them populous and powerful. More than half of Colorado's twenty-five largest cities are in the Denver metropolitan area. Denver directly abuts three other counties: Adams, Arapahoe, and Jefferson, each of which is among the most populous counties in the state (their combined population is three times that of Denver itself). Whenever Denver expands its boundaries, it must do so at the expense of one or another of these three counties. Denver, to repeat, is itself a county and, therefore, can grow only by taking pieces of other counties. Boulder County, northwest of Denver, is also considered by the United States Census Bureau to be a part of the Denver metropolitan area, although Boulder County has no direct border with Denver and is safe, at least for the present, from losing territory to Denver.

Within Adams, Arapahoe, and Jefferson counties there are more than two hundred units of local government, including about forty cities and towns. Some of these cities are very large in population and would shine more brightly if they were not standing in the glare of Denver. These cities include Aurora, Littleton, Englewood, Arvada, Lakewood, Wheat Ridge, and Westminster. Besides the governments just mentioned, there are about fifteen school districts in Adams, Jefferson, and Arapahoe counties, plus about 185 special districts. It is tricky to coordinate the efforts of all these units of government and to get them all working together on metropolitan-area problems.

The union of the City and County of Denver in 1902 produced a unitary government for the Denver metropolitan area that operated successfully in the first half of the century. In 1900 the city-county had about 140,000 people (fewer than the City of Colorado Springs today, and far fewer than the present-day Colorado Springs metropolitan area). In 1902 Denver encompassed only 58.72 square miles. For about forty years Denver remained comparatively free of overlapping units of government, although there was a separate school district and the Denver Water Board acted somewhat independently, even if officially part of the city-county government. In general, the metropolitan area was highly unified, systematic, and simple in form. Denver's city-county form was hailed as an ideal form of metropolitan government that avoided the problem of overlapping, competing governments.

That idyllic state of affairs does not prevail today. Since the Second World War, a proliferation of governments in the metropolitan area has resulted in strife and bickering over jurisdiction and gross deficiency in coordination and cooperation among them. Joint planning has been wholly inadequate. The city-county government has changed from the status of a single metropolitan government to one of many overlapping governments. Denver's status is now that of a *core city* surrounded and overlain with a profusion of competitors and neighbors. The present population of the Denver metropolitan area is well above 1.5 million, and over two hundred governments share authority, of which the City and County of Denver is only one.

Denver continues to provide some metropolitan services and to behave as the lion in the jungle. The Denver Water Board furnishes water to large parts of the metropolitan region outside Denver proper, and the City and County of Denver administers a variety of services benefiting the whole metropolitan area. For example, it maintains several mountain parks, provides a regional airport, and maintains large stadium facilities.

Efforts have been made since 1950 to bring order out of chaos by various plans for metropolitanwide government. Several successes have been chalked up (although they cannot be called complete successes): in 1960 the Metropolitan Denver Sewage Disposal District No. 1 was set up, which now handles sewage treatment in three-fourths of the Denver metropolitan area; in 1961 the Metropolitan Capital Improvement District (MCID) was established to provide capital improvements and capital equipment for Denver and three adjacent counties. The MCID, however, was ruled unconstitutional on grounds that the legislature lacks authority to give powers to a special district when those same powers have been reserved to home-rule cities by the state constitution. In 1969 an Urban Drainage and Flood Control District was set up, partly in reaction to flooding of the South Platte River. The district makes plans for preventing future floods and for handling storm water runoff. Also in 1969 the legislature set up a Regional Transportation District (RTD) to serve Denver, Adams, Arapahoe, Boulder, Jefferson, and Douglas counties. The transportation district has the duty of developing, maintaining, and operating a mass transportation system.

The foregoing agencies do not by any means constitute a complete answer to metropolitan problems in the Denver area. They touch a few problems, but not all. Each agency is a one-purpose special district, providing a single service. No all-encompassing agency has been established to coordinate them as more and more single-purpose local special districts are set up. Each district attacks a single problem piecemeal, which in itself creates a need for coordination. There are many who argue that the Denver region needs a multipurpose agency that can attack numerous problems, especially such problems as planning for growth, planning for land use, and dealing with tensions between the City and County of Denver on the one hand and suburban areas on the other.

Attempts have been made to set up regional government in the Denver area by amending the state constitution to allow such supragovernments to do numerous things now reserved to home-rule cities. A plan by the Governor's Local Affairs Study Commission to amend the state constitution to permit the legislature to set up "urban counties" was introduced in the general assembly in 1965 and 1966 but didn't pass. This plan would have swept away almost all special districts and consolidated their existing functions, plus various additional functions, into one government. The municipalities would have been retained, but with limited powers. A similar proposal was introduced in 1966 and 1967 to set up a multipurpose metropolitan service authority in the Denver area, but this, too, failed.

However, a voluntary association of local governments in the Denver region was set up in 1966, which is now called the Denver Regional Council of Governments (DRCOG). It is more of a confederation than a federation: that is, it is an organization in which member governments participate only while they continue to be so inclined: it is not the permanent, legal, and binding marriage that a federation should be. Because it is voluntary, the organization does not have the strength and internal cohesion to deal with controversial issues that a federation would have. While it does serve as an intergovernmental clearinghouse for mutual consultation and exchange of views and makes technical studies of such problems as drainage and population trends, it has very little decision-making authority.

In 1970, as noted earlier, an amendment to the Colorado Constitution directed the state legislature to enact a law providing for the creation of regional service authorities. Promptly, an attempt was made to get voters of the Denver metropolitan area to create a regional service authority (to be known as the Urban Service Authority). Unfortunately for its advocates, the proposal lost by a narrow margin in a 1973 special election.

In 1975 the federal department of Housing and Urban Development, among others, supported a study of the Denver metropolitan area that led to establishment of a Denver Metropolitan Study Panel, which, after a two-year study under the guiding spirit of the Denver Urban Observatory, recommended establishment of a Denver Metropolitan Council as a regional service authority with responsibility mainly in the area of comprehensive planning for Adams, Arapahoe, Denver, and Jefferson counties. The study panel tried to get the Colorado General Assembly to pass an act placing the issue on the November 1978 ballot. This narrowly failed in the legislature. There was considerable opposition from those who

feared the council might foreshadow a mighty regional government
superseding the powers of local governments on matters such as
zoning and schools. Many suburban county commissioners and
elected suburban municipal officials actively opposed the idea,
which on the other hand was supported by the *Denver Post,* the
Denver and the Colorado League of Women Voters, and the Denver
Chamber and Junior Chamber of Commerce. After their setback in
the legislature, proponents of a Denver Metropolitan Council then
tried to put the issue on the November 1978 ballot via the petition
route but were unable to get the twenty-two thousand signatures
needed.

In 1990 the Colorado General Assembly spent a lot of time
perfecting a bill to establish a Metropolitan Transportation Authority that would control most of the money for transportation development in the six-county Denver metropolitan area. As the bill made
its way through the legislature, it acquired more enemies than it
could survive. Provisions were written into the bill that would
earmark a certain proportion of the transportation money (including
hundreds of millions in federal urban transportation aid) to this or
that form of transportation. This bothered the people campaigning
for light rail, and it bothered the people campaigning for more
freeways. Insofar as the bill sought to finance light rail by transfer-
ring control of the proceeds of a .5 percent sales tax (about $10
million a year) away from the Regional Transportation District to
the new Metropolitan Transportation Authority, it naturally in-
curred the mortal hostility of RTD.

Worse, perhaps, was that part of the bill that would have given
the new Metropolitan Transportation Authority power to plan future transportation development in the metropolitan area. This
made sense, one would think. Certainly if you are going to set up an
agency to guide future transportation development, it would be
insane to deny it power to plan future transportation development.
But giving the proposed new Metropolitan Transportation District
planning authority would invade the turf of the Denver Regional
Council of Governments that currently has planning authority. Of
course, DRCOG's hostility by itself was no great threat to the bill.
DRCOG is only a feeble organization, a loose conglomeration of the
representatives of some forty local governments, with no power to
do anything but make recommendations. But behind DRCOG's

hostility was the pique of many mayors, city council members, and county commissioners within those forty governments. These elected local officials have enormous clout with state legislators. They were upset by the idea that a Metropolitan Transportation Authority would be just another competing and dominating layer of government above them. The bill, which did not consolidate but left existing agencies intact, failed to pass.

Parties and Pressure Groups 5

CHAPTER OUTLINE

The structure of parties in Colorado is a jungle of committees, assemblies, conventions, caucuses, and officers so complex that probably not one citizen in ten thousand could describe it. The apparatus of each party consists primarily of three hierarchical systems prescribed by state law: (1) the designating assembly system, whose purpose is to decide which names will appear on the party's primary election ballot, (2) the convention system, whose central purpose is to send delegates to the national presidential nominating convention, and (3) the committee system, which is mainly concerned with administering the party and campaigning for the party's candidates. Over and above the statutory party organization, each party has affiliates and auxiliaries such as the Young Republicans and Young Democrats.

THE PRECINCT CAUCUS

The foundation of the Colorado party structure is the precinct caucus. A precinct is the neighborhood political unit, containing up to one thousand registered voters, including those registered as

affiliated with a political party as well as those registered unaffiliated. Of course, only Republicans attend the Republican Caucus in
each precinct, and only Democrats the Democratic Caucus. The
precinct caucus leads to everything else in the party. Among its
duties are to elect two precinct committeepeople, select delegates to
party assemblies, and recruit election judges. Candidates for office
will often try to encourage their friends and supporters to attend a
caucus. At a caucus, these supporters can get themselves elected as
delegates to party assemblies, where they can help get the candidate
on the primary election ballot.

On the first Monday in April of every even-numbered year, the
registered voters of each party within each precinct may attend and
vote in the precinct caucus. (Any registered voter of a given party
who is present at that party's caucus is a voting member of it,
providing he or she has affiliated with that party at least two months
before the caucus and has lived in the precinct at least thirty-two
days.) It is not necessary to have an invitation to attend. The time
and place of precinct caucuses are announced by the county clerk
and are usually published in the newspapers. The headquarters of
each party in each county will also know when and where each
caucus in the county is to be held.

THE COMMITTEE SYSTEM

COUNTY CENTRAL COMMITTEE

The precinct committeepeople elected by each precinct caucus
belong to the county central committee. Other members of the
county central committee include the elected county officials of the
party; any elected state official, district attorney, state senator, state
representative, or United States senator or representative belonging to the party who resides within the county; plus the county party
officers. The county central committee meets between the first and
the fifteenth of February of odd-numbered years to organize. This
they do by selecting a chairman, a vice-chairman, and a secretary.

STATE CENTRAL COMMITTEE

The state central committee of each party consists of the chairman and vice-chairman of each party county central committee,

AN OVERVIEW OF
POLITICAL PARTY ORGANIZATION IN
COLORADO

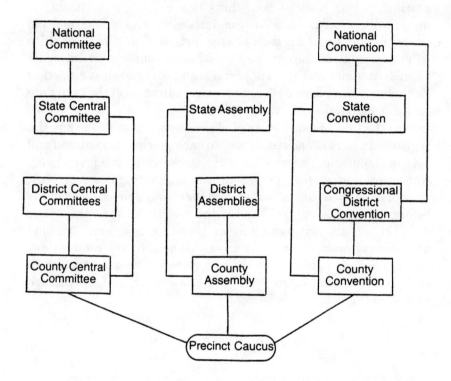

together with any of the following elected officeholders belonging to the party: United States senators, representatives in Congress, governor, lieutenant governor, secretary of state, state treasurer, attorney general, members of the Board of Regents, members of the state Board of Education, state senators, and state representatives. There is a bonus system for counties, geared to the size of the party's vote in the preceding general election. If a county party polled at least ten thousand votes for its candidate for governor or president, that county is allowed to send two additional persons to sit as members of the state central committee. And to sweeten the pot still more, two additional members are allowed for each additional ten thousand votes, or major portion thereof. These additional members are elected by the county central committee.

OTHER DISTRICT CENTRAL COMMITTEES

Each party within each election district has a district central committee. Thus, in addition to the county and state central committees mentioned above, there are congressional district central committees (for members of the state Board of Education, Board of Regents, and members of Congress), judicial district central committees (for district attorneys), state senatorial district central committees, state representative district central committees, and county commissioner central committees (in counties with five commissioners).

A degree of similarity in the composition of these various committees exists, but the details differ, and these details are defined with precision in Title I, Chapter 3 of the *Colorado Revised Statutes,* which may be found in most public libraries. These district committees are usually composed primarily of the chairmen and vice-chairmen of the various county party central committees within the district, and in some cases a county's representation on a district committee may be augmented by two bonus members for each ten thousand votes cast in that county for the party's candidate for governor or president.

ORGANIZATIONAL MEETINGS

All party central committees except the county central committee meet between February 15 and April 1 of odd-numbered years to organize by electing a chairman, vice-chairman, secretary, and vacancy committee.

WHAT DO THE CENTRAL COMMITTEES DO?

The party's state central committee has power (1) to pass upon and determine all controversies concerning the regularity of the organization of that party within any congressional, judicial senatorial, or representative district or within any county, (2) to pass on the right to use the name of the party, and (3) to make all rules for party government. The main function of the various central committees of the party is to advance the cause of the party through the organization and management of campaigns and by other means.

THE ASSEMBLY SYSTEM

Party assemblies are involved in what is sometimes called *preprimary nomination,* a practice not common in other states. In Colorado, the assemblies, to put it as plainly as possible, nominate (designate) party candidates for nomination. These candidates for a party's nomination, together with any others who become candidates for nomination through the petition process, go before the rank and file of party voters at the primary election. The rank and file decides who among the candidates for nomination shall become the party's actual nominee to run against nominees of other parties and organizations for each office. Thus, to get your name on the general election ballot it is ordinarily necessary to win designation by a party assembly and to win in the primary election. Then, to actually win the office, it is necessary to win in the general election. The first big hurdle in this laborious process is the assembly.

THE COUNTY ASSEMBLY

Delegates to county assemblies are elected at precinct caucuses on the first Monday in April in even-numbered years (known as *precinct caucus day*). The county central committee fixes the number of delegates from each precinct to participate in the county assembly. Then, on precinct caucus day, each precinct "elects" its quota of members. "Elects" is in quotation marks because in actual practice, most precinct meetings are so small that the problem is to find people willing to spend a day at the county assembly. A precinct caucus, often composed only of nine or ten people sitting in a schoolroom, will probably be conducted quite informally. Anyone who wants to go to the assembly simply says so. If there should happen to be more who want to go than the number allotted, then, while tea and cookies are served, it is decided who "really" wants to go, who "more or less" wants to go, and who "doesn't care." Finally, it's agreed that the individuals who "really" want to go will go, and if there are some seats left over, then a couple of those who "more or less" want to go will fill them. The "don't cares" are invited and often drafted to attend the county convention as alternates. There are as many alternates as there are delegates. Alternates do not vote unless one of the precinct's delegates fails to show up, in which case one alternate takes his or her place.

When only nine or ten people show up for a precinct caucus (a very common occurrence) and six delegates and six more alternates have to be chosen, there is usually opportunity for everybody to participate at the county assembly. Not every precinct caucus is so lightly attended, however. Some are well attended — by twenty or fifty or a hundred people, and in some caucuses factional lines are drawn, strict parliamentary procedure is followed, and seats at the county assembly are hotly contested. But that is the exception, not the rule.

If you are elected as a delegate to the county assembly, you very quickly find yourself courted by the various candidates of your party who seek county offices: candidates for sheriff, commissioner, clerk, treasurer, and so forth. Candidates for state representative and state senator are also interested in you — even candidates for state and national office — for reasons to be explained. The assembly will be held in some large hall, perhaps in a school auditorium.

There were about six hundred delegates at the Republican assembly that I covered. Together with alternates and miscellaneous other people, perhaps a thousand people filled the auditorium. The great hall was festooned with the political banners, placards, posters, and advertising of candidates for various state, county, congressional, and legislative districts. The candidates themselves were there, including several aspirants for state office, to shake the hands of delegates. Seekers after state office knew that several hundred of these delegates from the county assembly would soon be going to the state assembly and would have an influence on nominations there.

On every seat in the hall was a collection of political literature on candidates — some of it slick and interesting and clever and colorful, some of it dull and pedestrian. Presumably the delegates would read this literature and look at pictures of candidates during the long, dull hours of the all-day meeting. Inside the hall and at the doors and corridors leading to it hovered candidates and their helpers, passing out more literature, shaking hands, calling as many people by first name as possible. Some of the more prosperous candidates were represented by troops of good-looking girls clad in eye-grabbing uniforms.

The assembly opened, typically, with prayers, pledge of allegiance, and national anthem. During the course of the day Chairman Frank Klotz brought every candidate within sight to the platform to say a word or two. Most candidates have learned to be brief; one candidate for Congress limited his remarks to, "Hello, how are you?" When the hard-core business of the assembly commences, there are nominating speeches on behalf of candidates for various county offices, followed by seconding speeches. All the speeches proclaim the same thing: the candidate is honest, articulate, intelligent, a great guy (or gal), a good Republican (or Democrat, whichever assembly you're attending). If he is an incumbent seeking reelection, he is said to have done wonders while in office; if he is not an incumbent, he is said to be gravely needed in the office. He is said to be a good family man — his children are named and his wife introduced. (This drumbeat of hard-hitting speeches, all beginning with the words, "Fellow Republicans (or Democrats, as the case may be), it gives me great pleasure to nominate a . . . ," continues through the long hours until, with benumbed brain, you pick up some campaign literature off the floor and lazily draw elaborate designs on it. All this is made more thrilling if the air-conditioning system breaks down.

Voting is done, for the most part, by voice. Candidates must get at least 30 percent of the votes to put themselves on the primary ballot in August. The prize is getting *top-line designation* on the ballot. The candidate, say for sheriff, who gets the most votes (above 30 percent) at the county assembly is rewarded by having his name put first on the ballot, that is, at the top of the list. The names of others designated by the assembly for the same office are placed beneath his in descending order of the number of votes they received at the assembly. Top-line designation is important for two reasons, the most important of which pays tribute to the unawareness of many voters. Statistical evidence shows that about 20 percent of the primary election voters don't know one candidate from another and simply vote for the name at the top of the list. Top-line designation, therefore, sometimes sways an otherwise close contest. A second value of appearing first on the ballot is the knowledge held by a good many party members that top-line designation implies a strong endorsement by people at the county assembly who do know the candidates. This influences some voters.

In voice voting, the question is put to the whole assembly and usually everybody shouts "Aye!" The reason many votes are by voice and that everybody shouts "Aye" is that for many offices there is either an incumbent who is not challenged within his party or there is only one candidate for a vacancy. When there are two candidates seeking a place on the primary ballot, the assembly is often thrust into a tedious voting procedure. In the populous counties this is done by a call of the precincts. As each precinct is called, a committeeperson walks to a microphone in the aisle and reports how many votes there are in the precinct delegation for each candidate: "The 101st precinct: two votes for Jones, six votes for Smith," or something like that. Or the voting may be done by paper ballot, with elaborate procedures to assure that exactly the right number of ballots is handed out and that no one gets a ballot who isn't properly entitled to have one. When the candidates for county office have been designated for the primary ballot, the convention breaks up into representative and senatorial district assemblies.

REPRESENTATIVE AND SENATORIAL DISTRICT ASSEMBLIES

Representative and senatorial district assemblies are often held on the same day and at the same place as the county assembly because delegates to the county assembly are often also delegates to the senatorial or representative districts within which their precinct is located. The situation is somewhat more complicated where one of those districts includes parts of more than one county. In that case the delegates to those district assemblies are often forced to meet at some place and day other than the day of their county assemblies.

Often the legislative district assemblies are routine and uneventful. Ordinarily an incumbent legislator is not challenged in his own party, and the district assembly consists of nothing more than the standard nominating speech describing him in lofty terms and two or more seconding speeches. The whole business can be over in a jiffy.

The picture can be quite different, however, where there is a contest. One or two votes may spell the difference between getting the 30 percent required for designation or not getting it. Elaborate procedures may then be taken to see to it that no one is allowed to vote who is not a proper delegate or alternate and that no one votes more than once. Precautions in the voting procedure can at times overshadow everything — the entire assembly may seem to be little more than a tedious, tiresome, exasperating process of calling the roll of delegates precinct by precinct and placing a ballot in the damp palm of each and every individual entitled to vote.

CONGRESSIONAL DISTRICT ASSEMBLIES

Delegates to congressional district assemblies (and to the state assembly) are elected by the county assemblies from among their own members. But how do the huge assemblies of large counties such as El Paso go about electing several hundred people to serve at these higher assemblies? It would be out of the question to nominate and elect them one by one. The Democrats vote their preferences among candidates for the United States House and Senate and for governor. Then, with the results of this preferential vote known, the county assembly proceeds to apportion delegates to the state assembly and to the congressional district assemblies among candidates in proportion to the percentage of support won by those candidates. It is done as follows: first, those who support the various candidates gather in separate caucuses. Then, anyone who wants to attend the assembly (congressional district or state assembly, as the case might be) puts his or her name in a hat and the allocated number of delegates and alternates is drawn. Some special accommodation is given in this delegate selection process to the leaders and key workers of candidates.

Republicans of El Paso County use a somewhat more hierarchical mechanism for selecting delegates to state and congressional district assemblies. Not burdened by a principle of fair reflection, the decision is left up to party leaders who select people for the state and congressional district assemblies from among persons who had previously volunteered to go when the precinct caucuses were held. Each district leader and the precinct committee members of the district have a meeting to decide which volunteers would be named to attend the congressional district assemblies. The slates of all districts in the county are then combined, and one long slate of over two hundred names is put before the county assembly. The slate is usually approved without many attempts to refine it by nominations and deletions from the floor.

A congressional district assembly ordinarily has only one basic duty: to designate party candidates to run in the August primary election for the United States House of Representatives. If there is an incumbent member of congress of the party, he or she is not likely to be challenged, and the assembly turns into a campaign rally for him or her. This happened a while ago at the Fifth Congressional District Assembly of the Republican Party in Denver held the day before the Republican State Assembly. Bill Armstrong heard himself nominated in glowing terms as an honest man (as if honest men were almost unheard of), and many other fine things were said by those who seconded his nomination. There were standing ovations and waves of applause after each speech, especially after the candidate's acceptance speech. Then the campaign workers for Armstrong went to work mobilizing the assembly, or as much of it as possible: buttons, balloons, bumper stickers, pencils, lapel pins, and whatnot were distributed to each delegate, along with a card for use in volunteering time or money to the cause. The picture changed radically two years later when there was no incumbent, Bill Armstrong having vacated his seat in the lower house to run for the upper house of Congress. Kenneth B. Kramer of El Paso County and Robert Eckelberry of Arapahoe County battled it out for top-line designation. The assembly was wild and exuberant. It designated Kramer. But two years later the assembly shifted back to its campaign-rally mode when Kramer was redesignated. Research might show that contests for designation are more common in the majority party than in a minority party. The minority party may thank its lucky stars to have any candidate at all who is willing to fight an uphill and probably hopeless battle.

Occasionally, also, congressional district assemblies have other duties besides designating a candidate for Congress. There are several state elective offices wherein the election is limited to a congressional district. For example, the Colorado State Board of Education is made up of members elected from each congressional district of the state; likewise, the Board of Regents of the University of Colorado, although some members are elected from the state at-large.

THE STATE ASSEMBLY

Of the three levels of academic degree — B.A., M.S., Ph.D. — it is sometimes whispered that M.S. means "more of the same" and Ph.D. means "piled higher and deeper." The same might be said of the three levels of party gatherings: the county assembly, the state assembly, and the national convention. All are alike in character: the state assembly is like the county assembly of a large county only bigger, noisier, and more pompous. It is definitely "more of the same."

It was a sunny, hot July morning when I arrived in Denver to cover the a Republican State Assembly in Currigan Exhibition Hall. Outside the hall a frenzy of last-minute campaigning prevailed: giant placards, streamers, eager hands, and smiling faces doling out campaign literature to the throng of arriving delegates. Hank Brown workers gave everybody a "Brown bag" with a piece of fudge inside. Dave Sunderland's people offered oversized "Sunderland" pencils with which to properly mark one's ballot. There were badges, buttons, and stickers; there were booklets, pictures, and cards. Strickland people supplied bright red cowboy hats to all who believed in "TED," and it was a sea of red hats that later carried the day for Strickland. Joe Shoemaker advanced his gubernatorial hopes by thoughtfully providing plastic bags bearing his name in large letters. However, Bill Armstrong's giant hot-air balloon would not fit any of Shoemaker's plastic bags. Just as I arrived, a balloonist stepped aboard the gondola, the crowd retreated, a jet of roaring, flaming gas fed the bag, and the great sphere slowly ascended. Upturned eyes saw a mammoth Armstrong streamer unfold.

I finally turned away from these spectacles and walked into the lobby of Currigan Hall. But a similar hullabaloo was going on in there, too. Shoving my way through the lobby toward the doors of the exhibition hall, I was interrupted by a gracious Jack Swigert worker who offered me a bite-sized donut covered with powdered sugar. In my soaring imagination I could associate this tasty globule with the white moon around which astronaut-candidate Swigert sailed in the ill-fated Apollo XIII flight. Hours later, when Swigert's name was put in nomination, hundreds, maybe thousands, of small white plastic balls were tossed high by his many champions.

I was late for the invocation. This disappointed me; I wanted to see if the clergyman was again to be introduced as "one tremendous Republican," in the manner his predecessor four years previously had been introduced. However, I arrived in time for the "Star-Spangled Banner." Four years ago the entire crowd attempted to sing the anthem, high notes and all. This year it was done professionally by a high soprano who rendered it from the stage straight into a sensitive microphone that drove every decibel through the air like bullets, lancing ears and transfixing everyone with awe and terror. Finally the music ended, and the Pledge of Allegiance began, recited by five thousand less-piercing voices.

I sat toward the back of the hall in an area reserved for guests and alternates, who were strictly segregated from delegates seated in their own ghetto, well forward where they could see the platform. The hall enclosed enough of the cosmos to fly an airplane. From where I sat, people on the platform looked like ants. Powerful field glasses, or a telescope, would have been useful. However, the loudspeakers worked well (as did the air conditioners), and it was possible to follow proceedings in perfect comfort and clarity.

In general one cannot find fault with arrangements for this assembly, although it was thoughtless of the managers not to provide beds for delegates. Chairs were dangerous to dozing delegates, who risked striking their heads on the floor. At least alternates should have had beds. The peril to alternates was greater, as they had absolutely nothing to do during the long day but wait for the possible death or absence of delegates.

Some three thousand delegates were elected to the assembly, and another three thousand alternates. El Paso County elected 257 of each type. Believe it or not, every El Paso County alternate present for duty after 5:00 P.M. got to vote on candidates for five of the nine offices to be filled. This came to pass because the less glamorous offices (secretary of state, state treasurer, and three vacancies on the Board of Regents) were dealt with last on the agenda, after the sun had set and hundreds of delegates had gone home. Of course, many alternates were also AWOL. In fact, there were not enough El Paso delegates and alternates put together to cast all 257 votes. (The uncast votes were prorated according to votes cast.) Thus, no alternate who stuck it out to the bitter end was left with a feeling of utter uselessness when the closing gavel fell.

The most exciting time at the assembly came at dusk, after a long day of speechmaking and voting. A lonesome delegate stood and spoke into a microphone by the aisle. The great loudspeakers brought his voice seemingly from all directions: he could have been right or left, near or far. No matter. What he said thrilled the assembly. He proposed a change in the rules to speed things up: he proposed to combine five caucuses into one. The assembly, he said, should quit trying to caucus regarding each office separately, but should listen to all the nominating speeches for all the remaining offices (state treasurer, secretary of state, and three regents) and then have one omnibus caucus in which delegates would vote their preferences for all five vacancies. That would avoid four caucuses.

Caucuses were very time-consuming. It was, of course, easy for delegates from a county such as Mineral or Custer or Gilpin, with only three or four delegates, to caucus right in their chairs on the floor of the assembly. But counties such as Denver, Jefferson, or El Paso, with hundreds of delegates, had to get up and leave the convention hall and reassemble in another building across the street, where the roll of delegates had to be called, name by name. If any delegate was absent, an alternate had to be called to take his place. This procedure skirted the limits of sanity, and was, of course, tedious and lengthy. Hour upon hour was spent at it. After each caucus, the masses of delegates trooped back to the convention hall. Then began another tedious process: each county, one by one, had to report its vote.

By the time delegates had repeatedly filed back and forth to caucus on United States Senator, governor, lieutenant governor, and attorney general (the glamour offices), they were weary of it. And so came this voice from the floor, proposing to combine five caucuses into one. The house went insane with joy. It cheered, whistled, shouted, applauded as if the Denver Broncos had scored a touchdown. I was gratified to see such spirit. Indeed, I had waited all day for something like this, all day for some show of intense life, for some issue, cause, belief, or matter of deep faith that would stir the hearts of these delegates and release a tide of holy commitment. Here, at last, we had it! It came in the form of this lonely delegate whose motion said it effect, "Let's try to get the hell out of here at a reasonable hour."

Still, it was midnight before I got home. And I wondered why all nine caucuses couldn't have been combined into one, as they had been at the Democratic State Assembly in June, or why, in fact, the whole voting process couldn't be handled by mail ballot, avoiding the assembly altogether. If all those thousands of delegates and alternates who sit so many long hours at party assemblies would spend an equal number of hours helping candidates on the political front line, the party would be unconquerable.

THE CONVENTION SYSTEM

CONVENTIONS

When I first came to Colorado I was curious to know the difference between a convention and an assembly in Colorado. It seemed to me that the work of assemblies (that is, designating candidates for possible nomination to public office) was what I had always been taught is the work of conventions. When I asked people to explain the difference, they couldn't. I went to the county headquarters of a major party and asked to have the difference explained, and even they seemed hazy.

Possibly part of the reason for this confusion in many minds is that conventions in Colorado are held only every four years, and people tend to forget about them betweentimes. When they do meet, the delegates attending the conventions are often the same people attending assemblies. In fact, assemblies and conventions are often held at the same day and place to save time. Nor can it be claimed that the work of assemblies is totally different in nature from the work of conventions. Both have to do with the process of getting party candidates nominated. The big difference between assemblies and conventions is that the convention system is concerned only with the presidency and vice-presidency of the Untied States, while the assemblies are concerned with numerous state, congressional, and local offices.

In Colorado, the convention system is organized roughly like the assembly system: there are county conventions, congressional district conventions, and a state convention. But there are no representative district, senatorial district, or judicial district conventions.

PRESIDENTIAL PRIMARY

Heretofore, one purpose of the convention system has been to pick delegates to the national party convention (which, of course, nominates the party's candidates for president and vice-president). As we go to press, it is it not clear just what role, if any, Colorado's convention system will have in the selection of delegates to national party conventions in light of the new presidential primary law of 1990. The law seems to leave it up to each party to make use of the presidential primary results as they see fit, all to be governed by party rules.

The Colorado presidential primary will be conducted somewhat like other state primaries. The presidential primary elections of all political parties are held at the same time and at the same polling places and are conducted by the same election officials. The cost of the primary (that is, of running the election) is paid for by the county or state. In order to vote in such a primary, one has to be registered to vote and affiliated with a political party. Each voter may vote only for presidential candidates of the political party to which he or she is affiliated. Any political party that is represented by a candidate may participate in the presidential primary.

But just because you are, say, a Democrat, you can't just put your name on the presidential primary election ballot for the fun of it. To be placed on the ballot you have to be eligible to receive payments under the federal Presidential Primary Matching Payment Account Act, (26 U.S.C. 9031 et seq. and 11 C.F.R. 9033.3 [3]). To be eligible under that federal law, one must, among other things have raised $5,000 in each of twenty states in amounts of $250 or less. Furthermore, no political party may participate in the presidential primary unless it received at least 20 percent of the vote in the last presidential election. In Colorado, that means only the Democratic and Republican parties may have candidates on the presidential primary ballot. The names of candidates appearing on any presidential primary ballot are set in alphabetical order.

The purpose of Colorado's presidential primary is to help the political parties select delegates to the national party conventions at which candidates for president are nominated. Just how these results are used in the delegate selection process by each party depends on the rules of each party. Delegates selected by input from this primary are not pledged or bound to vote for the candidate to which they have been allocated, except to the extent that this may be permitted or required by party rules.

THE ELECTORAL COLLEGE

The state convention nominates candidates for a curious and little-understood elective office in Colorado: that of presidential elector. Presidents not only have to be nominated, but also elected, as everybody knows. Technically they are not elected by the people but by presidential electors, who are elected by the people. In

Colorado, the Republican state convention and Democratic state convention each nominates eight electors, and those two sets of electors (together with the slates of electors nominated by political organizations described on p. 112) run against one another in the general election. When the average voter casts his vote for his or her favorite presidential candidate, that voter is actually voting for one or another of those slates of eight would-be electors. Whichever slate gets the most votes is elected and those eight persons become officeholders in the sense that they hold the office of elector.

Colorado law requires each presidential elector to vote for the presidential candidate who receives the highest number of popular votes in the general election. However, this law is of doubtful constitutionality. The United States Constitution gives authority to the electors to decide who should be president, and they are free to vote for anyone they want. However, for reasons of party loyalty, electors almost invariably vote for the presidential nominee of their party's national convention.

The *electoral college,* composed of the electors of all states, elects the president. There is no general meeting of the college; each state's electors meet at the state capital in December of presidential election years and vote in the manner predicted by the election returns a month and a half before, in November. The office of elector is in practice honorary, and each party state convention will nominate people for the office who have served the party or contributed to the party in various outstanding ways. Recently one candidate for elector in the Democratic Party went to the microphone at a congressional district convention and told the assemblage that she thought she deserved to be nominated for the office of elector because she "had worked damned hard for the party and deserved the honor." She was promptly nominated but failed to become an elector because the Republican presidential nominee, not the Democratic candidate, carried Colorado that year.

The state convention does one other important thing: it elects two national committee persons (historically a man and a woman). These are important elections; the national committee is the supreme governing and administrative board of a party between national conventions.

PARTY PLATFORMS

Any party assembly or convention may adopt a platform for the political subdivision it represents. This is not customarily done with any thoroughness beneath the state level, although conventions and assemblies are fond of adopting resolutions from time to time on subjects that especially agitate them. At the state level, there is special machinery provided in the state election laws for adopting state party platforms. Briefly, the party's candidates for state and federal office, plus a party's incumbents in those offices whose terms continue on, and a few others meet every even-numbered year to draft a state party platform. Few people pay any attention to these platforms, and the platform is almost never mentioned in the course of a campaign. Most candidates prefer to run on their own platform, program, or position statement.

PARTY BALANCE

In Colorado there are two major parties: Republican and Democratic. In recent years about 34 percent of all registered voters in Colorado have been registered Democrats, 28 percent Republicans, and 38 percent unaffiliated. Democrats outnumber Republicans, although the number of unaffiliated voters exceeds the number of those registered with either party. It cannot be said that either party dominates in Colorado. Control of statewide offices and of the legislature and the United States senatorial and congressional seats, has shifted back and forth between the two major parties in recent years. Political parties other than Democratic and Republican that have run candidates in recent Colorado elections include La Raza Unida, Socialist Workers, American, Libertarian, Colorado Prohibition, and People's. None is technically qualified as a political party under Colorado laws; such parties are termed *political organizations.*

PRESSURE GROUPS

Who runs Colorado? Are there hidden forces steering the ship of state? Certainly there are forces. The extent to which they are hidden depends on how hard you look, but it is safe to say that most people in Colorado are, to some degree, ignorant of the forces at work. A good deal is hidden from all of us simply because we don't and can't know everything.

There are political forces everywhere, influences everywhere — groups, associations, clubs, firms, individuals. Barbers, for example, commonly want the state government to keep the number of barbers down and price of haircuts up. The organized professional barbers therefore quite naturally try to influence state legislators to establish a barber board with power to license barbers and set the minimum price of haircuts. To call barbers a hidden or sinister force may be stretching things, depending on how you view it and how keen you are about what's going on. Every organized profession, whether insect exterminators, brain surgeons, or municipal court judges, is a force. Anybody who wants anything from government and takes trouble to go after it is a force. Probably everyone reading this book wants something from government (say an education) and belongs to some group (say a student association) that attempts, among other things, to influence power holders. This is not necessarily sinister. It is simply politics.

Most politics in America and in Colorado have nothing to do with political parties; it is outside and beyond parties. It is called pressure politics: the attempt of people as individuals or as groups to get what they want from government through the exercise of influence. This kind of politics is not illegal, nor is it necessarily wrong, nor is it unconstitutional. In fact, it is protected by the First Amendment to the United States Constitution, which guarantees the right of people to assemble and petition their government. Colorado's constitution promises the same freedom. Pressure politics, interest group politics, all that vast realm of politics that goes on beyond parties and that dwarfs parties, is as American as apple pie. It is the heart of what we call representative government. Pressure politics is simply the process by which groups (sometimes individuals) go about the business of letting some part of the government know as forcefully as possible what they want, why they want it, and what they are prepared to do to get it.

A lobbyist spends most of his time educating power holders as to what he wants and why it is a good idea to let him (or the people he represents) have it. Being a lobbyist, by the way, is not a bad line of work for political science majors, both men and women; it involves knowing where power lies, how to manipulate and influence it, and how to organize and package information for the benefit of power holders.

Chapter 9 concerns pressure-group politics in the state legislature. But pressure groups do not limit themselves to pressuring the legislature; they attempt to influence every center of power in (and out of) government, and it is worth noting that those various centers of power in the government also lobby each other. Research might show that more lobbying, more pressuring, more political arm twisting, if you will, is done by government agencies than by private groups. It is absolutely false to imagine that pressure groups are simply private groups. In truth, the various arms, branches, and agencies of government are also pressure groups. Big business and big labor are not the most powerful lobbies in Colorado. Public state employees may have a more effective lobby than big business or labor. Bureaucrats lobby to protect and increase their own programs and have more power in the state than the governor. Many government agencies go so far as to employ professional lobbyists and pay tax money to join associations that lobby for them. Examples of such associations are Colorado Counties, Incorporated; the Colorado Municipal League; the Colorado District Attorneys Association. There are many others.

Professional lobbyists are required to register with the secretary of state. Each must give his name, business address, business phone, as well as the name, address, and phone number of any person by whom he is employed as a paid lobbyist. Professional lobbyists must also regularly file disclosure statements with the secretary of state reporting such things as the total sum of all payments personally received for lobbying during the calendar year, the name and address of everyone who has given the lobbyist more than $50 during the year for the purpose of lobbying, the name and address of everyone to whom an expenditure of $50 or more has been made in connection with lobbying, and the name of any official to or for whom expenditures of more than $50 have been made by the lobbyist for gift or entertainment purposes in connection with lobbying. None of this applies to volunteer lobbyists, or to citizens who lobby on their own behalf, or to state officials acting in their official capacity, or to political committees, or to individuals testifying as witnesses before legislative committees.

A recent list of registered professional lobbyists issued by the Colorado secretary of state includes the names of more than 350 individuals, representing some four hundred employers. An impressive fraction of these lobbyists is employed by public agencies, including, for example, the Aurora Public Schools, the Cherry Creek School District, the Colorado State University System, the Denver Police Department, the Denver Water Department, and so on. Additionally, each principal department of state government is permitted to designate one employee of the department to be in charge of lobbying for that department. There are approximately twenty such persons designated, and they coordinate the activities of a hundred or more assistants all told. Professional registered lobbyists, plus department designated lobbyists and their assistants, plus volunteer lobbyists add up to five hundred or more lobbyists roaming the hallways of state government. Lobbyists, to repeat, do not limit themselves to lobbying the legislature but touch every point in government, most of which are in the bureaucracy, where there is power to help their cause.

Some states of the American Union are so dominated by a single economic interest or by a tiny group of interests that all other pressures upon state government take second place. That cannot be said of Colorado, though it might be said of some local governments. We have no single overwhelming economic interest dominating the state as a whole (unless perhaps it is the state government itself, the largest employer in Colorado). The public bureaucracy (state and local) is undoubtedly the greatest force in Colorado politics, the greatest influence upon government, and will become even more influential as it becomes bigger and better organized. If one were to lay bets on which of Colorado's special interest groups is likely to show the largest growth of power and influence during the next generation, one might want to put money on the state's organized public school teachers. They are not only multiplying their power through organization but also through a new consciousness of that power and a new willingness to participate actively in politics. As a group they have prestige in the community and a great deal of knowledge about a great many things, including knowledge of how power is mobilized and used.

Interests that have spent the most money in recent legislative races in Colorado have been these, listed roughly in the order of the

magnitude of their campaign contributions: realtors, labor union-
ists, educators, home builders, brewers, commercial and industrial
firms, mine owners, doctors, construction trades, general contractors, chiropractors, dentists, public utilities, apartment house owners, oil companies, and ophthalmologists.

Elections 6

THE ELECTORATE

In Colorado, almost every citizen of the state who is at least eighteen years old, who has resided the requisite length of time in his or her precinct, and who is registered to vote is eligible to vote (*C.R.S.* 1–2–201 [1]). Even a person confined in a state institution for the mentally ill does not lose the right to vote simply because of such confinement, and in fact, such a person has a right, upon request, to be assisted in obtaining voter registration forms and in making application for an absentee ballot. A prisoner, on the other hand, who is serving a sentence may not vote, although a confined prisoner who is merely awaiting trial retains his or her right to register and vote. A person released from prison may also vote.

THE RESIDENCE REQUIREMENT

To register to vote in Colorado a person must, among other conditions, be a resident in the state and in his or her precinct for thirty-two days (*C.R.S.* 1–2–101 [1] [b]) before election day. Residence for purposes of voting means to be domiciled in the state and in the precinct. A person might have two or more places of residence but by law may have only one domicile. A domicile is where one lives with intent to make it a fixed and permanent home. A person who resides in two places may vote in only one, the place where he or she is domiciled.

Under Colorado law the residence of a person is the principal or primary home or place of abode of a person. That means a place in which a person's habitation is fixed and to which he, whenever absent, intends to return regardless of the duration of such absence (*C.R.S.* 1–2–102 [1] [a]). But students beware. This definition of residence does not necessarily apply to the determination of residence or nonresidence status of students for any college or university purpose (*C.R.S.* 1–2–103 [3]). Colleges and universities have their owns rules about such things. A residence is a permanent building, or part thereof, including a house, condominium, apartment, room in a house, or mobile home. Vacant lots are not considered a residence.

In determining the residence of a person, the following circumstances relating to that person are taken into account: business pursuits; employment; income sources; residence for income or other tax purposes; age; marital status; residence of parents, spouse, and children, if any; leaseholds, location of personal and real property; and motor vehicle registration (*C.R.S.* 1–2–102 [1] [b]). For purposes of voting in Colorado, no person gains residence by virtue of presence in the state for military service or presence as a student or presence for institutionalization, such as imprisonment. On the other hand, no one loses residence because of absence for military service, absence to attend school, or absence because of institutionalization (*C.R.S.* 1–3–103 [1]).

One purpose of a residence requirement is to give registration officials time to do paperwork connected with preparing a list of eligible voters. Another purpose is to prevent people from voting who are just visiting or passing through. A third purpose is to insure that those who vote are part of (and somewhat familiar with) the community for at least a while before they vote.

Some political scientists believe residence requirements should be kept short. The United States is a highly mobile society, and a large part of the electorate is disenfranchised by moving. (State and local residence requirements apply to national elections for national officers as well as local.) Although there may be merit to the contention that people should live in a community for a while before voting there, doing so would hardly be much help in preparing one to vote for national officers, unless one is a brand new United States citizen.

Colorado has in recent years reduced its residence requirements in the state from one year to thirty-two days (twenty-nine days for voting for president and vice-president [*C.R.S.* 1–8–201]), and from ninety days in the county to thirty-two days in the precinct. In the Voting Rights Act of 1970 (84 Stat. 314), Congress provided that any person who has lived in a district for thirty days is eligible to vote for national officers. Congress apparently thought thirty days was ample time to protect the state's interest in preventing fraud. The United States Supreme Court agreed with this in 1972 (*Dunn* v. *Blumstein,* 405 U.S. 330).

AGE

By tradition, a person ceases to be a minor and passes into the age of majority at twenty-one years. That has long been considered *full age,* the age at which a person is entitled by law to manage his own affairs and enjoy civic rights such as the right to vote. In recent years that tradition has been abandoned insofar as the right to vote is concerned. During the Second World War, Georgia lowered its voting age from twenty-one to eighteen. Part of the thrust for this came from the idea that if an eighteen-year-old can be drafted, he can vote. "Fight at 18, Vote at 18!" was the cry in Georgia. Some advocates of the lower age also argue that eighteen-year-olds are better educated today than in a former era and that the voting strength of the youthful portion of the population should be augmented because older voters are increasing in numbers and are more likely to take the trouble to vote than younger ones.

In 1971 the United States Constitution was amended (Twenty-sixth Amendment) to permit eighteen-year-olds to vote; to be precise, the amendment forbids the United States or any state to deny any person who is eighteen or over the right to vote solely on the basis of age. Colorado law provides that every person who, on the date of the next ensuing election, will be eighteen and who possesses the other qualifications for voting is entitled to vote (*C.R.S.* 1–2–101 [1]). If you are not quite eighteen but will be on the date of the next ensuing election, you may register to vote before your eighteenth birthday, provided you will have resided in the state of Colorado for thirty-two days as well as in the precinct for thirty-two days before the election (*C.R.S.* 1–2–101 [1] and 1–2–212.5 [2]) and are a citizen of Colorado.

CITIZENSHIP

Colorado, like all other states, requires a person to be both a United States citizen and a citizen of the state to be eligible to vote (*C.R.S.* 1–2–101 [1] [b]). In Colorado one must have been a citizen of the state for at least thirty-two days to acquire the right to vote in state and local elections (*C.R.S.* 1–2–101 [1] [b]) but only twenty-nine days to vote for president (*C.R.S.* 1–8–201).

LITERACY

The Colorado Constitution (Art. VII, Sec. 3) seems to invite the legislature to make an educational qualification for voting, but it has not done so. A Colorado voter need not know how to read or write in order to register to vote; he or she may sign the registration form with an X, if necessary. Thus, Colorado cannot be accused of race or class discrimination disguised as a literacy test, as have several other states.

Powerful arguments can be made for a literacy test, fairly and nondiscriminatorily applied. Illiterate people are not well equipped to inform themselves of issues or candidates and cannot even read the ballot. On the other hand, in this day of universal elementary and secondary education very few people are illiterate, and the trouble it takes to exclude them from voting far exceeds the damage they might do by voting. Furthermore, there is evidence that voters get most of their political information by watching television and listening to radio, not by reading.

REGISTRATION

There is a rather sterile dispute among political scientists as to whether registration should be included in the list of qualifications for voting, alongside age, residence, and citizenship, or whether registration should be considered merely a mechanism whereby persons already qualified to vote go about registering their names for future identification at the polls. No one may vote who has not registered. Obviously, whether you call registration a qualification or a mechanism, the result is the same.

Registration has not always been required in advance of casting a ballot. Although registration as a means of preventing voting frauds was used as early as 1800, most states (including Colorado) adopted registration procedures between the end of the Civil War and 1910. In that era, "good government" forces fought for voter registration as a means of verifying who was eligible to vote. The system substantially reduced voting fraud but did not end it.

Almost all states, including Colorado, have some variety of permanent registration, a system wherein once you have gone to the county clerk (or other official) and put your name on the list of eligible voters, your name stays on that list until, because of failure to vote or for some other reason, it is removed.

PURGING THE REGISTRATION ROLLS

Without a system for removing the names of voters who have moved away or who habitually don't vote, the registration rolls in the various precincts would soon be loaded with phantom voters. This opens the door to voting fraud wherein, for example, individuals posing as others who have died or moved away could cast many votes, especially where election officials are in cahoots with the fraud. As registration rolls grow larger by making registration easier, a speedy and efficient removal system (purge system) becomes all the more imperative. Besides inviting fraud, voter rolls inflated by phantom voters are expensive because additional names result in creation of more precincts with more paid officials and equipment. The costs of election campaigns are also increased. And in any case, voters are annoyed when strangers are shown as registered to their address. And good citizens by the hundreds despair when the voter turnout on election day is revealed to be so small a proportion of the total number of registered voters, not realizing that half the graveyard is still registered to vote. Voter turnout statistics grow more accurate as the purge system becomes more efficient.

Colorado now has a reasonably competent purge system (*C.R.S.* 1–2–222). Either of two events triggers the process of removing a voter from the roll of registered voters. The first trigger is initiated just before each primary election, when every registered voter is sent a nonforwardable information card. If that card is returned as "undeliverable," the name is flagged as "inactive." Later, if that person does not vote in the next general election, then he or she is mailed a nonforwardable "continuance" card. If that card is not filled out by the person and returned to the county clerk or if it is returned by the post office as undeliverable, the name is removed from the registration rolls.

A second thing that triggers the removal of a registered voter from the registration rolls is the failure of that voter to vote in the general election. Such a person is flagged as inactive. If such a person does not make current his registration information and does not vote in the next primary or general election, he will then get a nonforwardable continuance card. If that card is not filled out by the person and returned to the county clerk or if it is returned by the post office as undeliverable, the name is removed from the registration rolls.

AFFILIATION

In Colorado, one may be registered without stating an affiliation with any political party. Such a person is called *unaffiliated.* A person registered with a party is called *affiliated.* At present there are only two political parties with which one can affiliate. This is because no political organization can achieve the legal status of political party in Colorado unless its candidate for governor receives at least 10 percent of the total vote cast for that office in Colorado. Only the Democratic and Republican parties have achieved the needed 10 percent. One may state a preference for a *political organization* as opposed to a political party, but one may not affiliate with a political organization. If one states a preference for a political organization, he or she will be registered as *unaffiliated* (*C.R.S.* 1–2–205 [1]). Thus, one cannot affiliate with, say, the Communist Party. But, to repeat, one can register a political preference even while remaining unaffiliated. Thus, one could indicate a preference for the Communist Party if one chose to do so, and this preference would be entered on one's registration form. If in some future election the Communist Party or any other political organization were to achieve the requisite 10 percent in an election, then one could actually affiliate with that party.

The other variety of registration (not used in Colorado and little used elsewhere) is called *periodic registration.* Under this system the voter must periodically register, whether or not he or she regularly votes. It has the advantage of keeping the registration lists accurate and up-to-date but is expensive for the state and inconvenient for the voter. The periodic system also has the virtue — or vice — of discouraging the least diligent from voting. Because the least diligent are apt to be the poor and the young, it is said to favor conservatism. As a matter of fact, all forms of registration are to some degree deterrents to voting.

It is not always necessary to make a visit to the county clerk's office to register. Clerks in Colorado are authorized at their discretion to establish small branch offices (mobile registration sites) in temporary locations, where individuals may register (*C.R.S.* 1–2–212). One often sees these in shopping center malls and other convenient locations. Branches are open for several weeks preceding the registration deadline before primary and general elections. In addition to these branches, the Department of Revenue, through its driver's license exam facilities, is now required to provide each qualified elector who applies for the issuance, renewal, or correction of a driver's license an opportunity to register to vote (*C.R.S.*

1–2–215.5). The voter registration and the driver's license application are on the same piece of paper, providing a more forceful invitation to register than one sees in states where "motor voter" registration consists only of making the voter registration form available to those who ask for it. About a dozen states now use some form of motor voter registration.

The last date to register to vote in primary and general elections is twenty-five days before the election (*C.R.S.* 1–1–113), but one must still have been a resident of the precinct for thirty-two days (*C.R.S.* 1–2–101 [1] [b]).

REQUIREMENTS THAT COLORADO DOES NOT HAVE

It may be of interest to mention a few voting requirements with which Colorado is not and has not been afflicted. First among them is the literacy test, discussed above. Also, we do not have poll taxes, which are unconstitutional if payment is a prerequisite for voting. The Twenty-fourth Amendment to the United States Constitution, adopted in 1964, made such poll taxes unconstitutional in all elections for national office. And in 1966 the Supreme Court declared the use of poll taxes in elections for state officers unconstitutional. Colorado did not have a poll tax and was not affected. Nor does Colorado impose any requirements relating to the morality or character of the voter, such as the "good character test" once used in several states to inhibit voting by certain minority races. Nor did Colorado ever have "white primary" laws, which operated on the theory that political parties have a right to exclude anyone they wish from party membership and thus from the primary. Such laws were held unconstitutional by the Supreme Court in *Smith* v. *Allwright*, 321 U.S. 649 (1944). Colorado was not troubled by the decision.

WHO MAY RUN FOR OFFICE

In Colorado, state, county, and district offices carry different qualifications, but one qualification is common to all: no person except a qualified voter may be elected to any office in the state. From there on the requirements differ.

Member of the General Assembly (both House and Senate): No person may be a state representative or senator who is not at least twenty-five years old and who has not lived at least one year before election within the district wherein he or she is a candidate.

Governor: Must have resided within the limits of the state two years preceding election and be at least thirty years old.

Lieutenant Governor: Must have same qualifications as governor.

Secretary of State: Must have same qualifications as governor, except for age. He or she must be at least twenty-five years old.

State Treasurer: Must have same qualifications as secretary of state.

Attorney General: Must have same qualifications as secretary of state, and must also be a licensed attorney of the Colorado Supreme Court.

Regents of the University of Colorado: Must be at least twenty-one years old and be qualified electors within the congressional districts they represent, if they are district members.

District Attorney: Must be at least twenty-one years old and be a qualified elector of the district he or she represents and must have been licensed to practice law in Colorado for at least five years.

County Officers: Must have resided in the county for one year preceding election.

State Board of Education: Must be qualified electors within the congressional districts they represent, if they are district members.

THE PRIMARY ELECTION

Occasionally, when voters go to the polls to vote at a primary election, they are slightly annoyed when asked what party they belong to. (Primaries occur on the second Tuesday in August of even-numbered years [*C.R.S.* 1–4–101].) Such a voter may have been taught that the ballot is supposed to be entirely secret, that people shouldn't have to tell anyone what party's candidates they intend to vote for. However, the primary election, as opposed to the general election that comes later, is strictly a party affair. It is an occasion when the members of a political party vote to decide who shall be the party's nominees for whatever offices are to be filled. It is entirely reasonable then, at an election of this sort, for election

1	**OFFICIAL BALLOT FOR DEMOCRAT PRIMARY ELECTION EL PASO COUNTY, COLORADO TUESDAY, AUGUST 14, 1990**

FOR UNITED STATES SENATOR **VOTE FOR ONE**	JOSIE HEATH	137 ▶
	CARLOS F. LUCERO	138 ▶
FOR UNITED STATES CONGRESS DISTRICT 5 VOTE FOR ONE	CAL JOHNSTON	140 ▶
FOR GOVERNOR VOTE FOR ONE	ROY ROMER	142 ▶
FOR LIEUTENANT GOVERNOR VOTE FOR ONE	MIKE CALLIHAN	144 ▶
FOR SECRETARY OF STATE VOTE FOR ONE	AARON HARBER	146 ▶
FOR STATE TREASURER VOTE FOR ONE	GAIL SCHOETTLER	148 ▶
FOR ATTORNEY GENERAL VOTE FOR ONE	DUANE WOODARD	150 ▶
FOR REGENT OF THE UNIVERSITY OF COLORADO AT LARGE VOTE FOR ONE	GUY J. KELLEY	152 ▶

A portion of a sample ballot; primary election, El Paso County, August 14, 1990, as it appeared on voting machines.

officials to find out who are Republicans and give them a Republican primary ballot and who are Democrats and give them a Democratic primary ballot. If a person is registered but not affiliated with a political party at the time of a primary election and nevertheless wants to vote in the primary, it is possible to do so by declaring a party affiliation at the polls on primary election day (*C.R.S.* 1–2–205 and 1–7–201 [2]).

The primary election is not the only way candidates are nominated, but today it is the most common method in the United States in elections above the municipal level. In Colorado, all party candidates for state, judicial district, county, and congressional offices are nominated in this manner, except when there is a vacancy of nomination and the party assembly vacancy committee has to do the job (*C.R.S.* 1–4–903). Independent candidates (*C.R.S.* 1–4–801) and the candidates of political organizations other than political parties (*C.R.S.* 1–1–104 [17]) are nominated by petition.

The primary election system of nominating party candidates was first used statewide by Wisconsin in 1904. The turn of the century was an era of electoral reform, wherein attempts were made to purify politics by curbing the influence of party leaders and expanding the influence of rank-and-file party members through such devices as the referendum, the initiative, the primary, and the recall. Thus, the primary system of nominating candidates gradually replaced the convention system. Prior to such reforms, party conventions had been held in which the party leaders decided who the party's nominees would be in the forthcoming general elections. This process had become ever more corrupt as contractors and other interests sought to buy the votes of convention delegates. Reformers said the best way to restore honesty to the nominating process was to let all the party members do the nominating instead of the party leaders — a whole party couldn't be bribed. Colorado adopted the primary system in 1910.

The primary has not been totally successful in curbing the power of party bosses in the nominating process. This is partly because so few people bother to vote in the primaries. Party activists do bother to go to the polls and are therefore able to sway the outcome of the nominating process. Party activists are, in turn, somewhat influenced by party leaders, who thus continue to hold some vestige of power. This is particularly true in Colorado, where party assemblies largely determine who appears on the primary ballot.

OPEN AND CLOSED PRIMARIES

Colorado has a *closed primary*. In a closed primary voters are given the primary ballot only of the party to which they have previously registered or to which they have declared their affiliation at the polls. In an *open primary* (not used in Colorado), voters may help nominate the candidates of whatever party they please, choosing their party in the secrecy of the voting booth without ever announcing a party affiliation in advance.

Professional politicians tend to prefer the closed primary for the obvious reason that it keeps outsiders from intruding. However, there are many people who do not want to reveal their party affiliation to employers or to anyone else. This makes the open primary attractive to such persons, who register as "independent" but in the privacy of the voting booth exercise a role in the nominations of the party to which they are secretly attached.

To vote in a primary election in Colorado, affiliated registered voters must have resided in their precinct for thirty-two days (*C.R.S.* 1–2–101 [1] [a]) and been affiliated with their party for at least twenty-five days (*C.R.S.* 1–2–202 [1] and 1-2-205 [1]) as shown on the registration books before they will be given the primary ballot of that party (except those who have just turned eighteen). However, to repeat, any unaffiliated registered voters may declare a party affiliation at the time they present themselves to vote at a primary election and may receive the ballot of that party (*C.R.S.* 1–2–205 [1]) and 1–7–201 [2]).

GETTING ON THE BALLOT

In Colorado, only political parties may use the primary election for nominating candidates. As we have seen, the term *political party* has a limited definition in Colorado law (*C.R.S.* 1–1–104 [18]). The statutes speak of political organizations (*C.R.S.* 1–1–104 [17]) and political parties. A political organization becomes a political party when at a general election its candidate for governor receives 10 percent or more of the total vote cast for governor, and a party ceases to be a party when it fails to get the said 10 percent (*C.R.S.* 1–1–104 [18]). When we talk of getting on the primary ballot, we are talking about people who want to be nominated by a political party. There are two ways to get on the primary ballot. One is by designation of candidates by what we call party assemblies in Colorado. The other is by petition. A political organization may not put its candidates on the general election ballot by caucuses or nominating assemblies.

They are forced under present Colorado law to petition (*C.R.S.* 1–1–104 [17]) to place candidates onto the general election ballot.

DESIGNATION BY PARTY ASSEMBLY

Party assemblies are discussed in detail elsewhere in this book. The designating assemblies of the various political parties must complete their work of designating candidates for the primary ballot no later than sixty-five days before the date of the primary (*C.R.S.* 1–4–601 [1]). No assembly may designate for nomination a candidate who has not been affiliated with the party holding the assembly for the period of time required by rule of the candidate's own political party (*C.R.S.* 1–4–601 [2]). The assemblies are forbidden to declare that any one candidate among those who receive the necessary 30 percent vote in the assembly has received the nomination. Assemblies, to repeat, do not nominate, they only designate candidates for possible nomination.

PREPRIMARY DESIGNATING ASSEMBLIES

The preprimary designation of candidates for nomination by party assemblies (or some variation thereof) is used in a few other states besides Colorado, including New Mexico, Utah, and Rhode Island, but it is not the most common method of placing names on the primary ballot. The more common way, the way used in most states, is by petition. This method is used in Colorado only by party members not designated by assemblies. (Independent candidates and the candidates of political organizations cannot use primaries for purposes of nomination and hence have no preprimary designations system. However, they are nominated for the general election ballot by petition.)

The Colorado system gives a great deal of power to the regular party organization, in other words, to the party activists and party leaders. The primary election system was designed to break the power of just that group. But when party regulars in Colorado were forced to accept introduction of the primary election system in 1910, they simultaneously pressed for and got a preprimary designating system. It cannot be said, however, that the power of party bosses is as firm and centralized under the post-1910 system as it was before 1910. Reformers gained a great deal of ground on that front.

There is something to be said for giving party regulars a large, but not complete, voice in the selection of candidates. Regulars are likely to know the strengths and weaknesses of candidates better than rank-and-file voters. Furthermore, if party responsibility is a virtue (as some modern reformers insist), then party leaders and regulars need some measure of control over the standard-bearers of the party.

DESIGNATION BY PETITION

Any person who has been affiliated with a political party for at least twelve months (*C.R.S.* 1–4–603 [5]) may petition onto the primary ballot of his party for that office, provided that person was not a candidate for designation at the party assembly and failed to get 10 percent of the assembly's vote for the office sought (*C.R.S.* 1–4–603 [5.5]). Such a person should not be confused with a member of a political organization (not a political party), who cannot use the primary election system at all and must get on the general election ballot by petition rather than by primary. Remember, we are talking about getting on the primary ballot, not the general election ballot, by petition. The law is not very friendly to those who want to petition their way onto a party primary ballot. The number of signatures required is high and, therefore, laborious and expensive to get. The exact number depends on what office is sought.

Every petition in the case of a candidate for any county office must be signed by electors resident within the county commissioner district or political subdivision for which the officer is to be elected, and such petition must have signers equal in number to 20 percent of the votes cast in the political subdivision at the last preceding primary election (*C.R.S.* 1–4– 603 [2] [a]). No person may sign a petition who is not a registered voter of the political subdivision for which the officer is to be elected and who is not affiliated with the party named in the petition (*C.R.S.* 1–4–603 [3]).

Roughly similar principles for designating party candidates by petition apply to other elective officers. In the case of a candidate for member of the General Assembly, district attorney, or any district office greater than a county office, the petition must be signed by not less than one thousand electors resident within the district for which the officer is to be elected or the petition must have signers equal to at least 30 percent of the votes cast in the district at the last primary election (*C.R.S.* 1–4–603 [2] [b]). In the case of statewide offices, the petition must be signed by electors in a number equal to at least 2 percent of the votes cast in such district at the previous general election for the party's candidate for the office in question (*C.R.S.* 1–4–603 [2] [c]).

It is not easy to collect all those signatures. The job is made even more difficult in Colorado, where each person who signs must state to the circulator (right there on the doorstep, where most people do sign) that he or she has been affiliated with the political party named in the petition for at least two months, that he intends to vote for the candidate at the ensuing primary election, and that he has not signed any other petition for any other candidate for the same office (*C.R.S.* 1–4–603 [3]).

THE PRIMARY ELECTION

Nominations for most statewide, county, district, and congressional offices are made by primary election. There are three exceptions to this rule. One applies to presidential electors, who are not nominated by primary election but by party convention. A second exception is that candidates, to be elected at special elections, to fill vacancies in unexpired terms of representatives in the United States Congress may also be nominated by party committee. A third exception applies to independent candidates, who are nominated by petition, inasmuch as the primaries are reserved for parties and are not used by independents.

Though both political parties use separate ballots, they hold their primaries at the same time (the second Tuesday of August in even-numbered years) and same place, conducted by the same election officials. The primary is accomplished in the same way as general elections; election officials at primaries do essentially the same thing as election of officials at general elections. Although a primary election is for the use of political parties, the cost of these elections is not borne by parties but by the public treasury, in the same manner as general elections.

Candidates designated by a party assembly for a particular office are placed on the primary election ballot in the order of the number of votes received at the assembly. Beneath those names appear the names of candidates nominated by petition, in an order established by lot (*C.R.S.* 1–4–605).

Any registered elector desiring to vote in the primary election must write his name and address on a form available at the polling place and give this form to one of the receiving judges, who then announces the name. An election judge will look in the registration book or the computer list to see if the would-be voter is registered. If the name is found, the election judge likewise announces the name. If the registered elector's party affiliation has already been recorded on the registration sheet and his signature, initials, or properly witnessed mark and the date appear thereon, or if the computer list shows party affiliation, he will be given the party ballot of the party affiliation last recorded. If unaffiliated, the registered elector must openly declare to the judges of election the name of the political party with which he wishes to affiliate himself, and the name of that party will be written on the registration sheet or on the approved form for voter registration information changes in the space provided. Declaration of affiliation with a political party must be separately dated and signed by the registered elector in a manner so that he clearly acknowledges that his party affiliation has been properly recorded. Thereupon, the election judges deliver to the registered elector the appropriate party ballot, and the voter is allowed to enter the immediate voting area. If the registered elector declines to state a party affiliation, he is not entitled to vote at the primary election (*C.R.S.* 1–7–201 [1] [2]). The ballots are cast in the same manner as in general elections. The voter designates his choice of candidates on his party ballot and may not vote for more candidates for each office than are to be elected thereto at the general election as indicated on the ballot (*C.R.S.* 1–7–201 [5]).

SOME OBSERVATIONS ABOUT PRIMARY ELECTIONS

Earlier it was said that the primary election system had not been entirely successful in breaking the power of the bosses, partly because of the preprimary designating assemblies and partly because the primary election itself generally attracts mainly party activists. A large percentage of eligible voters is apathetic about the primary. Lack of interest in the primary is caused partly by the length of primary ballots. Voters know in their hearts they cannot very intelligently judge among all candidates and issues. Secondly, there is seldom any burning contest. Popular incumbents running for reelection tend to have the confidence of the rank and file of their party, if for no other reason than that they are proven winners.

Incumbents are generally sufficiently popular in the party to discourage challengers in the general elections as well as in the primaries. The absence of contest in most primaries increases the voters' sense of futility in taking the time and trouble to go to the polling place on election day. Also, many voters think the main action is in the general election, not the primary election.

Some people in our society are more likely than others to take the time and trouble to vote. Statistics show that property taxpayers are more likely to vote than others, conservatives are more likely to vote than liberals, older persons are more likely to vote than younger persons; the higher one's income and the more formal education one has, the more likely one is to vote.

One criticism of primary elections is that they add to the expense of elections. From the point of view of the taxpayers, it would be cheaper to nominate candidates by the convention system. As for candidates, they are often faced with having to spend money campaigning to win a primary election, whereas under the old convention system there was no campaigning, although it was necessary to win delegates to a convention. Another criticism of the primary election system is that it tends to produce serious and open conflicts between factions of a party. A primary divides parties. A convention tends to draw them together.

WRITE-IN CANDIDATES

Any voter, instead of voting for a candidate whose name is printed on his party ballot, may vote for any other eligible person who is a member of his political party and who has filed an affidavit of intent to be a write-in candidate pursuant to *C.R.S.* 1–4–1001 by writing the name of the person in the blank space immediately following the printed names of candidates for the office (*C.R.S.* 1–4–201 [6]).

GETTING ON THE GENERAL ELECTION BALLOT

Primary election winners go on the general election ballot, as do other independent candidates who are able to get on the general election ballot through the petition process.

INDEPENDENT CANDIDATES

In Colorado, independent candidates and the candidates of political organizations must petition to be placed on the general election ballot. The petition for each office must be signed by registered electors residing within the district or political subdivision in which the officer is to be elected. Many signatures are required, and this always makes the petition route difficult and expensive. The petition must have at least five-thousand signers for the office of president of the United States, one thousand for statewide office, five hundred when the office is to be filled by the registered voters of a congressional district. For member of the General Assembly, district attorney, or district office greater than a county office, at least one thousand signers are required or 20 percent of all the votes cast in the last preceding general election in the district for the office for which the petition is circulated, whichever is less. And when the nomination is for an office to be filled by the registered electors of a county, the petition must have at least six hundred signers, or 20 percent of all the votes cast in the county for the office for which the petition is being circulated, whichever is less (*C.R.S.* 1–4–801 [b]). No one may be placed in nomination by petition who has not been registered as unaffiliated for at least twelve months prior to the date of filing of the petition (*C.R.S.* 1–4–801 [i]).

GENERAL ELECTION BALLOT

Both the general election and the primary election ballots are *Australian,* meaning secret. We thus honor the Australians, who first introduced the secret ballot in the English-speaking world. Political scientists generally categorize ballots into two types with regard to arrangement of names on the ballot: *office block* (used in Colorado) and *party column.* The terms are fairly self-explanatory. In an office block ballot, the names of candidates are grouped together by the office they seek. In the party column ballot (not used in Colorado) candidates are grouped by party rather than by office: all the candidates of one party for all offices are listed in a single column, making it very simple for voters to pick their party and then go down the list checking every name. In some states where the party column ballot is used, a voter may vote for everybody in the column by simply making one X at the top. Obviously, party leaders often prefer the party column ballot because it fosters straight party voting.

1			
	OFFICIAL BALLOT FOR **THE GENERAL ELECTION** **EL PASO COUNTY, COLORADO** **TUESDAY, NOVEMBER 6, 1990**		

FOR **UNITED STATES** **SENATOR** **VOTE FOR ONE**	HANK BROWN	REPUBLICAN	43 ▶
	JOSIE HEATH	DEMOCRAT	44 ▶
	EARL F. DODGE	COLORADO PROHIBITION	45 ▶
	JOHN HECKMAN	CONCERNS OF PEOPLE	46 ▶
FOR **UNITED STATES** **CONGRESS** **DISTRICT 5** **VOTE FOR ONE**	CAL JOHNSTON	DEMOCRAT	48 ▶
	JOEL HEFLEY	REPUBLICAN	49 ▶
	KEITH L. HAMBURGER	COLORADO LIBERTARIAN	50 ▶
FOR **GOVERNOR/** **LIEUTENANT GOVERNOR** **VOTE FOR ONE PAIR**	JOHN ANDREWS LILLIAN BICKEL	REPUBLICAN	52 ▶
	ROY ROMER MIKE CALLIHAN	DEMOCRAT	53 ▶
	DAVID AITKEN MICHAEL L. FOLKERTH	COLORADO LIBERTARIAN	54 ▶
	WM. DAVID LIVINGSTON EARL W. HIGGERSON	COLORADO PROHIBITION	55 ▶

A portion of a sample ballot: general election, El Paso County, November 6, 1990, as it appeared on voting machines.

The Colorado office block ballot used in the general election divides each block into two groups, although only the trained eye can detect the distinction. In the first group, at the top of each block, are listed the names of the candidates of the two major political parties. Candidates for governor are listed in alphabetical order

jointly with their running mates. All the other major party candidates are listed on the ballot in an order chosen by lot (*C.R.S.*
1–6–403 [1]). In a second group, beneath the two major party
candidates but still within the same office block, the same scheme
is used for listing the candidates of political organizations that are
not considered political parties under Colorado law (*C.R.S.* 1–6– 403
[1]). Space is provided on the ballot for write-in candidates. Write-in
votes will not be counted unless the person voted for has filed an
affidavit of intent that he desires the office and is qualified to assume
its duties. This must be filed at least five days before election day.
The system for listing candidates on voting machines is somewhat
different (*C.R.S.* 1–6–404).

MUNICIPAL ELECTIONS

Elections in Colorado cities and towns are nonpartisan. There
is no party primary and, therefore, no formal preprimary party
designation system. Nominations are by petition on forms provided
by the city clerk. No voter may sign more than one petition for each
office to be filled. The office block ballot is used. The names of
candidates for each office appear on the ballot in alphabetical order
without any party identification or designation of the candidates'
business or profession. Spaces allow for write-ins.

Nonpartisan elections are common in the United States at the
local level. It is generally reasoned that there is no Republican or
Democratic way of collecting trash and that political parties introduce an unnecessary divisive element into elections. However, a
number of people argue that there is a Republican and Democratic
way of collecting trash and that differences of party philosophy
apply to the local level of government no less than to other levels.

METHODS OF VOTING

Three methods of voting are used in Colorado: the paper ballot,
voting machines, and electronic voting equipment (punch cards).
Whatever method is used, elaborate and precise measures are
taken to protect the integrity of the voting system. For paper
ballots, these procedures are set forth in *C.R.S.* 1–7–301 through

311; for voting machines, *C.R.S.* 1–7–401 through 407; for electronic voting equipment, *C.R.S.* 1–7–501 through 507.

VOTING MACHINES

If machines are used, they must by law afford voters an opportunity to vote in absolute secrecy, must be closed during the process of voting so that no one can know the number of votes cast during the progress of voting, must prevent voters from voting on any candidate or issue they are not entitled to vote on, must allow voters to vote on all they are entitled to vote on, must prevent voters from voting more than once, and must allow write-ins. Judges of election in each precinct meet forty-five minutes before the polls open to inspect voting machines and see to it that no votes have been cast — that the machine registers zero. If a voter asks for instructions concerning the manner of voting after entering the machine, two judges (of opposite political parties) are to give instructions. Each voter has three minutes in the voting machine, but judges in their discretion may allow a voter more time. Similar protections are applied to voting by punch card or other paper ballot.

ELECTRONIC VOTING EQUIPMENT (PUNCH CARDS AND BALLOTS)

Electronic voting is simply a system in which ballots are capable of being counted electronically (rather than mechanically as voting machines do, or manually as with paper ballots). This is often done with punch cards, by which the voter, using a small punching device, pushes a tiny hole next to the name of the candidate he or she wishes to vote for or next to the answer he wishes to give to a ballot issue. If punch cards are not used, then a ballot is used that is somewhat similar to a paper ballot but is marked by a marking device that can be read electronically. An X is marked next to the name of the candidate for whom the voter wishes to vote or next to the answer he wishes to give on a ballot issue.

Again, elaborate procedures are used to assure integrity of the system, procedures that involve the audible announcing of names and numbers by election judges both before and after the voter votes, et cetera. The voter is handed a ballot in a privacy envelope, goes into a closed booth, punches or marks his ballot, puts his ballot back in the privacy envelope so that the marks thereon are concealed and the stub can be removed without exposing any of the contents of the ballot or punch card, walks out, and lets an election judge tear off the stub. Then the voter deposits the ballot in the ballot box (*C.R.S.* 1–7–503). These ballots are then counted electronically by systems very precisely laid out by law (*C.R.S.* 1–7–505 through 507). If a voter has marked or punched more names than there are persons to be elected to an office, or if for any reason it is impossible to determine the choice of any voter for any office, his ballot is not counted for that office (*C.R.S.* 1–7–506 [c]).

If a voter spoils a ballot, he may successively obtain others, one at a time, not exceeding three in all, upon returning each spoiled one (*C.R.S.* 1–7–504).

VOTING BY ABSENTEE BALLOT

It is possible to vote by absentee ballot in any primary, general elections, or congressional vacancy election. Any registered elector of Colorado who expects to be absent from his precinct from 7 A.M. to 7 P.M. on the day of any such election, or who, by reason of his work or the nature of his employment, is likely to be absent or fears he will be, or who because of serious illness or handicap, elderliness, or because he will be abroad on said day, or because his residence within the precinct is more than ten miles from his polling place, or for religious reasons is unable to attend the polls, may cast his ballot by absentee ballot (*C.R.S.* 1–8–102).

Requests for an absentee ballot may be made orally or in writing (*C.R.S.* 1–8–103 [1]) and must be filed with the county clerk and recorder of the applicant's county of residence not earlier than ninety days before the election nor later than the close of business on the Friday immediately preceding the election (*C.R.S.* 1–8–102 (4)). The ballot has to be in the hands of the county clerk no later than 7 P.M. on the day of the primary, general, or congressional vacancy election. It is not sufficient merely to have it postmarked by then — it has to be in the clerk's hands (*C.R.S.* 1–8–114). The absentee ballot has to be signed in the presence of a notary public (or other person authorized to administer oaths) unless the voter is handicapped (*C.R.S.* 1–8–115).

VACANCIES IN ELECTIVE OFFICES

Vacancies in elective offices may be caused by death, impeachment, resignation, and/or (in the offices of the governor and lieutenant governor) conviction of a felony, or (in the office of lieutenant governor) by succession to the office of governor. All vacancies in state or county offices except that of member of the United States House of Representatives are filled initially by appointment, but all those appointed must have the qualifications required by law for election to such office.

When a Colorado vacancy exists in the **United States House of Representatives**, a special congressional vacancy election is called by the governor to fill the vacancy, but such an election may not be called within ninety days of a regularly scheduled general election. Major party candidates are nominated by conventions convened according to procedures determined by the state party central committees. Other candidates are nominated by petition.

If a seat in the **United States Senate** falls vacant, the procedure is much simpler: the governor merely appoints someone to fill the vacancy until the next succeeding general election, when an election is held to fill the remainder of the unexpired term (*C.R.S.* 1–12–101). The governor is not required to appoint a person of the same political party as the former member. A governor may appoint himself to the vacancy.

If a seat in the **Colorado General Assembly** (Senate or House of Representatives) falls vacant, it is filled by majority vote of the party vacancy committee of the same political party and of the same district represented by the former member, and it remains so filled until the next general election after the vacancy occurs, when the seat is filled by election (*C.R.S.* 1–12–103 [1]). The committee has ten days to make a selection, otherwise the governor makes the appointment (*C.R.S.* 1–12–103 [2]). Party vacancy committees are established every even-numbered year at the organizational meeting of each senate and house district party central committee.

Vacancies in **statewide elective offices** or in the **office of district attorney** are filled by appointment by the governor until the next general election after which the vacancy occurs, when it is filled by election (*C.R.S.* 1–12–104).

Vacancies in other **county elective offices**, except that of county commissioner, are filled by appointment by the board of county commissioners until the next general election, when the vacancy will be filled by election (*C.R.S.* 1–12–105).

The procedure for filling a vacancy on a board of **county commissioners** depends on whether the commissioners are elected by the voters of the whole county or by voters of a district. In either case, it is a party vacancy committee that fills the vacancy — a vacancy committee of the same political party as the former commissioner. If the former member was elected by voters of the entire county, then the vacancy is filled by a vacancy committee made up of members selected by the party county central committee of the former member's party. If, however, the former member was elected by a commissioner district, then it is the party vacancy committee of that district that appoints a successor. In either case, if the vacancy committee fails to fill the vacancy within ten days, the governor fills it by appointment. If the former member was unaffiliated, then the governor fills the vacancy with a registered unaffiliated voter. Any person appointed to fill a county commissioner vacancy holds the office until the next general election, when the vacancy is filled by election (*C.R.S.* 1–12–106).

Vacancies on most **municipal governing councils** are filled by individuals appointed by the council.

If the office of **governor** falls vacant, the lieutenant governor becomes governor, but if the office of lieutenant governor is also vacant, then the first named of the following officials who is of the governor's political party becomes governor: (1) president of the Senate, (2) speaker of the House, (3) minority leader of the Senate, (4) minority leader of the House. If none of the above four is of the governor's political party, then the first named of the four becomes governor.

Whenever there is a vacancy in the office of **lieutenant governor**, the governor nominates a new lieutenant governor, who takes office upon confirmation by majority vote of both houses of the General Assembly. This same procedure applies if the lieutenant governor accedes to the office of governor.

A vacancy in the state **judiciary** is filled by the governor from a list of names given to him by a judicial nominating commission and is subject to voter approval at the next general election.

Whenever there is a vacancy on the **Board of Regents of the University of Colorado**, the governor appoints a successor, who serves until the next general election, when the vacancy is filled by election (*C.R.S.* 1–12–104).

Whenever there is a vacancy on the **State Board of Education**, the governor appoints a successor, who serves until the next general election, when the vacancy is filled by election (*C.R.S.* 1–12–104).

CAMPAIGN FINANCE

To campaign for any office can be expensive. The cost depends on (1) the size of the election district, both in population and in physical area, (2) the strength of the opposition, and (3) whether there is a contest in the primary and/or general election. The cost of recent campaigns in Colorado for governor and United States senator by majority-party candidates has been roughly $2 million to $3 million. Candidates for state treasurer, secretary of state, and attorney general may spend in the neighborhood of $70,000 to get elected. The cost of campaigns for state legislature depends on various circumstances; $15,000 would get a candidate through the average state senatorial or state representative campaign. Some cost less, some far more. A large proportion of all campaign money comes from a wide variety of political action committees (PACs). In recent years this source has accounted for over half the money spent in campaigns for the Colorado General Assembly.

ANONYMOUS STATEMENTS CONCERNING CANDIDATES

To help trace the flow of campaign money, and for other reasons, Colorado law forbids anyone to publish or distribute material about a candidate that does not bear the name of those responsible. This applies to material concerning any person, whether a self-declared candidate or one declared to be a candidate by others without denial.

REPORTING CAMPAIGN EXPENSES

The Campaign Reform Act of 1974 is designed to assure public confidence in the representative government of Colorado through a more informed electorate. The act provides for public disclosure of campaign financing as well as regulation of certain campaign practices. There is no limitation on the amount that a candidate may accumulate or spend for a political campaign, but the Colorado law does require reporting of what is accumulated and spent. Most candidates for public office, and committees supporting or opposing candidates and ballot issues, must make a full and complete disclosure of contributions and expenditures. Also, the name and address of anyone who contributes over $25 must be reported, and so, too, must the name and address of anyone to whom an expenditure of $25 is made (*C.R.S.* 1–45–108 [4] [b]). All contributions of money received by a candidate or political committee must be deposited in a financial institution in a separate account whose title includes the name of the candidate or political committee. After the election, if there is any money left over, it may be contributed to the county or state central committee of the candidate's political party or to any other political committee on file with the secretary of state; or the candidate may keep the money for some future campaign, but it must be reported to the secretary of state every year until there is nothing to report. Likewise, campaign debts must continue to be reported every year until the debt is settled. No campaign contributions may be spent on any private purpose not reasonably related to the campaign.

All campaign statements filed with the secretary of state and the county clerk are subject to audit. Failure to file campaign statements in careful compliance with the act could result in civil and criminal penalties. All disclosure statements are available to the public for inspection. The Colorado Campaign Reform Act of 1974 does not apply to any federal office (such as United States senator), but candidates for federal offices are subject to the Federal Election Campaign Act of 1971 and its disclosure requirements.

HOW ARE ELECTIONS WON?

It may have been Senator Everett Dirksen of Illinois who said, "money is the mother milk of politics." Money is generally more important in large election districts than small. In small districts, small in population and compact physically, candidates can, if they really try, personally meet a large percentage of their constituents. In the larger districts, such as a congressional district, a state, a large city, or a large county, it is impossible for a candidate to come anywhere near meeting everybody face-to-face. In large districts candidates have to rely on the media of mass communication, an expensive proposition.

Winning an election involves communicating with the voters and prevailing on them to do the one thing you want them to do upon election day, namely, to go into a polling booth and vote for you. Psychologists, political scientists, politicians, and others have all sorts of theories about what makes people vote the way they do. Experts do not by any means agree on what motivates voters, and it is beyond the scope of this book to delve into the question. Many candidates believe voters are more likely to vote for someone they know (providing they know the candidate favorably) than for an unknown. It won't do to be known as an infamous bank robber, although it is said that in politics it is better to be infamous than unknown. In ordinary circumstances, in a contest between ordinary candidates, almost nothing is worse than being unknown. Most campaigns boil down to a matter of making as many voters as possible feel they know the candidate favorably.

This thrusts candidates into public relations programs with themselves as star performers. If the election district is fairly small, candidates can probably do themselves good by tramping around the district door-to-door, introducing themselves and handing out literature with their name, picture, life history, and statement of what they hope to do when elected. It is not easy to ring the doorbells of thousands of registered voters — that's a lot of walking. Of course, in the primary elections there's little point in going to the houses of people who aren't registered to vote or are registered in the other party. That still leaves thousands of front doors — a monumental, time-consuming, exhausting, and boring job. If the candidate wins in the primaries, then later, in the general election he or she can possibly afford to limit doorbell-ringing to unaffiliated voters, but even that adds up to several thousand doors. Doorbell-ringing does not seem a glorious or statesmanlike path to political victory, but political victory (especially in small election districts) is manufactured out of just that kind of menial work by the candidate and by the candidate's helpers.

To win, a candidate needs help, primarily with humble work. He or she does not need speechwriters as much as people to stamp, address, and seal envelopes; or intellectual work as much as physical work distributing leaflets door-to-door on election eve. College students sometimes shy away from the servile work of a campaign, wishing to do loftier things such as making speeches. Actually, candidates, when they can spare the time, must do the speech work themselves. What they need more than a speechwriter (and how many candidates need a speech written anyway?) are people who will hold coffee gatherings for them. A coffee has important value: just the process of phoning fifty or sixty people in a precinct and inviting them to a coffee makes them feel good about the candidate and at least draws his or her name to their attention. If only two or three people show up, a few might be willing to join the campaign or at least to put bumper stickers on their cars.

No candidate ever feels he or she has done enough in a campaign. There is always more to do and the need for more workers. From the point of view of the workers, it is a good way to learn something about politics and to do something about the ills of the world. A big part of winning an election is recruiting a large number of workers and keeping them busy; without their help, victory is unlikely. There is plenty of opportunity for any American to help change conditions by working for the election of good candidates. It is better to work in the campaign of a good candidate (or to be a candidate oneself) than to do nothing in the electoral system other than complain about its result.

RECALL ELECTIONS

The recall election is one of the reforms that came in side by side with initiative and referendum (discussed elsewhere) at about the turn of the century to restore democracy and purity in government. Every elective public officer in the state of Colorado except United States senators and representatives (who are national officers rather than state officers) may be recalled from office.

If you want to recall a public officer in Colorado, the exact procedure for doing so depends on which of several recall laws the officer falls under. If he or she is a state officer, such as governor, the state constitution describes in detail how to proceed; if a county officer, school district officer, or special district officer, various separate articles of the *Colorado Revised Statutes* apply; if a city or town officer, then the procedure depends on whether the city or town has a home-rule charter. If there is a home-rule charter, the charter prevails — if not, the *Colorado Revised Statutes* prevail. Every home-rule charter in Colorado is required to include provision for recall of officers.

Although there are separate laws providing for recall of state, county, statutory municipality, home-rule municipality, school district, and special district officers and although there are some differences among those laws, they are substantially alike in the procedures they provide for recall. The procedure for recall of officers in a city or town that does not have a home-rule charter is roughly illustrative of how all recalls in Colorado are accomplished. A recall election is initiated by petition. When the recall petition is circulated, it is supposed to include a statement for signers to read presenting the reasons why the recall is sought. This statement is limited to two hundred words. When the actual recall election is held, the same two hundred words appear on the ballot, and the officer being recalled may also publish on the ballot his side of the story in three hundred words or less. The reasons given by the pro-recall side need not necessarily be reasonable. No one may go to court challenging the reasonableness of the reasons.

The recall petition must be signed by enough people to equal 25 percent of the number of ballots cast for all candidates running for the office in question in the last preceding election. All signers must be registered to vote for the successor of the recalled officer. If the pro-recall side is successful in getting enough signatures on its petition, then a special recall election is called. The recall ballot is very simple. Voters are asked to decide two things. First, whether to recall the officer filed against and, second, whom to elect in his place. The recall and the election for a successor take place on the same ballot. The ballot presents the question, "Shall (name of person against whom the recall petition is filed) be recalled from the office of_____?" "Yes." "No." The aforesaid brief statements pro and con appear on the ballot. Also on the ballot are the names of persons nominated to succeed the officer filed against. It is not legal for a voter to vote for a successor unless he or she also votes either for or against recall. Nor is it permissible for the person filed against to be a candidate to succeed himself.

Recall is not easily accomplished. Securing the necessary signatures requires herculean efforts, not to mention additional signatures for the petition to nominate a successor. Surely any group contemplating the recall of an elected public officer would want to consider waiting for the next election to defeat their antagonist. After all, his or her term may be only two years. However, the increasing prevalence of four-year terms may make recall more worthwhile, providing it is instituted almost immediately after the officer is elected. Usually it takes a couple of years for an officeholder to make enough mistakes to warrant the mighty effort to accomplish a recall. In Colorado it is illegal to recall officers until they have held office for at least six months; this does not apply to members of the state legislature, who may be filed against five days after the legislature has convened, an exception that may go back to the time when the legislature met only once every two years for brief periods.

Some argue that it is a mistake to allow any procedure for recalling elected public officials: it gives powerful, well-financed special interest groups a threat to hold over the heads of public officials, depriving them of freedom of thought and action. If the threat of recall doesn't make public officials the tools of special interests, say the critics, it makes them slaves to the whims of public opinion.

Defenders of recall argue that the recall procedure is usually too difficult to make officeholders slaves of public opinion and that the existence of a recall procedure tends to make elected public officials more alert to the public than they might otherwise be. Possibly the existence of recall procedures has caused some people to favor four-year terms for public officers.

DIRECT LEGISLATION

Oddly enough, the constitution of Colorado begins its article on the legislative department (Art. V) with a lengthy section on how the people can act as their own legislature. In a sense, all the voters of Colorado constitute one huge legislature. When the constitution was first written in 1876, no such provision was included. The mechanisms for direct legislation by the people were added to the Colorado Constitution in 1910, partly as a result of thirteen years of agitation for such provisions by Populists, and partly because it was the style in that period to favor the *initiative* and the *referendum*. There was a good deal of popular distrust of government in that period — suspicion that it was controlled by special interests — and people needed a way to legislate directly, without interference by corrupt legislators and officeholders.

The direct legislative power that the people reserve to themselves is (1) the power to initiate, that is, to propose and enact state or municipal laws and state constitutional amendments and (2) the power to approve or reject any state or municipal legislation. The first is called the initiative and the second is called the referendum. Neither process is very easy.

THE INITIATIVE

Anyone who wants to propose a state statute or constitutional amendment directly to the people without first taking it to the legislature must be joined in proposing it by a substantial number of registered voters — enough to equal 5 percent of the number of votes cast for all the candidates running for secretary of state in the last general election in which that office was filled. The 5 percent must sign a petition, and the petition then has to be presented to the secretary of state at least three months before the election at which the initiative is to be voted upon (Art. V, Sec. 2). (See p. 148 for municipalities.)

Anyone who has tried to get signatures on a petition for anything knows how difficult it can be. To get hundreds of signatures long before the onset of election enthusiasm is doubly difficult. Ordinarily, securing that many signatures within the allotted time is not a job for an amateur. Still, the initiative has been used. Well over one hundred statutes and amendments (mostly amendments) have been proposed since 1912. Statistics show that roughly one in five constitutional amendments proposed by initiative has passed, but the passage rate was much greater in former times than it has been recently. Use of the initiative has somewhat declined in modern times, possibly because of the expense or because the legislature is more responsive to public pressures. Because it requires no more effort to amend the constitution by initiative than to enact a statute, there is not too much incentive to settle for a mere statute. Furthermore, the legislature is free to change initiated statutes.

THE REFERENDUM

The second legislative power the people reserve to themselves is the power to approve or reject acts of the General Assembly, the referendum. If the legislature has passed a bill, the bill or any part of it can be brought to a vote of the people by the presentation of a petition with the signatures of enough voters to equal at least 5 percent of the number of votes cast for secretary of state in the last general election when that office was filled. It has to be done not more than ninety days after the final adjournment of the session of the General Assembly that passed the bill (Art. V, Sec. 3). One small limitation has all but liquidated the referendum by petition: the Colorado Constitution prohibits use of the referendum for bringing to popular vote any bill that is "necessary for the immediate preservation of the public peace, health or safety, and appropriations" (Art. V, Sec. 3). The legislature routinely includes the aforesaid words in a so-called *safety clause* at the end of almost all bills, thus largely foreclosing the possibility of referendum, though perhaps not for that purpose.

From time to time the General Assembly seems to want to remove the burden of responsibility or blame for a certain controversial measure from its own shoulders and put it directly upon the shoulders of the voters. In such cases the legislature can refer the measure to the people; this is a second form of the referendum. Such referral requires no petition, although the bill must first pass the General Assembly in the usual fashion. To refer a constitutional amendment (and all such amendments must be referred), it is necessary for two-thirds of the members elected to each house to pass the amendment. Once the measure, whether statute or constitutional amendment, goes to the voters, it requires only a simple majority vote of the people to pass. Once passed by the people, the governor has no power to veto it.

INITIATIVE AND REFERENDUM IN MUNICIPALITIES

In Colorado, the voters of every statutory city, town, and municipality have the power of initiative and referendum with regard to municipal legislation of every character. Although the general laws of the state prescribe the manner of exercising those powers, municipalities themselves may decide, through ordinances or charters, on procedures for using initiative and referendum locally. Not more than 10 percent of the voters may be required to sign a petition to order a referendum, nor more than 15 percent to propose a measure by initiative in any municipality.

CRITICISM OF INITIATIVE AND REFERENDUM

At first blush, one wonders how any right-thinking person could find fault with initiative and referendum systems. When those electoral mechanisms first came upon the scene, they were hailed as the people's answer to corrupt legislatures and as a restoration of the people's power in the face of growing centralization of government. They were thought to be the perfect answers to the cry for more democracy. But the initiative and referendum have not been as wonderful as the dreamers dreamed. The system has its deficiencies and its opponents. It has always had its opponents, but today they can point to a half century's experience to support their criticism. First, they say, these mechanisms of direct democracy produce a long ballot. Voters find themselves confronted at the polls with a long list of proposals, concerning which they know practically nothing and in which they are often not interested.

Also, no matter what the issue, the public's understanding of it undergoes considerable bombardment during the campaign by slick advertising for or against the proposition, advertising mounted by special interests, which may spend hundreds of thousands of dollars. Such propaganda may create more heat than light; whichever side spends the most money is likely to win. In 1982, more than $1 million was spent by opposing sides on an initiative requiring a minimum refund value on all beverage containers (which failed to pass).

Another criticism is that the authors of initiative proposals often fail to write a proposal that says what they really want it to say or accomplishes what they want it to accomplish. To correct this kind of sloppiness, the authors of initiative proposals are now required to meet with the director of the Legislative Council to receive advice (which they need not take). Also, a board composed of the secretary of state, attorney general, and head of the legislative bill drafting service has authority to set an appropriate title and submission clause for the measure and to write a summary of the proposal, which is included with petitions circulated for signatures.

Opponents of direct democracy say this is not the way America was intended to be governed, that it is not the job of voters in a representative democracy to rule but only to choose those who are to rule. Furthermore, they complain that direct democracy promotes radicalism because the masses do not have a proper respect for, or understanding of, property rights.

CHAPTER OUTLINE

PIONEER JUSTICE

In Colorado before the gold rush of 1858, white man's justice usually came out of the barrel of a gun. Within the fur-trading posts there was law and order; outside the posts every man made and enforced his own law, although technically the territorial governments of Kansas, Nebraska, Utah, and New Mexico governed in what we now call Colorado. But none of those governments had effective control in Colorado. After the stampede of gold seekers to Jackson's Bar and the Gregory Diggings, mining camps mushroomed. There were killings, claim jumpings, horse thefts, and whatnot. The miners set up extralegal miners' courts, farmers set up claim clubs, and the larger nonmining settlements set up unauthorized people's courts to protect property and public orders. These vigilante courts gave way to regular authority when Colorado became a territory in 1861. In 1876 Colorado became a sovereign state with regularized courts and law.

RELATIONSHIP OF FEDERAL AND STATE COURTS

Colorado law and Colorado courts are not the only courts and law operating within the state. Federal law also operates here, as it does in all states, and there are federal courts. Each state of the Union has within its boundaries at least one United States District Court (the lowest level of the federal three-step court system). The district court in Colorado sits in Denver. The next higher federal court also sits in Denver, the United States Court of Appeals, which serves Colorado and neighboring states within a certain federal judicial district called the Tenth Circuit. There are eleven such courts in the nation, each serving a separate circuit. At the very top of the federal court system is the United States Supreme Court in Washington, D.C.

Which cases go to federal courts and which to state courts? To put it simply, controversies between states, controversies between citizens of different states involving a certain sum of money, cases in which the United States is a party, and cases involving federal law generally go to federal courts. When a case does not have those characteristics and involves state law, it generally goes to state courts. Both state and federal courts are charged with upholding the United States Constitution, and therefore a case may be started either in federal courts or in state courts (at plaintiff's discretion) if the case involves a claim that a state law or state action is contrary to the United States Constitution. Cases involving the Constitution

that are started in the state courts may ultimately be appealed to
the United States Supreme Court.

The ordinary citizen of Colorado is more likely to have contact
with state courts than with federal courts; most of the law touching
common activities — driving a car, getting married, buying a sofa,
assault and battery, public drunkenness — are governed by state
law or local ordinances. Federal laws tend to regulate matters that
most of us are less likely to be involved in, such as kidnaping or
interstate commerce.

STRUCTURE OF THE COLORADO COURT SYSTEM

The Colorado court system consists of the state supreme court,
the court of appeals, district courts, county courts, and municipal
courts. A separate probate court, juvenile court, and superior court
exist in the City and County of Denver.

Which one of the various Colorado courts is the lowest-level, or
bottom-level, court in the state system? At first glance, looking at
the organization chart (p. 153), municipal courts appear at the
bottom. This is deceiving. The bottom of the court system is different
for different kinds of cases. For example, a case involving a civil suit
in tort for damages below a certain number of dollars could begin in
a county court, whereas if the claimant were asking for damages
above a certain limit, the case would have to begin in the district
court. Even the court of appeals may be thought of as a bottom-level
court of record for appeals from the actions or awards of the Industrial Commission in workers' compensation cases. However, the
adjudicatory actions of administrative agencies are often considered
to be judicial or at least quasi-judicial. Therefore, one might say the
bottom of the court system is not even within the court system in
cases involving adjudicatory actions of agencies. The Colorado Supreme Court itself is the bottom of the court system for some
varieties of judicial action: the state supreme court has original
jurisdiction to issue, hear, and determine certain remedial writs.
However, in most matters, despite these curiosities, the hierarchical
relationship of Colorado courts to one another is more or less as
shown in the diagram on p. 153.

COLORADO COURT SYSTEM

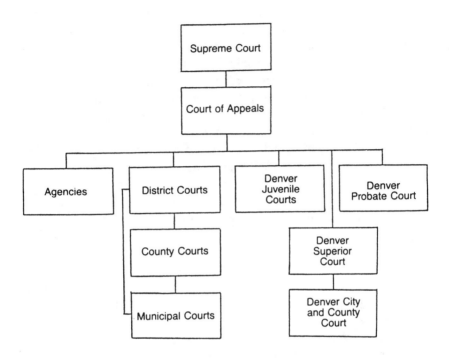

MUNICIPAL COURTS

Every city or town in Colorado may create a municipal court to hear cases involving violations of the ordinances of that city or town. The most common cases before municipal courts are traffic violations. If you are cited for violation of a city traffic ordinance, you go to a municipal court, but if you are cited for violating a state traffic law, you go to a county court. If the traffic violation is both a state and a municipal offense, the court you go to usually depends on whether the officer chooses to cite you under the municipal ordinance or under the state law, although drunk driving, hit and run, and license violations must go to county court.

Municipal judges of statutory towns and cities are appointed by the council. One municipal judge of each town or city is designated a *presiding judge* and his term must be at least two years. Most cities and towns do not have more than one municipal judge, but if there are more than one, those other than the presiding judge may be hired for terms less than two years.

The minimum qualification for a municipal judge is the same as that for a county judge in a Class D county (see p. 155), that is, he or she need not necessarily be licensed to practice law. However, state law requires that municipalities give preference, whenever possible, to the appointment of a municipal judge who is licensed to practice law in Colorado, or at least someone who is trained in law, if not licensed. Some home-rule cities have enacted ordinances requiring that their municipal judges be licensed to practice law in the state. Still, a substantial number of municipal judges in Colorado have never attended college and are not lawyers.

In most respects home-rule cities are not bound by state statutes in the establishment or governance of their municipal courts. Home-rule cities are, however, bound by state statutes governing judicial procedure, appeals, and payment of judges. The statutory rules for pay do not set an amount but provide that judges of municipal courts must be paid a salary on an annual basis and may not receive compensation or be paid fees based on the number of cases handled. This stipulation removes all motivation for a local judge to stimulate prosecutions in order to increase his or her pay. Municipal courts, like all other courts in the state, are subject to the rules of procedure governing the operation and conduct of courts promulgated by the Colorado Supreme Court. Specific municipal court procedures have been adopted. The municipal court may add refinements of its own as long as the refinements do not conflict with those rules or with other laws governing court procedure. Home-rule cities are bound (except in the procedure, appeals, and pay matters just mentioned) by their own city charters and ordinances in all matters concerning municipal courts and may provide for any reasonable method of selecting judges and allow them any reasonable term of office.

Some small Colorado municipalities have not established a municipal court. County court judges in Class C and D counties (see p. 155) may serve simultaneously as municipal court judges. Very few municipal courts are heavily burdened with cases; many municipal judges are virtually unemployed. Most of the 150 or so municipal judges in Colorado are part-time. Some hold judicial posts in two or three municipalities at the same time. Only a handful of cities maintain full-time judges — a few have more than one full-time judge. Most such full-time judges also maintain a private law practice on the side.

Approximately half of municipal court cases involve traffic violations, with the other half a mixture of violations involving dogs, trash, disturbance, zoning, and the health code. A fine is the predominant sentence, although jail sentences are also used. Defendants before municipal courts have the right to trial by jury, but few people bother.

A municipal court may or may not be a *court of record;* the decision is up to the city council of each city. A court of record is one that keeps a verbatim record of trials and all other proceedings, usually by electronic means. Appeals from a municipal court go to the county court and are heard *de novo* if the municipal court is not a court of record. De novo means the entire case will be heard again and a decision made on both the fact questions and the law questions. If the municipal court is a court of record, appeals go directly to the district court and are not heard de novo. The district court looks at the record of the trial in the municipal court and decides largely on the basis of that record.

COUNTY COURTS

Every county has a county court. The number of county judges in each county except Denver is set by the state legislature. About ten of Colorado's counties have more than one county judge. El Paso County, for example, has six at the moment, while Denver has sixteen. All county judges serve four-year terms. The qualifications one must have to be a county judge differ from county to county. The legislature determines those qualifications and, for this and other purposes, has put each county into one of four categories: A, B, C, and D, according to size of population. In A and B counties, county judges are required to be attorneys licensed to practice law in Colorado. While serving as county judge, they may not actually practice law but must give full time to their judicial duties. Class A and B counties include Adams, Arapahoe, Boulder, Clear Creek, Denver (the only class A county), El Paso, Douglas, Jefferson, La Plata, Larimer, Mesa, Pueblo, and Weld. Judges in Class C and D counties are not required to be attorneys but must at least be high-school graduates. If they are attorneys, they may engage in the practice of law in courts other than the county court. Those county judges in C and D counties who are not attorneys are required to attend an institute supervised by the state supreme court on the duties and functioning of the county court, unless attendance is waived by the Colorado Supreme Court. Several county court judges are not attorneys. The number, manner of selection, qualifications, term of office, tenure, and removal of Denver county judges is determined by the charter and ordinances of the City and County of Denver. Colorado has about one hundred county judges among its sixty-three counties.

COUNTY COURT JURISDICTION

Original and Appellate. When lawyers speak of the kinds of cases that may come before a particular court, they use the term *jurisdiction.* The jurisdiction of a court is normally subdivided into, as lawyers say, *original jurisdiction,* and *appellate jurisdiction.* These terms are fairly self-explanatory. Naturally, every case has to start in some court somewhere and be heard and decided there originally before it can be appealed to a higher court. Courts in which cases may be started are called courts of original jurisdiction. Some courts, like the Colorado Supreme Court, seldom hear a case originally and have little original jurisdiction. The supreme court of Colorado hears almost nothing but cases on appeal that have been initially decided by some lower court. A county court, being the lowest court for many matters, has mostly original jurisdiction. County courts have appellate jurisdiction insofar as they hear appeals from municipal courts. Municipal courts have nothing but original jurisdiction.

Criminal and Civil. The jurisdiction of courts is subdivided another way: criminal versus civil. A court has *criminal jurisdiction* when it can hear a case in which someone has been accused of committing a punishable public offense, for example, theft. A civil case, on the other hand, is one in which someone has committed a wrong not necessarily punishable as a public offense but nevertheless a wrong against someone, a noncriminal wrong. Whoever is hurt by such a wrong may go to court and sue for damages or other remedy if the wrong has been declared a civil wrong. Laws that give people the right to sue each other for such noncriminal wrongs are called civil laws, and courts deciding such cases are said to have *civil jurisdiction.* Most American courts have both criminal and civil jurisdiction. Some courts, like probate courts (which decide matters concerning the property of dead persons) have chiefly civil jurisdiction.

County courts have both civil and criminal jurisdiction. Their original jurisdiction in civil and criminal cases is limited to fairly minor matters. In civil matters a county court is not permitted to decide any case involving more than $10,000. A party initiating a suit involving less than $10,000 may originate it in a county court or in the next higher court, the district court. Because either court may take the case, we say (again, in lawyers' talk) that the district court and the county court have *concurrent original jurisdiction* in civil cases not exceeding $10,000. County courts are also forbidden to take cases involving probate, mental health (including commitment, restoration to competence, and the appointment of conservators), divorce, annulment of marriage, separate maintenance, matters affecting children (including custody, support, guardianship, adoption, dependency or delinquency), matters affecting boundaries or title to real property, and most matters concerning injunctions. The civil matters mentioned above must go, on original jurisdiction, to the district court. The district court judge may, however, appoint the county court judge as a referee in cases involving such matters. A referee is an advisor to a judge, who, in gathering evidence on which to base his advice, acts very much like a judge in court. The criminal jurisdiction of county courts is limited to misdemeanors, in which it has concurrent original jurisdiction with district courts. A misdemeanor is an offense less atrocious than a felony.

Traffic cases constitute the bulk of the work of county courts. The number of these cases has decreased somewhat lately, owing to legislation in 1975 that allowed fines for nearly all but the most serious traffic offenses to be paid by mail.

Most county courts have only one judge, but about a dozen counties have more than one. The number of county judges is set by the legislature, except that Denver sets its own number. Where there is more than one judge on a county court, the judges sit separately for the trial of cases.

Small Claims Court. Small claims courts are, in reality, a division of each county court, where trials involving small sums may be held as inexpensively, speedily, and simply as possible. Parties may file civil actions in which the debt, damage, tort, injury, or value of personal property does not exceed $2,000. Juries are not used in small claims courts, nor may either party be represented by an attorney. The judge or referee is not bound by formal rules of procedure or evidence other than those adopted by the state supreme court specifically for the small claims courts. Evening and Saturday sessions are often held, and clerks are expected to give friendly assistance to the public. Parties file all the papers themselves and present their own cases to the judge. The court, however, does not take cases involving libel, slander, forcible entry, or injunction. Nor does it take class suits or criminal cases. If you are sued in small claims court and wish to be represented by a lawyer, you can accomplish this by petitioning to have the case heard in the county court, where you may have a lawyer, even though the case will be conducted under the relaxed rules of small claims procedure.

DISTRICT COURTS

The next step up the Colorado judicial ladder is the district court. There are twenty-two districts in Colorado, each with a district court of one or more judges who serve six-year terms. District courts have both original and appellate jurisdiction. We have just discussed the county court and noted the limitations on the kinds of cases it can take on original jurisdiction, such as felonies, probate cases, juvenile cases, cases involving more than $10,000, and others. Most of those matters must be started in the district court. As for the district court's appellate jurisdiction, it extends to all final actions of the county courts, both civil and criminal. Also they have appellate jurisdiction to review the judgments of certain municipal courts that are courts of record. The caseload of district courts consists chiefly of civil, domestic relations, juvenile, criminal, probate, and mental health — in about that order.

The geographical districts of district courts are required by the state constitution to be formed of compact territory bounded by county lines. Every county court is therefore completely within the territorial jurisdiction of a district court. It is not easy to change district lines. The legislature can do so only by two-thirds vote in each house. The legislature also determines how many district judges shall be in each district; to increase or diminish the number of judges again requires a two-thirds vote in both houses. If the legislature decreases the number of judges, no judge may be removed from office by that means until the end of his or her term. All this fosters judicial independence by making the judge and the judge's district fairly secure from unnecessary legislative meddling.

District court judges in Colorado have numbered about one hundred in recent years. Some districts have more judges than others, depending on the amount of judicial business. Denver's Second District has many more judges than any other.

In each of the twenty-two judicial districts a district attorney is elected by the voters of the district. He or she serves four years. The main job of a district attorney is to prosecute violations of state law.

WATER COURTS

Colorado may be the only state in the Union with water courts. The state is divided into seven water divisions according to drainage patterns of rivers. In each division there is a *water judge,* appointed by the state supreme court from among the district court judges. The water judges and water records of the seven divisions are located in Greeley, Pueblo, Alamosa, Montrose, Glenwood Springs, Steamboat Springs, and Durango. One goal of the water courts is to simplify the legal process of having a water right established so that an attorney might not be necessary. Another purpose is to establish a more accurate tabulation of all water rights. Each year, five or six hundred water cases are filed.

COURT OF APPEALS

The court of appeals exists to help lighten the caseload of the Colorado Supreme Court. Except in cases where the constitutionality of a law is at issue, the court of appeals has initial appellate jurisdiction over appeals from the district courts and from the Denver probate, juvenile, and superior courts. It reviews actions of the Industrial Commission, the Banking Board, the Board of Medical Examiners, the Board of Dental Examiners, the commissioner of insurance, and the Board of Education, chiefly in cases where

The Supreme Court Chamber.

those boards have refused to grant a license or have revoked a license. The court of appeals is composed of ten judges who serve eight-year terms. The judges usually sit in divisions of three.

SUPREME COURT

The Colorado Supreme Court consists of seven justices who serve ten-year terms. The chief justice is chosen or elected by members of the court themselves and serves as chief as long as they wish. He or she is not only the presiding officer of the supreme court but is also the executive head of the entire Colorado judicial system. As executive head of the judicial system, the chief justice is in charge of carrying out the supreme court's superintending function and has power to appoint the chief judges of every one of the twenty-two district courts, who serve entirely at the pleasure of the chief justice. The chief judge of each district court exercises such administrative power over the district court and over the several judges who may be attached thereto as the chief justice of the supreme court directs. The chief justice may, when necessary to expedite judicial business, temporarily assign county or district judges to work in jurisdictions other than their own and may call retired judges to temporary duty.

The supreme court has initial appellate jurisdiction over cases in which the constitutionality of a statute, municipal charter provision, or an ordinance is in question; cases concerned with decisions or actions of the Public Utilities Commission; writs of habeas corpus; and certain water cases. The supreme court also has certiorari review over appeals that lie initially to the court of appeals. Also, the Colorado Constitution requires the supreme court to give its opinion upon important questions put by the governor or by either house of the legislature. The court must sit together to hear any case involving the United States or Colorado constitutions but may sit in departments (subdivisions) in other kinds of cases, each department having full power and authority of the court if concurred in by at least three of the seven members of the court. The state supreme court, in addition to being a court, also exercises general superintending control over all inferior courts, under such regulations and limitations as the state legislature prescribes.

The Colorado Supreme Court hears most of the cases filed with it. Though the court is very busy, it is not as avalanched by appeals as the United States Supreme Court, which attempts to serve the whole nation. The Colorado court is not forced to be as picky about the cases it takes as is the United States Supreme Court. Nevertheless, by 1970 the Colorado Supreme Court was so overwhelmed by its caseload that a court of appeals was created in that year to free the supreme court from some of its civil cases. Of course, some cases are eventually appealed from the court of appeals to the Colorado Supreme Court. Such appeals are handled by a recently adopted certiorari procedure. (A *writ of certiorari* is a court order by which a higher court takes — at its discretion — jurisdiction of cases from inferior courts.) Such transfers from the court of appeals constitute only about 10 percent of the work of the supreme court.

The total caseload of the supreme court is about one thousand cases a year. The court writes about three hundred opinions a year (roughly forty per judge). The court is not always unanimous in its written opinions, and judges occasionally write dissenting opinions in which they state why they would have decided the case in a different way than the majority decided it. These minority opinions sometimes foreshadow tomorrow's majority.

THE COURTS OF DENVER

Denver presents a special case in the Colorado judicial system. Its most unusual feature is the three special courts not found elsewhere in the state: a juvenile court, a probate court, and a superior court. Most of the jurisdiction of these three courts is carved out of what elsewhere in the state is within the jurisdiction of district courts. Judges of the Denver probate, juvenile, and superior courts have much in common with district court judges — same length of term, same requirements for retention in office, same qualifications basically, and same manner of appointment. Why does Denver have a system of courts separate from, and duplicating, the state court system? This is a political feature reflecting the special power and position that Denver historically has occupied in Colorado. Also, Denver is the only county in Colorado that is also a city.

JUVENILE COURT

The Denver Juvenile Court has exclusive original jurisdiction in the City and County of Denver to handle all matters concerning children, such as delinquency, need for supervision, dependency and neglect, adoption, and support payments. The court has three judges who serve six-year terms.

PROBATE COURT

The Denver Probate Court has exclusive original jurisdiction within the City and County of Denver over adjudications involving the mentally ill and over probate matters. The word *probate* originally related to proof (from the Latin *probatio,* meaning proof, and *approbatio,* meaning the approbation given by a judge to proof). In Anglo-American legal language, the word *probate* refers to the proof of wills, that is, proof that the document alleged to be the last will and testament of a deceased person is such in reality. In more recent times a *probate matter* has come to mean matters pertaining to the settlement of estates of deceased persons and other matters customarily handled by probate courts. The Denver Probate Court is a forum for proving wills. The court administers the estates of deceased persons, appoints conservators of estates, and reviews the guardianship and supervision of minors. In most matters, appeals go initially to the court of appeals. Probate matters are handled by the district courts everywhere in the state except in Denver County.

SUPERIOR COURT

The Denver Superior Court, which has one judge who serves for six years, has original concurrent jurisdiction with the Denver District Court in civil cases involving $1,000 to $10,000 (not involved in probate). It also has exclusive appellate jurisdiction in cases appealed from the Denver County Court. Review of superior court judgments by the state supreme court and court of appeals is identical to review by those courts of district court judgments.

APPOINTMENT OF JUDGES

Not long ago almost all states elected judges: judicial candidates ran for office. Many states still use that system. Electing judges has its pros and cons. One of the greatest objections to electing judges is that it forces judges to be politicians. One cannot help wondering whether an elected judge has one eye on the next election when he decides controversial cases. A judge should be free, impartial, and above suspicion. He should "call 'em as he sees 'em." No matter how impartial an elected judge may be, one cannot escape the suspicion that he slants his decisions for political reasons, and the shorter his term the greater the suspicion if he or she is elected. Justice should not only be fair but should have the appearance of fairness. It is almost as bad for a justice to appear unfair as to be unfair. And there is always the question of whether voters know the difference between a good judge and a poor judge and whether voters are qualified to choose judges.

An alternative to election of judges is appointment, which doesn't seem to be much of an improvement. Customarily, where states use the appointment system, the governor does the appointing, and there is a long history of appointments made for reasons of political favoritism rather than for reasons of merit. Furthermore, an appointed judge may not be very responsive to the people. Though we may not want a judge who is too dependent on popular good will, neither would we want a judge who is too independent of public opinion.

Each federal judge from top to bottom of the federal judicial system is appointed by the president with consent of the United States Senate. And those who are appointed to the United States Supreme Court, a United States court of appeals, or a United States district court have life tenure, or, to be precise, serve during good behavior. The appointment system has worked reasonably well at the federal level; nominees for judicial posts are screened by the American Bar Association, the Justice Department, and others. The prestige of the federal judiciary and the care with which it is staffed exceeds that of the judiciary in most states.

In recent years, several states have tried to devise systems for selecting judges by some method that combines the virtues of appointment with the virtues of election, while avoiding the vices of both. That seems like a tall order, but the compromise system, generally referred to as the Missouri System, appears rather successful so far. In 1967, Colorado adopted a version of the Missouri System — prior to that, county, district, and state supreme court judges were elected. The Colorado system is described below.

JUDICIAL DISTRICT NOMINATING COMMISSIONS

In each judicial district of Colorado there is a *judicial district nominating commission*. When a vacancy occurs on a district court or on any county court within the district, the commission submits to the governor a list of two or three nominees, one of whom the governor appoints to fill the judicial vacancy. For the state supreme court and court of appeals there is a *supreme court nominating commission,* which likewise submits a list of three nominees to the governor, who makes an appointment from the list.

Care is taken in the composition of these nominating commissions, but the governor has perhaps too much to say about who the commissioners are, in view of the fact that he makes the final judicial appointment. In the case of district nominating commissions, four of them are appointed by the governor; the other three are appointed jointly by the governor, the chief justice of the supreme court, and the attorney general. The four appointed by the governor are laymen (not lawyers), and the other three must be licensed to practice law in the state of Colorado. With regard to the three members of the bar, it is provided that in districts having fewer than 35,000 inhabitants, fewer than three members of the nominating commission are required to be members of the bar if the governor, chief justice, and attorney general think it justified. No more than four of the seven may be of the same political party. There is an eighth, ex officio, member: one justice of the Colorado Supreme Court sits on each district nominating commission as a nonvoting chairman. He is appointed by and serves at the pleasure of the chief justice. As there are twenty-two districts, each of the justices chairs several commissions.

The supreme court nominating commission is chaired by the chief justice, who serves as a nonvoting, ex officio member of the commission. There are ten voting members of the commission, two from each of the five congressional districts. One member from each congressional district must be licensed to practice law; the other is not licensed. The governor appoints all nonlicensed members; licensed members are appointed jointly by the governor, chief justice, and attorney general.

Members of both the district commissions and the supreme court commission serve six-year, overlapping terms. Reappointment is not permitted. They may not hold elective governmental or political party offices while serving on a commission. No lawyer member of the supreme court nominating commission is eligible for appointment as a justice of the supreme court or the court of appeals while on the supreme court nominating commission, or for three years thereafter. Likewise, no lawyer member of a district nominating commission is eligible for appointment to judicial office in that district while on the commission, or for one year thereafter.

After a judge has been appointed by the governor from the list supplied him by the commissioners and has served a provisional term of two years, he may, if he wishes to retain his office, run in the next general election. If he is a state supreme court justice or an appeals court judge, the voters of the state at-large vote on the question of his retention in office; in the case of a district court judge, electors of his judicial district do the voting; in the case of a county court judge, the voters of the county elect him (the Denver County Court is not covered by any of this procedure; county ordinances govern the personnel of the Denver County Court). A judge or justice does not run against anyone in this election. He runs on what is called a *noncompetitive ballot;* the voters simply vote "Yes" or "No" on the question, "Shall Justice (Judge) _____ of the Supreme (or other) Court be retained in office?" If elected, he or she serves a full term and may run again for successive terms until, at the age of seventy-two, he reaches mandatory retirement for judges in Colorado. Most judges are appointed to the bench in their late forties through their middle fifties and retire between the ages of sixty-eight and seventy-two.

REMOVAL OF JUDGES

The Colorado Constitution provides a system for removing or disciplining judges for willful misconduct in office, willful or persistent failure to perform his or her duties, intemperance, or violation of any canon of the Colorado code of judicial conduct. The same system allows a judge to be retired for permanent or potential disability that interferes with performance of duties. This is done by the Colorado Supreme Court upon recommendation of a commission on judicial discipline. The commission consists of two judges of district courts and two judges of county courts, each selected by the Colorado Supreme Court, plus two lawyers and four citizens (who are neither lawyers nor judges) selected by the governor with the consent of the Senate. Members of the commission serve four-year, overlapping terms.

The commission may conduct an investigation of any judge on any Colorado court of record. (Federal judges are not within its power.) All proceedings of the commission and all papers filed with it in connection with any investigation are confidential, and the filing of papers with the commission and the giving of testimony is *privileged*. (The judge under investigation cannot base a defamation suit on such testimony or papers.)

The commission itself does nothing more than make a recommendation to the state supreme court in those cases where it wants to remove, retire, suspend, censure, reprimand, or in some other way discipline a judge. The supreme court then decides in a separate proceeding what to do and may, if it likes, wholly reject the commission's recommendation. Some judges will resign or retire before such proceedings reach their conclusion. Obviously, however, not every resignation or retirement is the result of a commission investigation.

PROSECUTIONS

Prosecution means accusing someone of a public offense and instituting judicial or other proceedings to determine guilt or innocence. A prosecutor does this in the name of the government. Prosecutions before municipal courts of Colorado are handled by the city attorney, prosecutions before county courts and district courts are handled by the district attorney of the district in which the court is situated, and prosecutions before the court of appeals and the Colorado Supreme Court are handled by the state attorney general.

THE DISTRICT ATTORNEY

Each of Colorado's twenty-two judicial districts has a district attorney. His job is to appear on behalf of the State of Colorado and/or on behalf of the county government of any county within his district in all indictments, suits, and proceedings wherein the state or any county of his district may be a party. (This, by the way, does not prevent a county from hiring its own legal counsel to appear, prosecute, or defend in any proceeding.) Another duty of the district attorney is to give his opinion in writing upon the request of any county officer regarding that officer's duties. The district attorney is most commonly known for his role as prosecutor.

The district attorney is elected for a four-year term and must have the same qualifications as district court judges, that is, be qualified to vote in the district and have been licensed to practice law for five years. He has deputies to help him; they hold office at the pleasure of the district attorney. The salary of the district attorney is set by the legislature and is, in part, paid by the counties within the judicial district he or she serves, each county paying according to its proportion of the total population of the district. Expenses of the office are similarly financed.

THE ATTORNEY GENERAL

The main job of the attorney general is to appear for the state of Colorado and to prosecute and/or defend in all actions or proceedings, civil and criminal, in which the state is a party or is interested. He appears for the state in all cases before the Colorado Supreme Court involving the state. In general, he (with his staff) is the lawyer for the state. He does things lawyers commonly do, such as prepare drafts of contracts and give legal opinions. He is the legal counselor for every department, board, bureau, and agency of the state government. When asked by the governor or other high state officials or the state legislature, he or she will give a legal opinion in writing upon any question of law.

GRAND JURY

A grand jury is a jury of inquiry summoned by criminal courts to receive complaints and accusations in criminal cases, hear the evidence adduced on the part of the state, and bring indictments (charges) in cases where a trial appears justified. *Grand* juries are so called because they ordinarily comprise more jurors than an ordinary trial jury, called a *petit* jury. By tradition, grand juries consist of either twelve or twenty-three persons. Colorado counties with a population of 100,000 or more must have a grand jury, which is drawn to attend the sitting of the court beginning at the first term of the court. In all other counties a grand jury may be called by the court on its own motion, or upon the motion of the district attorney, to sit for as long as the court wishes.

The grand jury usually consists of twelve persons, although if the district attorney asks, a jury of twenty-three may be convened. If the grand jury finds the bill (list) of accusations against a party to be sustained by the evidence laid before it and is satisfied of the truth of the accusation, it endorses (signs) the bill of accusations; this implies that it is a "true bill" so far as the grand jury is concerned. If, on the other hand, the jury is not satisfied that the accusations against a party are sustained by the evidence, it may return "not a true bill." To return a true bill in Colorado, nine of the twelve jurors must assent, or, where there are twenty-three jurors, twelve must assent.

The court selects grand jurors from the first seventy-five names on a list of jurors, or from such other lists as the court may order. The court appoints a foreman. A grand jury hears only witnesses on behalf of the people. The reason for such a one-sided hearing is that the purpose of a grand jury is not to determine guilt or innocence but only to determine whether there is sufficient evidence against the accused to justify bringing the case to trial.

In addition to county grand juries, there are statewide grand juries. When the attorney general deems it in the public interest to have a grand jury with jurisdiction beyond the borders of one county, he may petition the chief judge of any district court, who may impanel a grand jury with statewide jurisdiction. Such a grand jury also has twelve or twenty-three members, but no more than one-fourth of them may be from any one county.

Use of grand juries is declining. They were entirely abolished in England in 1933, and the Colorado Constitution practically invites the legislature to abolish their use. After barely mentioning the grand jury, the Colorado Constitution hastens to say, "PROVIDED, the General Assembly may change, regulate or abolish the grand jury system." (Art. II, Sec. 23.)

CRIMINAL PROCEDURE

Criminal procedure is the procedure by which a person who has committed, or is thought to have committed, an offense is brought to the point of being found guilty or innocent. Every public offense in Colorado is either a felony, a misdemeanor, a petty offense, or a traffic offense. The exact lines between these four species of wrong are cloudy. The legislature has subdivided felonies into five classes, misdemeanors into three classes, petty offenses into two classes, and traffic offenses into four classes. Each class is defined in terms of the maximum and minimum punishment for each. For example, the minimum punishment for a Class 1 felony (murder) is life imprisonment, and the maximum penalty is death. There is a certain amount of overlap in severity of punishment between the least heinous felony (Class 5, which includes bigamy) and the most heinous misdemeanor (Class 1, which includes theft of a trade secret). The shortest term of imprisonment for a felony is one year, while the maximum imprisonment for a misdemeanor is twice as long, two years. However, there is a clarifying shaft of sunlight: the Colorado Constitution defines the term felony. It says, "The term felony shall be construed to mean any criminal offense punishable by death or imprisonment in the penitentiary, and none other." (Art. XVIII, Sec. 4.) We are forced to conclude, therefore, that misdemeanors and petty offenses are any and all offenses not thus punishable: that is, not punishable by death or imprisonment in the penitentiary. In accordance with such reasoning, the Colorado legislature has enacted a law saying that no term of imprisonment for conviction of a misdemeanor shall be served in the state penitentiary unless served concurrently with a term for conviction of a felony. Thus, now that the death penalty seems all but abandoned, it appears that the one immaculate distinction between a felony and all other public offenses has to do with the geographic location of imprisonment.

INDICTMENT; INFORMATION

The word *indictment* stems from the Latin *indictio,* meaning a declaration or proclamation. An indictment is an accusation in writing presented by a grand jury charging a person with a punishable public offense. An *information* resembles an indictment but is filed at the discretion of the prosecutor rather than at the discretion of the grand jury.

ARREST

An officer may without a warrant arrest anyone who has committed a punishable offense in the officer's presence. When an offense is committed elsewhere than in the officer's presence, he may arrest without a warrant only if he has probable cause to believe an offense has been committed and provided that the person he or she wants to arrest is the offender. In cases where a warrant is required, a judge issues a written order directing a peace officer or other specifically named person to arrest the person named in it who is accused of an offense. That written order is the warrant. However, suspects may be briefly detained without a warrant.

When arresting someone, police should immediately tell the suspect that he or she has certain constitutional rights — the sooner the better from the standpoint of prosecution. Statements made by a suspect between the moment of arrest and the moment of being told his or her rights will be excluded from court. The United States Supreme Court in *Miranda* v. *Arizona,* 334 U.S. 436 (1966) said the police must tell the person being arrested (1) that he or she has a right to remain silent, (2) that whatever he says can and will be used against him in court, (3) that he has a right to consult with counsel prior to questioning and to have counsel present during questioning if he desires, (4) that if he fails to request counsel, his failure does not constitute a waiver of the right to have counsel at any time, and

(5) that if he (the accused) is unable to secure a lawyer, one will be appointed for him.

A summons such as one gets in most traffic violations is not an arrest; at least, it is not a custodial arrest. A summons is simply an order, issued by some representative of the court such as a police officer, commanding the person named in the summons to appear at a certain time in court and answer the charges against him or her.

RIGHT TO COUNSEL

Any person in custody must, under Colorado law, be allowed to consult with an attorney as often and for as long as he or she wishes, within reason. Any police officer (or other person) violating the duty to allow someone in custody to see a lawyer may be ordered by a judge to pay monetary damages to the person in custody.

PRELIMINARY HEARING

After arrest (or after being accused of an offense) the person in custody may request a preliminary hearing before a judge to determine whether probable cause exists to believe the person in custody committed the offense alleged. If there is no probable cause, the person in custody is released. At the preliminary hearing the court again advises the defendant of his or her right to counsel and other procedural rights.

BAIL

Any person in custody prior to conviction has a right to be released on bail, except in the following circumstances, where the presumption of guilt is great and to grant bail would place the public in significant peril: (1) when the person in custody has allegedly committed a capital offense and (2) when the person in custody has allegedly committed a crime of violence while on conditional release from confinement, or after two previous felony convictions, or after one previous felony conviction if the previous conviction was for a crime of violence.

ARRAIGNMENT

After an indictment, information, or complaint is filed and after preliminary hearing, the defendant is brought to court to answer the matter charged. This is *arraignment*. The accused is called, the indictment, information, or complaint read to him, and he or she is asked whether he wishes to plead (1) guilty, (2) not guilty, (3) nolo contendere (no contest), or (4) not guilty by reason of insanity. Refusal to plead is considered a plea of not guilty. If the defendant pleads guilty and if the court accepts the plea of guilty (after satisfying itself that the plea was not made under duress and is justified), the plea (of guilty) is equal to conviction for the offense and constitutes a waiver of right to trial. Sentencing follows the plea of guilty.

THE TRIAL

Jury Selection. Every person charged with a public offense has a right to trial by jury, although no one is required to be tried by jury. Any defendant, except someone accused of an offense punishable by death, may waive his right to trial by jury. The jury consists of twelve persons if the offense charged is a felony or Class 1 misdemeanor. In matters involving misdemeanors other than Class 1, the accused is entitled to a jury of six. If the matter involves a petty offense or traffic offense there are three on the jury, although the defendant may ask for a jury of six.

Jury duty is served by persons eligible for jury duty chosen at random from a list of everyone who lives in the county. To be qualified for jury duty one must have the right to vote; be at least eighteen years old; be a resident of a county within the area served by the court; be a citizen of the United States; and be able to read, speak, and understand the English language. The list is updated once a year. The chief judge of the district court appoints a jury commissioner in counties with a population of more than 50,000, to maintain the list and to draw persons from the list as needed for potential jury duty. This work is done in counties of under 50,000 by the clerk of the district court. The clerk or jury commissioner procures the names of all persons within the jurisdiction of the court who are qualified to serve as jurors. At such times as directed by the judge, the jury commissioner summons persons by an impartial method from the list of persons qualified to attend court for possible service as jurors. No one who is eligible for jury duty is excused except those who have physical or mental disabilities that would affect their ability to serve. But in extraordinary circumstances the time of one's service may be deferred.

The bailiff seats the requisite number of prospective jurors in the jury box. Then begins the so-called *voir dire* (meaning, in French, to "speak the truth"): this is the process in which prospective jurors are examined in order to select a jury reasonably satisfactory to both the prosecution and defense. Attorneys for each side are entitled to a certain number of peremptory challenges, meaning they may challenge and cause to be removed from the jury a certain number of prospective jurors without offering any reason, relying on intuition, if nothing else. Also, the attorney for each side may challenge for cause an unlimited number of prospective jurors; any facts indicating bias are sufficient to excuse a juror for cause.

Opening Speeches and Presentation of Evidence by Prosecutor. The trial opens with statements by the two opposing attorneys outlining what they will try to prove during the proceedings. Then the prosecutor begins with presentation of evidence. He calls his witnesses one at a time. Each witness may be cross-examined by the defense attorney to probe the honesty and accuracy of the witness. It is the responsibility of the prosecutor to make what is known in legal circles as a *prima facie case* (Latin, meaning "at first view"). The prosecutor must, in other words, present sufficient proof of the guilt of the accused to support a finding of guilty if evidence to the contrary is disregarded. Because at this stage the defense has not yet begun to present its proof, the judge has a clear view of the prosecution's case. If the prosecution's case looks weak, the defense attorney may move at this stage that the accused be acquitted on grounds that the evidence was not sufficient to make a prima facie case. If the judge agrees, he may conclude the trial and release the defendant.

Presentation of Evidence for the Defense. If the prosecution has made a prima facie case, the trial continues, and it becomes the turn of the defense to present evidence and call witnesses. The accused may, if he wishes, decline to take the stand inasmuch as the constitutions of both the United States and Colorado guarantee that no person "shall be compelled to be a witness against himself" in a criminal case. However, the accused does have a right to appear and testify, if he or she wishes.

Final Arguments. After the prosecution and the defense have presented their evidence, each side has an opportunity to make closing statements, summarize the evidence, and comment on its significance.

Instructions to the Jury. When the prosecuting attorney and defense attorney have finished their concluding statements, the judge has a chance to instruct the jury with regard to certain matters of law that should affect their deliberations. For example, jurors may be reminded that in criminal cases an accused is presumed innocent until proven guilty. Other matters of law may be mentioned, such as the legal definition of the crime of which the defendant is accused. This is a touchy moment in the course of a trial because lawyers resent it when the judge's instructions to the jury seem to lean toward one party or the other. Many court decisions have been reversed on appeal because judges' instructions were unfair. To help avoid the pitfalls of biased or ambiguous jury instructions, judges keep a large book, *Colorado Jury Instructions,* at their fingertips. It contains sample jury instructions, which judges are required to use when applicable.

Jury Deliberation and Verdict. After the jurors receive their instructions from the judge, they retire to the jury room (taking a written copy of their instructions with them), where they discuss the case and vote. The verdict must be unanimous in criminal cases. Some juries take several ballots, only to decide they will never come to an agreement, in which case they come out and tell the judge. The judge will probably tell them to go back and deliberate some more; if they still fail to reach a verdict, it is said to be a *hung jury,* and the judge ends the trial. The prosecutor may then institute a new trial on the same grounds as before. The jury decides only fact questions, that is, whether the accused in fact actually did what he or she was accused of doing. All law questions, as opposed to fact questions, must be decided by the judge.

Sentencing. If the accused is found innocent by the jury, the trial ends. If found guilty, the next step (after a presentence investigation) is sentencing. In this, the law generally allows some discretion to the judge. Before deciding on the sentence, the judge will hold a hearing for the purpose of gathering information about the accused. Medical, psychiatric, and sociological data helps the judge to arrive at a sentence appropriate for the accused, and one that serves the best interests of society as well.

Motion for New Trial and Appeal. Only a small percentage of all convictions is appealed. A case cannot be appealed solely because the defendant wants to appeal. The finding of the jury is a finding of fact considered final unless it can be clearly shown that the jury made an error in its finding. Seldom can it be shown that the jury made a clear error. Appeals almost always rest on grounds that there was some sort of legal (as opposed to factual) error in the trial, an error in selection of the jury, for example, or in admission of evidence, or instructions to the jury. The appellate court does not have a jury because it does not review fact questions but tries to stick to law questions, insofar as law and fact can be untangled. The appeals court bases its decision on the record: that is, on what is to be found in documents such as the indictment, minutes of proceedings, and transcript of the trial testimony. If the appeals court sustains the conviction, there is still the possibility, however remote, of appeal to the governor for a reprieve (delay), a commutation (reduction of penalty), or a pardon (release from punishment), which in the eyes of the law leaves the offender as innocent as if he or she had never committed the offense.

There is much public criticism of the courts based on a general belief that too many people accused of crime are set free by the courts and that even if an offender is found guilty in the trial court, often he or she will go free after an appeal on a technicality. The facts do not support such a belief about Colorado courts. In Colorado, over 90 percent of persons brought to trial for criminal offenses are convicted and only about 5 percent of those found guilty at trial have their convictions reversed.

PUBLIC DEFENDER

The practice of providing court-appointed defense attorneys for indigent defendants is not new. (*Indigent* means someone who does not have enough property to furnish him or her a living and has no one to whom he or she is entitled to look for support.) Although court-appointed lawyers for the indigent are not new, the practice of representing accused indigent persons by means of an institution within the state government just for that purpose is fairly new. Colorado has such an institution, called the Office of State Public Defender, an agency within the judicial department. The state public defender is appointed by the Colorado Supreme Court and serves one or more five-year terms. The first state public defender in Colorado began his term in 1970. The defender has his office in Denver and employs assistant public defenders in regional offices who serve all the courts of the state.

In some instances the public defender comes into a case at the request of a defendant and in other instances at the order of a court. If the court so orders, the public defender may decline, in which case the court may appoint an attorney other than the public defender to represent an indigent person. Although public defenders may prefer to enter only felony cases, their duty under Colorado law is to defend against misdemeanor charges as well as felony charges. Because the word *indigent* is not precise, the public defender must decide who is indigent and who is not, among applicants for service. The state supreme court provides guidelines, and the public defender's refusal to classify someone as an indigent is subject to court review.

CIVIL PROCEDURE

A civil case is an action by one party to compel another party to do a specific thing, such as pay money. The defendant in a civil case is not charged with commission of a punishable offense but with a private or personal wrong, such as failure to pay a debt or to honor a contract. A civil case begins with (1) a summons and (2) a complaint. If A is suing B for nonpayment of a debt, A goes to the court (usually through a lawyer except in small claims cases) and asks the court to issue an order (summons) directed to the defendant, requiring him or her to appear at a certain time and to defend. The summons names the parties and includes a brief statement of the sum of money or other relief demanded by the plaintiff. If a copy of the complaint does not accompany the summons, then the defendant must be supplied with a copy within ten days. The summons may be delivered by the sheriff or by any person over eighteen years old not a party to the action. There are detailed rules about what constitutes actual service of the summons.

When the *complainant* (or *plaintiff*, the person who starts the suit) asks for a summons, he or she also files a complaint. In the complaint, the one who is suing tells the defendant all material facts that support the plaintiff in his demand. The defendant is then entitled to ask for a *bill of particulars* describing the complaint in greater detail. After a set period of time, the defendant must answer the complaint or lose the suit by default.

If either side wants a jury trial, a jury will be called in much the same manner as in criminal cases. The trial proceeds in essentially the same way as a criminal trial, although there are several key differences. First, in a civil case, because there is no crime involved, the defendant is obligated to take the stand and testify (although he has a right not to answer questions that might tend to incriminate him). Second, in a civil case proof of the charges need not show the defendant's guilt (or fault) beyond a reasonable doubt; the standard of proof is less rigid. Proof supporting a civil complaint need only add up to a *preponderance of evidence;* in other words, the evidence must make it look more probable than not that the demands of the complainant are justified. Third, the findings of juries in civil cases need not be unanimous. The verdict of a majority is sufficient unless the parties stipulate some number greater than a majority. The jury in a civil case consists of six persons unless the parties agree to a smaller number, not less than three. The jury does not have the right to decide everything; they may only decide fact questions, not law questions, a distinction easier to mention here than to explain. If neither party wants a jury, then all issues are decided by the judge. Jury or no jury, the judge always decides all law (as opposed to fact) questions.

LAW IN COLORADO

COMMON LAW

One of the skills for which we pay lawyers is their ability to "find" the law. In the common-law world, finding the law is difficult. You see, lawyers have a secret; it is that no one in the common-law world really knows what the law is — only what the law was. This is because 90 percent of American (and Colorado) law consists of cases decided in the past, which lawyers read hoping to guess what the court (any court) will decide in the future. Because American judges are by tradition wedded to the principle of *stare decisis* (Latin for "let the decision stand," the principle of deciding future cases the way similar cases were decided in the past), we can occasionally predict decisions with some accuracy. That is what you pay a lawyer to do.

Cases decided in the past constitute a body of law called *the common law*. It is what law students spend most of their time studying in law school. An important part of being a successful lawyer is knowing how to find your way through the heap of past decisions and putting your finger on the right cases and the right commentaries on cases (there are a thousand law journals making comments) relevant to the cases at bar. It is beyond the scope of this book to describe how to find the common and statutory law; there are volumes on the subject. One of the best is *How to find the Law,* edited by Morris I. Cohen and Robert C. Berring and published by West Publishing Company, St. Paul, Minnesota, 1983.

STATUTORY LAW

In addition to common law, there is *statutory law*. A statute is an enactment of a legislative body such as the state legislature, a county board, or city council. Acts of the Colorado General Assembly are codified (that is, arranged by subject matter) in the *Colorado Revised Statutes,* which is well indexed and easy to use. For other statutory law, such as city ordinances, the place to find them is in the offices of the government whose law you are interested in.

EQUITY

Colorado courts also possess what we call equity jurisdiction, under which they dispense a category of justice not governed by common law. In an equity case the court often tries to prevent a future wrong rather than to remedy a past wrong. When exercising their powers of equity, courts commonly employ the *writ of mandamus* (a court order to a public official demanding that he perform a ministerial, or routine function), or the *writ of injunction* (a court order forbidding some act that threatens irreparable harm).

RULES AND REGULATIONS

Keep in mind that rules and regulations made by Colorado regulatory agencies also have the force of law. Rules made by agencies of the state government are codified and published in the *Code of Colorado Regulations.* Local governments generally do not codify their rules; to find them, go to the offices of the regulatory agency itself.

The rise of administrative rulemaking throughout America and in Colorado has presented the courts of this land with a great challenge in the field of constitutional law: how to assure fair procedure by agencies as they go about limiting people's personal and property freedoms. Every rule, even if only a rule in a state park that states where you may or may not pitch your tent, denies personal liberty and often denies property in the sense of prohibiting people from using their tents, or whatever, in certain places and ways. All rules, in a sense, are a great onslaught on liberty — but that is true of all law. At the same time, law is the greatest protector of liberty.

Both the Colorado and United States constitutions emphatically prohibit denials of "life, liberty or property without due process of law." Over the generations of American and Colorado history, the courts of the United States as well as the courts of Colorado have tried to spell out what constitutes a denial of life, and of liberty, and of property, without due process of law. (The term *due process* seems to have been boiled down so that it means "fair.")

The struggle to keep the multitudinous agencies and their flood of rules within the law has fallen chiefly upon the courts. An important course in every law school, Administrative Law, deals with judicial limits on the rulemaking powers (and adjudicatory powers) of agencies. But Congress and all the state legislatures, including Colorado, have been jittery about this heaving ocean of rules, this massive realm of lawmaking going on outside the capitol, far from the House and Senate, all of it done by people who are not elected by anybody (though they are permitted and sanctioned by legislative bodies to do it). Legislatures across America have yearned to get a handle on all this — to make a stab at controlling the Frankenstein they have created — control of that mass of beyond-the-capitol lawmaking.

One by one all the states over the past half century have enacted administrative procedure acts that spell out what the legislature conceives to be "fair rulemaking procedure" that must be uniform for all agencies in the way they go about making rules. The United

States Congress set the ball rolling in 1946 with its famous Administrative Procedure Act. Colorado's administrative procedure act, though not officially titled as such, may be found in *C.R.S.* 24–4–102, 103, 104, 105, and 106. This bundle of laws, like the typical administrative procedure act, deals not only with rulemaking procedure but also with the procedure agencies must follow when they give or take away a license (say to practice medicine) and the procedure they must follow when they hold other kinds of adjudicatory hearings, hearings upon which they base determinations about anyone's rights or property. And, like most other administrative procedure acts, this bundle of laws also sets forth how the courts are supposed to approach their frequent job of reviewing the legality of agency rules and the legality of agency adjudications when their legality is questioned in court.

But this alone has not satisfied the legislatures, has not satisfied the Colorado General Assembly. Colorado state senators and representatives (like those of a number of other states) in recent years have wanted to have a say about this ocean of rules. But this seems almost hopeless — like getting your hands on a mile-wide swarm of gnats. But still, there has been an ever-present, ever-rising rumble from all sorts of people who think they've been wronged by this or that rule and who think there's nowhere they can turn for recourse except to the very bureaucrats who made them. State senators and representatives are asked, "Isn't there something *you* can do? You're the legislature, aren't you?"

These swarms of rules are not limited to regulating where, for example, you may spit. They control all manner of things, including the operations of banks, insurance companies, electric companies, and all sorts of giant economic interests. (See p. 275 for a list of things regulated by the Colorado Department of Health alone.)

A sense of concern settles over the legislature about all this. How can they really oversee the flood — is it too massive, too complex? After all, a legislature usually gives an agency the power to regulate that which is too technical (hospital sanitation standards) for the legislature itself to cope with. Yet, there is constant urging for legislatures to become more involved with all those rules and regulations made by state agencies that have the force of law. Lately, such involvement on the part of legislatures in many states, including Colorado, has taken the form of some sort of hands-on review of rules before such rules become effective.

The Colorado law (*CRS* 24–4–108 [7]) gives this hands-on review job to the legislature's own standing Committee on Legal Services. The committee is directed to set up a system for annual review of rules and regulations to determine whether any of them conflict with state statutes. Here is how the system works: every rule adopted or changed by an executive agency is first reviewed by an attorney in the Office of Legislative Legal Services to determine whether the rule is within the power delegated by the legislature to the agency and is in other ways consistent with state statutes. If the attorney thinks there is a problem with the legality of the rule, it is then reviewed by the Committee on Legal Services at a public hearing. If, after the hearing, the committee thinks the rule is illegal, it will take steps to terminate the rule.

Rule termination works this way: by law, all rules (except those of regulatory agencies within the Department of Regulatory Agencies) expire on July 1 of the year following their adoption by the agency *unless* the General Assembly adopts a bill that postpones their expiration. Each year members of the Committee on Legal Services sponsor a bill to postpone expiration of all the thousands of rules subject to this procedure that have been made by all the agencies of the state government of Colorado. The doubtful ones are allowed to expire. Rules made by the many regulatory agencies of the Department of Regulatory Agencies are not subject to this procedure; rather, they are reviewed under sunrise/sunset procedure when the entire agency, together with all of its rules, may be terminated if their value is found wanting by the Sunrise and Sunset Review Committee and by the legislature. (See p. 255 for sunset procedure.) But there is much to question about any given rule besides its mere legality. There is also, for example, the question of whether it is a stupid rule. The Committee on Legal Services does not, however, review for stupidity, only legality.

Legislative oversight of agency rules does not end with the Committee on Legal Services. It continues in random probings by practically every committee of the legislature, in investigations of this and that, in sunset reviews, in audits, in the budget process, and in the general questioning of bureaucrats about their agencies.

This sort of haphazard intermittent peering into the guts of agencies may be the best way for the legislature to determine the wisdom and good sense of new rules.

POLICE

It is essential to mention police in a chapter on courts and law. After all, the criminal process usually begins when the police arrest a suspect. Police are so essential to the process of justice that they have been called the "initial ministers of justice." Neither judges nor juries make as many decisions as police concerning the behavior of individuals — for example, whether that behavior is within the law or outside the law, whether or not it deserves the attention of a judge. The judgment of a police officer precedes the judgment of a judge, and for most people the judgment of police is the most fateful judgment of all.

Police officers represent the law in the eyes of many people, and they represent the prestige of the law. It is the police officer who is the contact point between citizens and the criminal law. Police officers are doubly important because it is they who decide which among the endless number of laws shall be enforced vigorously, which sporadically, and which shall be ignored altogether; they haven't time to enforce them all, even if they wanted to. You may well ask, what is the education and training of police officers in Colorado and what is their pay? These questions cannot be answered here, but they are crucial to the Colorado system of justice.

Legislature — Organization and Functions

8

WHAT DOES THE COLORADO LEGISLATURE DO
BESIDES MAKE LAWS?

PARTICIPATION IN ADMINISTRATION

Confirmation of Appointments. The Colorado Constitution, like the constitutions of most other states, gives the state Senate authority to participate in the appointment of all nonelective officers (except officers where the appointment is by law otherwise provided for). This is called the consent power, and the constitution says the offices just mentioned shall be filled by the governor "by and with the consent of the Senate." (Art. IV, Sec. 6.)

Structuring the Executive. The legislature has power to prescribe the exact internal organization structure of the executive branch. Departments (such as the Department of Health) and their major divisions are created by statute and given a great deal of individual attention in the long appropriations bill. An administrator's discretion over how work is to be organized within departments is greatest beneath the division level.

Oversight of Administration. Inasmuch as the legislature creates much of the state's organizational structure and gives money to the various agencies of the bureaucracy, it feels it has a right to look into how they are doing and how well the money is being spent. Such examination is called legislative oversight of administration. It is one of the most important jobs of the legislature, especially in an era of growing executive power.

Legislatures today are reverting to the oversight role they played in Europe centuries ago, before modern legislatures were born. In the beginning (roughly the thirteenth century) they were gatherings of lords (for example, the Norman Magnum Concilium) who met to give counsel to the king and petition him, and to lodge formal complaints against him and/or his administrators. Gradually they gained a voice in decision making, but their main role was to keep an eye on the bureaucracy, particularly upon tax levies. The modern role of legislatures — declaring the law — developed much later and is almost a product of modern times. But modern legislatures have abandoned so much lawmaking power (that is, regulatory and rulemaking power) to the executive branch, have authorized such a vast bureaucracy to carry out the work of government, that today legislatures around the world have regressed somewhat toward their thirteenth-century beginnings, focusing more and more upon oversight of administration.

In Colorado, each department of the executive branch falls within the oversight jurisdiction of one committee in the House and one committee in the Senate. The Department of Administration, for example, is the responsibility of the Appropriations Committees of the House and Senate. Joint Rule 25 of the Colorado General Assembly charges the "committees of reference of the House and Senate to keep themselves advised of the activities, functions, problems, new developments, and budgets of the principal department or departments of the executive department of state government which are within the subject matter jurisdiction of each committee. . . . The chairman of a committee shall, from time to time, invite the principal personnel of the respective . . . departments under the committee's jurisdiction to appear before the committee to keep members so advised. Such personnel shall also provide the committee with additional information as may be requested."

Oversight committees do not spend a great deal of time in what one would call formal oversight; they don't sit down and say, "Now we are going to oversee the administration." Oversight is largely a by-product of everything else they do, and, in fact, all the committees of the legislature become involved in peering up the skirts of every agency at random as they make laws pertaining to those agencies. The appropriations function naturally leads the legislature to look over the shoulder of every administrative agency to see what it is doing and how well.

Some critics question the ability of the legislature to do a good job of systematic and professional oversight, as few members of committees are likely to know enough about any one agency to do more than a hack job. Legislative terms are short, and there is high turnover among members, some of whom may have little incentive to do a professional job of oversight, even if they have the time and ability. And, of course, zealous oversight can become a threat to committee members insofar as the process may infuriate miscellaneous interest groups enjoying cozy relationships with agencies being investigated. In addition, legislative oversight can be politically motivated — partisan or personal. If the legislature is of one party and the governor of another, nothing is more natural than legislative detective work to ferret out as much damaging evidence as possible. Personal rivalries and turf wars inside and outside the bureaucracy can have more to do with the course of legislative oversight than anything lofty and professional.

Oversight of Administrative Rulemaking. Today most of the statutory law at all levels of government in the United States (and Colorado) is made by administrative agencies in the form of rules. Oddly, the state legislature does not make as much state law as do the administrative agencies. The volume and complexity of legislation required in our era is so great that legislative bodies have delegated a great deal of quasi-legislative power to administrative agencies, which make their laws in the form of rules. These rules have all the force and effect of law and are ultimately enforced by courts. Rules of state agencies vastly outnumber the acts of the Colorado General Assembly. Lately, legislatures in many states, including Colorado, have tried to become more involved. This involvement usually takes the form of some sort of hands-on review of rules before they become effective. The Colorado law, *C.R.S.* 24–4–108 (7), gives this hands-on review job to the legislature's own standing Committee on Legal Services. (See p. 181 for how this is done in Colorado.)

ERRAND RUNNING

Legislators receive many requests from constituents for help in solving problems with state agencies or in getting answers to questions. This is called *legislative casework.* Legislators spend hours running errands for their constituents. One of the services legislators can or should be able to offer their constituents is a good understanding of who does what in the bureaucracy. They can help put a constituent in touch with the right people in the executive apparatus, or they can address inquiries to any agency regarding the status of a constituent's case, or in some other way find an answer to the constituent's problem. This activity makes legislators almost a part of the administration, for such errand running is as much administrative as legislative in nature.

CONSTITUTION MAKING

The *constituent function* is the power of the legislature to submit proposed constitutional amendments to the voters. In Colorado, amendments to the state constitution may be proposed by the state legislature, but each house must approve such amendments by a two-thirds majority of its total membership. A proposed amendment is then submitted to the voters for adoption by simple majority vote. If the legislature should decide the time is ripe, it may recommend to voters that a constitutional convention be convened to revise the constitution. A two-thirds vote in each house of the legislature is required to propose a convention, and a majority vote of the people to approve it. The convention, if approved, would then meet and probably draft revisions to the constitution. These revisions would then be submitted to the voters, to be adopted as part of the constitution by majority vote.

JUDICIAL POWERS OF THE LEGISLATURE

Judge of Members. Each house of the Colorado legislature has power to discipline its own members (and other persons as well) for contempt or for disorderly behavior in its presence; with the concurrence of two-thirds of the entire membership of the chamber, either house may expel one of its members.

Impeachment. Although most people mistakenly believe *impeachment* means removal of someone from public office by a legislative body, the word actually means "to accuse," or "to charge." A charge of impeachment is not the same thing as trial of an impeachment. Impeachment occurs when the Colorado House of Representatives decides by majority vote to bring charges against an officer or judge, alleging that he or she is guilty of a high crime or misdemeanor or malfeasance in office. Bringing charges is, to repeat, not the same as trial of charges. Trial of the articles of impeachment takes place in the Colorado Senate. When senators are sitting for the purpose of trying a case of impeachment, they are in every sense judges and as such are put upon oath to do justice according to law and evidence. The House of Representatives is somewhat like a prosecuting attorney, and the Senate is the court. When the governor or lieutenant governor is on trial, the chief justice of the Colorado Supreme Court presides, and it requires a two-thirds vote of all the senators elected to the Senate to convict.

If convicted, a judge or executive officer may be removed from office and disqualified to hold any office of honor, trust, or profit in the state. Conviction (or acquittal) of impeachment charges does not in any way prevent later prosecution, trial, judgment, and punishment in the regular courts of law for the same offense for which the officer was impeached — there is a suggestion of double jeopardy in such a case.

Impeachment is threatened more than used. So rarely is it used that some members of the legislature cannot say for sure whether anyone has ever been impeached in Colorado. Actually, it was last used in 1938, when articles of impeachment were passed against two members of the state civil service commission who shortly thereafter left office. Also, according to George E. Warren, state archivist, seven articles of impeachment were passed in 1935 against the serving secretary of state, which resulted in the secretary's resignation.

LAWMAKING, AND LIMITS ON LAWMAKING

We come now to what is supposedly the most important function of the legislature — lawmaking. There are those who maintain that real lawmaking decisions lie outside the legislature in most (or many) cases and that the legislative lawmaking function is merely a ceremonial one — to bless and make legitimate those decisions arrived at elsewhere. But let's assume for the sake of this discussion that legislating is the main function of the legislature.

The legislature is a place where competing interests meet to do battle over what shall prevail as law. The law that results is not the highest law in the state: it is subordinate to state and federal constitutional law. The ultimate battle over what shall prevail as law is fought over what shall be in the constitution and who shall interpret the constitution and how it shall be interpreted. On the other hand, laws of the legislature are superior to laws of local governments in matters of statewide concern. You will remember, however, that the Colorado Constitution permits cities and towns to acquire home rule. Municipalities have power to adopt a city charter (the basic organic law of the city), and insofar as that charter concerns only local municipal matters, it (and all ordinances made pursuant to the charter) is superior to any state statute in conflict therewith. It is not, however, crystal clear what is a statewide concern and what is a local concern, and the courts must decide cases of dispute.

RESTRICTIONS ON LEGISLATIVE POWER

THE BILL OF RIGHTS

Essentially, the whole state constitution is a limitation on the state government generally, including the legislature. Some provisions of the state constitution seem aimed more specifically at curbing legislative power than others — the Bill of Rights for example. Most people think of the Bill of Rights in terms of the United States Constitution, not the Colorado Constitution. But if you read the Colorado Constitution, almost the first thing you run into is a bill of rights, longer than the federal bill. It guarantees almost everything guaranteed in the federal bill, and more. In some cases the General Assembly of Colorado is restricted by name, for example, "No ex post facto law . . . shall be passed by the General Assembly." (Art. II, Sec. 11.) In most cases the General Assembly is not specifically named but is assumed to be limited along with other arms of state government and local instrumentalities. For example, when Art. II, Sec. 25 says "No person shall be deprived of life, liberty or property, without due process of law," the General Assembly is not mentioned but is clearly included in the restriction.

The Colorado Bill of Rights is, in substance, a duplication of the federal bill. Both the federal and state documents limit the legislature. The federal Bill of Rights, although originally directed at Congress and the federal government, is now applied to the states through the Fourteenth Amendment to the Constitution. If you are denied religious freedom by Colorado state law, for example, you could attack the law with two hammers: (1) the federal Bill of Rights and (2) the State of Colorado Bill of Rights. One hammer would be entirely sufficient — two is poetic.

SPECIAL LEGISLATION

It seems that for every no-no in society, human ingenuity finds a way around it. Children and legislators seem to have a special knack for that art. An example is the prohibition against *special legislation*. The Colorado Constitution is quite clear on the subject of special legislation. It says, "Where a general law can be made applicable, no special law shall be enacted." (Art. V, Sec. 25.) This means the legislature may not, for example, grant a specific couple a divorce but must make a general divorce law (if it wants any such law at all) stating the conditions under which anyone who seeks a divorce may obtain one. Or, to use another example, the legislature may not declare a specific individual to be of age — that would be special legislation, a special law — but may pass a general law that anyone who reaches a certain age shall be deemed "of age." The prohibition applies to towns and cities as well as individuals.

The way to get around a prohibition against special legislation is to write general laws that are so specific that in effect they could apply to only one place. For example, if the legislature wants to legislate for Denver and only Denver it could pass a law to the effect that "all city-counties in the state of Colorado must do the following," Denver being the only city-county in the state. The Colorado Constitution (Art. V, Sec. 25) enumerates certain areas in which the legislature may not make special laws, thus making doubly sure there will be no special legislation (regulating county affairs, for example, is listed). Those double-sure enumerations have not extinguished the brilliance of the legislature in writing general laws that go like a rifle shot to special targets. Because of these prohibitions against special legislation, the state legislature is not as free as Congress to entertain private bills.

Incidentally, the state constitution itself indulges in exactly the kind of special legislation that it specifically prohibits to the legislature. Denver is mentioned by name in numerous places. And in 1972 the people of Colorado wrote a piece of special legislation into their supreme law by specifically prohibiting state financial support for the 1976 Winter Olympic Games (Art. XI, Sec. 10).

DEBT

Owing to their experience with corrupt and irresponsible legislatures in generations past, almost all states of the Union have enacted constitutional provisions attempting to prevent the legislature from plunging the state hopelessly into debt. Article XI of the Colorado Constitution (which runs several pages) is designed to set up firm defenses against certain kinds of fiscal irresponsibility. It flatly forbids the state to contract any debt whatsoever by loan except to provide for casual deficiencies of revenue, to erect public buildings for the use of the state, and to do a few other things related to war, defense, and suppression of rebellion. Therefore, in most

The Senate Chamber.

things the legislature must work within the perimeter of its anticipated revenue. (See p. 309 for more on this subject.)

OFFICIAL DESIGNATION

About half the states of the Union officially call their state
legislatures the State Legislature. Quite a number of states, including Colorado, call the legislative body the General Assembly. A few
other states use such names as Legislative Assembly, and General
Court; and Nebraska calls its one-house legislature the Senate.

The upper house is everywhere referred to as the senate. The
lower house is usually called the house of representatives, as it is in
Colorado. A few states call their lower house an assembly, a general
assembly, or a house of delegates. The terms *upper house* and *lower
house* are general terms, not the official names of these houses. The
branch with the greater number of members is the lower house —
in Colorado, the House of Representatives, with sixty-five members.

The House of Representatives.

The term *lower house* is a carryover from British tradition. At the time the United States was founded, the British Parliament had two houses, as it still does today: a House of Lords representing the nobility, who, naturally, are "upper" in a social sense; and a House of Commons representing commoners, who are "lower." The British House of Commons has more (active) members than the House of Lords. In the United States, houses of representatives, having the greater number of members, are considered closer to the people and have thus inherited the title "lower house" (although you would think that in a democracy, where the people are supposed to be sovereign, the lower house would be the upper house!). As for the senates, they possess several attributes of the British House of Lords. First, like the House of Lords, most, if not all, American senates try impeachments. (The American senates and the House of Lords differ, however, as to other judicial powers: the House of Lords functions as the supreme court of England, whereas in the United

States, direct judicial power has been denied to the federal and state senates — with the exception of impeachment trials).

Another reason why American senates are called the upper house is that in old English law a lord was a member of the royal council, that is, he was the king's councilor (and counselor). American senates, both national and state, also have a counseling function not shared by the lower house. For example, in Colorado the senate must approve many of the governor's appointments. The United States Senate holds a similar power over appointments; it is also the body that ratifies treaties.

For many years the United States Senate was comparatively distant from the people because senators were not elected directly by the people. It was not until 1913, 124 years after the founding of the Republic, that the Seventeenth Amendment provided for direct popular election of United States senators. Members of most state senates have always been directly elected, generally for longer terms than members of the House, as are United States senators. The term of a member of the Colorado House of Representatives is two years, that of a Colorado senator four years; a member of the United States House of Representatives is elected for two years, a United States senator for six years.

BICAMERALISM

From time to time, proposals are voiced to create a unicameral (one-house) legislature in Colorado. Several years ago Representative John Carroll introduced a resolution to amend the Colorado Constitution to combine the House and Senate into a unicameral General Assembly. Carroll said the two-chamber system is "expensive duplication" and an "unneeded luxury." He said there was historic justification for a two-house Congress but no similar historic justification for a two-house general assembly in Colorado. The original justification for a two-house Congress was that small states feared political domination by larger states. The need was perceived for one house based on population and another house based on geographic size. Carroll believed the authors of the Colorado Constitution blindly and needlessly followed the federal example. Actually, unicameralism is the most common form of legislative body in America if you count those of local governments.

A two-house legislature is called *bicameral,* a Latin word drafted into the English language by Jeremy Bentham (a British philosopher) to describe a system wherein the legislative body is divided into two chambers. *Bi* means "two," and *camera* in old English law means "a room, or chamber." (Lawyers use the term *in camera* to describe a hearing that goes on in the judge's private rooms or chamber — the case is said to be heard in camera.)

The important issue regarding bicameralism is not where the word comes from but (1) why we have a two-house legislature rather than one house and (2) whether it is better to have two houses than one. The second question makes a good topic for university debate teams because the arguments on both sides are compelling. As for the first question, the primary reason we have two houses at the state level is probably the force of tradition. The founders of the United States Constitution took bicameralism straight from the British Parliament. When the authors of the Colorado Constitution sat down to design a system of government for this state, they did what constitution writers in most other states did — they started with a copy of the United States Constitution and copies of the constitutions of several other states (which in turn had also been written by people moved by tradition and example).

Some arguments for bicameralism are these. First, the people of a state, and even their legislators, are apt to do hasty and stupid things if swept suddenly by some excitement or passion. Requiring every bill to be dragged through the processes of two houses slows things down and gives time for the rebirth of reason along the way. Second, because members of the upper house serve longer terms, they can better afford to ignore popular excitement than can members of the lower house. Third, it is said that lobbyists find it harder to control two houses than one. Also, the members of each house represent different constituencies, the main difference now being that senatorial districts are more populous.

A few arguments for unicameralism are these. It is cheaper (fewer legislators to pay). It is more efficient because, with only one house, it isn't necessary to do everything two times. Furthermore, with only one house to watch and try to understand, the people can keep a better eye on what the legislature is doing. Also, it is claimed that two houses fall into rivalry and competition with one another, and this serves no public interest.

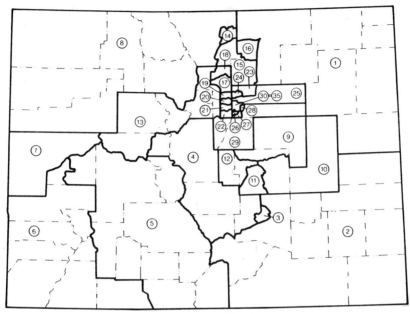

Colorado Senate Districts.

APPORTIONMENT AND REAPPORTIONMENT

Legislative apportionment means apportioning legislative seats to various parts of the state: dividing up the state into legislative districts. *Reapportionment* means periodic revisions of such legislative district boundary lines. At bottom, the issue in all apportionment and reapportionment battles is who will gain (or lose) power. If the boundaries of a legislative district are deftly drawn to include more Democrats than Republicans, then such an act gives power to Democrats to elect a legislator in the district. The reverse would give power to Republicans. If the district has more rural people than urban people, then rural power prevails. If it has more blacks than whites, then black power prevails. And so on. When district lines are deliberately drawn to give power to one group over another it is called *gerrymandering,* a word invented from the strange appearance of one cleverly drawn district long ago that reminded someone of a salamander with arms and legs and a twisting torso, an apportionment designed to bring into the district just the right people and leave out the rest.

Wherever there are districts, there is apportionment, and usually

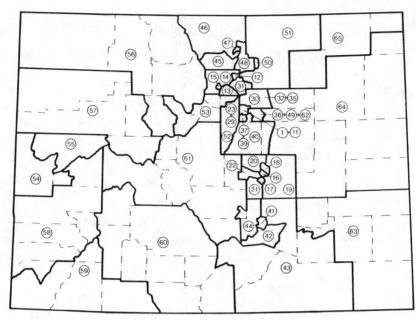

Colorado House Districts.

there is some kind of conscious or unconscious gerrymandering. This applies to city council districts, county commissioner districts, state legislative districts, congressional districts and every other kind of district. Where and how district lines are drawn determines who controls the district.

The Colorado Constitution now (in response to United States Supreme Court decisions) provides that each legislative district, both House districts and Senate districts, have a population "as nearly equal as may be." (Art. V, Sec. 46.) Of course, Senate districts have to be larger than House districts because there are fewer of them. Furthermore, the constitution now requires these districts to be "as compact in area as possible" and to be composed of "contiguous [touching] whole general election precincts." (Sec. 47.) The legislature was required by the constitution to revise the boundaries of these districts after each ten-year federal census in order to keep districts equal and compact. And the state constitution put a pistol to the head of the legislature by saying that if the legislature should fail to revise the boundaries after forty-five days into the first legislative session after publication of a federal census, the salary of legislators would be cut off, and worse yet, no legislator could serve another successive term until such revision was made.

Because the General Assembly is likely to fall into serious and time-consuming controversy every ten years over reapportionment, as it did after the 1970 census, a constitutional amendment was added to the Colorado Constitution in 1974 to spare the legislators this ordeal. The amendment gives the power to revise legislative district boundaries to an eleven-member reapportionment commission. The commission consists of the speaker and the minority leader of the House and the majority and minority leaders of the Senate, three appointees of the governor, and four appointees of the chief justice of the Colorado Supreme Court. No more than six of the eleven members of the commission may be affiliated with the same political party. The Colorado Supreme Court is charged with reviewing the commission's final reapportionment plan and would be called on in case the commission could not reach agreement on a plan. The sponsors of this amendment believed it would take partisan politics out of reapportionment and thus reduce the gerrymandering of legislative districts. But it is difficult to take politics out of anything.

The Colorado Reapportionment Commission had its maiden flight in 1981, when it divided up the state's legislative districts to conform with 1980 census figures. Candidates in 1982 ran in the new districts. Asked whether he experienced any pressure as chairman of the commission, Robert E. Lee said, "That depends on how you define pressure. We certainly had a lot of sales jobs."

COMMITTEES OF REFERENCE

Each bill introduced into the House of Representatives is referred by the speaker to one or more committees of reference, whose duty it is to consider the merits of the bill and decide whether to kill it or to change it and send it on to the House for further consideration. The ten House committees of reference are:

1. Agriculture, Livestock, and Natural Resources
2. Appropriations
3. Business Affairs and Labor
4. Education
5. Finance

6. Health, Environment, Welfare, and Institutions
7. Judiciary
8. Local Government
9. State Affairs
10. Transportation and Energy

The House and Senate Appropriations Committees are committees of reference for the limited purpose of evaluating the fiscal (financial) impact of bills upon the state government, whether that impact be for better or worse.

Sometimes it is doubted whether the appropriations committees should be called committees of reference. Nevertheless, House Rule 25 and Senate Rule 21 each lists its respective appropriations committee as a committee of reference. (See the June 1989 *Colorado Legislator's Handbook.*)

Theoretically, bills having no financial impact upon the state government do not go to an appropriations committee. We say "theoretically" because apparently, from time to time for political reasons, bills are referred to appropriations committees for reasons that have nothing to do with appropriations.

Except in a few instances Senate committees are identical in name to House committees. The ten Senate committees of reference are:

1. Agriculture, Natural Resources and Energy
2. Appropriations
3. Business Affairs and Labor
4. Education
5. Finance
6. Health, Environment, Welfare, Institutions
7. Judiciary
8. Local Government
9. State, Veterans, and Military Affairs
10. Transportation

Committees of reference also have oversight responsibilities, which means they are supposed to watch over the shoulders of Colorado's administrative departments of government and try to evaluate their performance. (See p. 230 for more on committees of reference and see p. 184 for more on the legislature's oversight responsibilities.)

JOINT COMMITTEES

Joint committees, composed of members from both the House and the Senate, are more or less permanent committees that do jobs of value for both houses. Some of them provide legislative services to the General Assembly and are critical to the daily functioning of the legislature: the Joint Budget Committee, Committee on Legal Services, Legislative Audit Committee, Legislative Council. These are discussed elsewhere in this book. (See index.)

SESSIONS

The term *General Assembly* in Colorado is not only the name of the legislature but is also a specific two-year period of time. Each General Assembly lasts two years. To determine what General Assembly is currently sitting, count the years since 1876 (the year Colorado was admitted to the Union) and divide by two. In 1991 the 58th General Assembly is meeting. Each General Assembly runs simultaneously with the terms of members of the Colorado House of Representatives, all of whose members are elected in November of even-numbered years and begin their two-year terms when the legislature convenes in January of odd-numbered years. Every General Assembly is composed of two regular sessions, a first session the first year and a second session the second year. There may also be some special sessions (more on this later).

REGULAR SESSIONS

Attempts have been made in various states to prevent the legislature from meeting too long. Some of these attempts sprang from an era of popular suspicion of legislatures when it was felt that "no man's life, liberty, or property is safe while the legislature is in session." The shorter their sessions, the less damage legislators could do. In Colorado, the General Assembly begins its regular session at 10 A.M., no later than the second Wednesday of January of each year. Regular sessions of the General Assembly may not exceed 120 calendar days.

Colorado's 120-day session was adopted by constitutional amendment in 1988. Prior to then, the constitution allowed the legislature to meet as long as it wanted in odd-numbered years but limited sessions in even-numbered years to 140 days. Sessions in both odd- and even-numbered years are now limited to 120 days. For several decades prior to the 120-day amendment, the average number of days the legislature met annually was about 145, yet it always had the option of meeting as long as it wanted when necessary in odd-numbered years, and sometimes the legislature needed this freedom in order to get its work done. Now the axe falls at 120 no matter what.

Some legislators think 120 days is simply not enough time to address the issues that need attention every year. One hundred and twenty days is an inflexible deadline that limits the number of issues that can be considered, limits the time necessary for thorough consideration of the issues, restricts public testimony and input, reduces time to exercise vital legislative oversight of the state's vast administrative apparatus, and increases the power of bosses in the legislature to set the course and agenda of the sessions.

Backers of the 120-day limit speak of preserving the "citizen legislature" and of avoiding a legislature composed of full-time politicians. The longer the legislature meets, the more its members must give up their hometown life and abandon their professions, occupations and businesses. It is said that legislators become less representative of their communities when they are forced to abandon life in those communities and opt for full-time service at the capitol.

And yet, shortening sessions may not really shorten them at all. If a legislature cannot get its work done during the session, it creates special sessions which it or the governor may call, or it pushes work onto interim committees. All this, in effect, extends the session, involves members beyond the session, and defeats the goal of retaining citizen legislators with plenty of time to spend at home with their other life.

No doubt a legislature can improve its efficiency by adhering to ironclad procedural deadlines (as the Colorado legislature does) and by limiting the number of bills that may be introduced in any one session by a legislator (as, again, the Colorado legislature has done — the limit usually being about four per member). Yet, the hard truth may be that the idyllic citizen legislature of bygone days is no longer possible in today's world of complexities that need governmental attention. Colorado is growing, and the larger a state grows, the bigger becomes the job of governing that state and the longer the legislature usually ought to meet. America's most populous state, California, now has a legislature that, for all practical purposes, never adjourns.

SPECIAL SESSIONS

In Colorado a special session of the General Assembly may be called upon the written request of two-thirds of the members of each house, but the session may consider only those subjects specified in the request. The governor may also call special sessions for specified subjects. They are most often called when the legislature is unable or unwilling to deal with a problem during its regular session. Sometimes a governor will call a special session to focus public attention on some issue he regards as vital to the state but which the public and the legislature has neglected. State senators and representatives, once settled down after the regular session, are not always happy to have their lives disrupted by special session calls, especially sudden ones called to serve the governor's political resolve.

INTERIM COMMITTEES

Interim committees work between sessions to study important questions, take testimony, and write bills for the forthcoming session. In Colorado there are usually three or four of these every year. For example, right now (September 1990) there happen to be four, one each on the following subjects: (1) the Two Forks Dam debate, (2) child abuse and maternal substance abuse, (3) the changing role of school principals, and (4) the accountability of government boards and commissions. Each will be permitted to introduce four (no more) bills at the forthcoming regular session.

Incidentally, in addition to interim committees, numerous other committees of the so-called citizen legislature are meeting in the interim, including three committees of the Legislative Council, which are studying (1) long-range planning, (2) economic development, and (3) the structure of state and local government. Furthermore, several standing committees that work year-round continue to meet in the interim (though not technically as interim committees). They include the Capitol Development Committee, the Highway Legislative Review Committee, the Joint Sunrise and Sunset Review Committee, the Colorado Commission on School Finance, and the Joint Review Committee for the Medically Indigent.

COMPENSATION

The basic pay of Colorado state legislators is presently (1990) $17,500 a year, plus $.20 per mile ($.24 for 4-wheel drive vehicles) for one roundtrip home a week during regular and special sessions, plus $99 daily ($45 for Denver-area legislators) for living expenses during regular and special sessions and for committee or official business between sessions. This usually brings the pay of most Colorado legislators to around $30,000 a year, assuming only a 120-day regular session, with no between-sessions payments. Legislative leaders in both houses are paid extra money. The president of the Senate, the speaker of the House, and the majority and minority leaders of both houses each receive $99 more for each day of legislative business.

Legislators find it politically embarrassing to raise their own salaries. Raising per diem payments is less of a problem because most voters don't have the slightest idea that legislators get per diem money. But one has to be careful about per diem payments, too. Anything above a reasonable amount could touch off some sort of notoriety in the press.

The pay of state legislators seems to bear some relation to the population of a state; big states usually pay more. The 1990 basic pay of New York legislators was $57,500, of California legislators $40,816, of Mississippi legislators $10,000, of New Hampshire legislators $100 (yes, $100). It is often debated whether legislators should work for nothing, should be well paid, or should be modestly paid. Some argue that it costs money to run for office, and if a candidate can't pay this out of his salary as a legislator, he or she is going to get it from special interests. Others say he is going to get it from special interests anyway, whether he has a salary or not. It is also argued that you cannot expect competent people to spend their time working for nothing, or even for a little, and that if you want to attract good people to the legislature you have to make it worth their while.

No doubt, some validity attaches to these arguments but perhaps not as much as is sometimes claimed. Other compensations besides money attract people to public office, such as power and prestige. Also, many legislators are able in some greater or lesser degree to continue practicing their private professions, businesses, and occupations between, as well as during, sessions of the legislature. In some cases service in the legislature helps their private occupation. This is often true, for example, of young lawyers, whose legal practice may be improved by the prestige, publicity, and influence acquired through election to the legislature and service there.

PERSONAL BACKGROUND OF COLORADO LEGISLATORS

Colorado has exactly one hundred state legislators, sixty-five in the House of Representatives and thirty-five in the Senate. Among the hundred members there are a variety of human types — some are smart, some are dull; some are honest, some are clever; some are quick, some are slow; some aggressive, some docile; some courteous, some rude; some clean, some vile; some vengeful, some forgiving; some courageous, some cowardly. These characteristics prevail in any sizable group, whether it be a troop of soldiers, the inmates of a prison, the faculty of a university, the brothers of a monastery, or the members of a legislature.

Like the members of any group, legislators tend to have some things in common. For example, they all more or less want to be members of the legislature; most have a common desire to remain members and to maximize their power. It is this characteristic that governs a good deal of what they do in the legislature. To keep getting elected, you have to keep doing what is necessary to win elections, especially the next immediate election: pleasing people, winning respect, and attracting potential campaign fund contributions. Besides a common wish to serve in the legislature, statistics show that legislators tend to have other things in common as well. Legislators as a group tend to be in a substantially higher economic class than the constituents they represent, and likewise a greater percentage of them hold college degrees. Most legislators are of the majority race, although each of Colorado's major ethnic minority groups usually has members in the legislature. It can no longer be said that legislators are almost always men: the number of women in the legislature has sharply increased during the past quarter century. In recent years about a third of all members of the General Assembly have been women.

Most Colorado legislators are between the ages of thirty-five and forty-five; few are younger than thirty-five. It is commonly thought that most members are lawyers. This is not true of the Colorado legislature, where about a quarter are lawyers and the rest are likely to be ranchers, teachers, or business people, some retired. In recent years teachers have constituted about 10 percent of the legislature.

TURNOVER

Turnover is faster in the lower house than in the upper house owing to the difference of terms (two years versus four years). The reasons for this turnover are several. One is financial. Legislators, most of whom are in that upwardly mobile period of life, find their careers interrupted by service in the legislature. For a lawyer, the process of running for office once or twice and serving a term or two helps establish a practice, or at least a reputation, but five months absence from a law practice every year can be ruinous. Furthermore, the pay of legislators is not great, and the costs of campaigning can be high. Service as a legislator is never a secure job, and even in states where a legislator's pay is high, turnover continues to be high because there are still political casualties — and high pay will not necessarily cover costly political campaigns.

The effect of high turnover, according to some observers, is a reduction in the quality of legislation. It may take several terms for a legislator to become really effective, and only a fraction survive that long. However, the exact effect of turnover is uncertain. A legislator who doesn't intend to run for reelection may be better, or may be worse, because of it. On the one hand, it makes a legislator more independent and more likely to use his or her own head rather than hewing to the line of others. On the other hand, legislators who don't plan to run again can get away with disregarding the opinions of voters.

As if turnover were not already a problem in the Colorado legislature, the sovereign people adopted a constitutional amendment in 1990 that limited the number of terms a member of the legislature may serve. Senators may serve two four-year terms, Representatives, four two-year terms. This helps decapitate the legislature by removing leaders, delivers it more into the hands of special interest lobbyists, produces unresponsive last-term lame ducks, and deprives the people of their right to choose.

Still, in Colorado and across the nation, defeating incumbent elected officials at the polls is next to impossible. Incumbents have all sorts of natural advantages: they spend their entire term campaigning for reelection and attract name recognition and money. In some states such as California where the pay of legislators is high, most want to stay. The same is true of Congress. Incumbents win 95 or 96 percent of the time. But in Colorado the attractions of legislative service are less alluring, and turnover comes naturally without the help of a term limitation.

OFFICERS OF THE LEGISLATURE

One might say there are six officers of the legislature in the sense that they are members of the legislature who get extra pay for their duties. Two of these are the speaker of the House and the president of the Senate. The other four are the majority leader and the minority leader of House and the majority leader and minority leader of the Senate. These latter four jobs are party jobs. The majority and minority leaders and their assistants are mainly busy trying to pull fellow partisans together on bills thought to be important to their respective political parties. Why this party work should make them officers of the legislature is not clear.

The only two real officers of the legislature are the speaker of the House and the president of the Senate, who, properly speaking, are not elected to be party agents but to be managing agents of their respective houses in getting legislative work done. They are the super business managers of the two houses. But, in truth, they, too, go about their duties in a highly partisan manner, so that the line between a party officer and a nonparty officer is thin indeed.

SPEAKER OF THE HOUSE

The speaker of the House is the chief officer of the House. If you should visit the House, you will see either the speaker presiding or someone he has called to the chair to preside temporarily. The speaker is supposed to take the chair at the hour scheduled for the House to convene, and when he sees the presence of enough members to make a quorum, he calls the meeting to order and proceeds with business.

As presiding officer, the speaker performs the traditional duties of a presiding officer. He or she is supposed to be the head police officer of the House and, with the help of the sergeant at arms, has power to order everybody out of the House in case of disturbance and to control the doors, halls, and approaches to the House. Needless to say, as presider he applies the rules of parliamentary law and decides questions concerning the rules of procedure — provided that the House itself, which makes the rules of procedure in the first place, can change them at any time and can overrule the speaker's decisions with regard to the rules and their application. He announces the results of all votes taken in the House.

Sessions of the legislature attract many representatives of the public, press, radio, and television: the speaker *accredits* those persons (that is, he determines which among them are permitted to have seats in the House chamber and tells them where to sit). He performs other minor or major duties (you can't tell when a minor duty will turn out to be a major duty), such as signing subpoenas, administering oaths, receiving messages addressed to the House, and signing bills passed by the General Assembly.

The speaker is the most powerful member of the House. Perhaps the greatest of the speaker's powers is authority to appoint all committees of the House. The magnitude of this power comes into focus when you realize that the legislature does most of its business through committees. Committees are the eyes, ears, hands, and brain of the legislature. No one can have a sophisticated understanding of any state legislature, or of Congress, without understanding the role of committees. He who controls legislative committees controls the legislature. Nothing is more important to a member of the legislature than membership on a committee. It is a sign and source of the speaker's power that he appoints all committees of the House, whether reference committees, joint committees, or special committees. Members of the House request their committee assignments and chairmanships through the speaker. In practice, minority party members of committees are usually selected by the minority leaders.

The speaker refers each bill to the appropriate committee, and this adds to his or her power. If any bill might conceivably, by virtue of its vague subject matter, warrant consideration by several committees, the speaker can ordain the fate of the bill by consigning it to a friendly or to an unfriendly committee. Being speaker of the House does not prevent him from speaking, as other members, on general questions before the House, although to do so he must call some other member to the chair temporarily. (See Chapter 9 for more discussion of the speaker's role in the House.)

PRESIDENT OF THE SENATE

In 1974 the people of Colorado added an amendment to the state constitution that removed the lieutenant governor as president of the Senate and allowed senators to choose their own presiding officer. Traditionally the role of the lieutenant governor in almost all states has been to serve as presiding officer of the Senate. The vice president of the United States has a similar role as presiding officer of the upper house of Congress. The new Colorado amendment was tried out in 1975, when the Colorado Senate for the first time elected its own presiding officer.

In the past, the lieutenant governor as president of the Senate was something of an outsider in the Senate. He was not, after all, elected by the Senate itself to preside but presided whether the Senate liked it or not. This was his duty under the Colorado Constitution (almost his only duty). Because he was, one might say, thrust upon the Senate, he was not ordinarily a powerful figure by comparison with the speaker of the lower house, who is the chosen leader of that house and therefore an officer of power.

The presiding officers of the two houses are now quite comparable. They are both elected by, and preside over, their respective houses; they refer bills to committees; they have a lot to say about who serves on standing committees; and their work is similar in many ways. The president of the Senate is usually less an autocrat than the speaker of the other house because the Senate is a cozier, clubbier body, with only thirty-five members, who serve four-year terms. The House, with its sixty-five members, is less cozy, and they are all in a constant frenzy of reelection because of their short two-year terms. Sociologists might conclude that big, insecure groups always need a stronger captain at the helm than small, secure groups.

STAFF OF THE LEGISLATURE

Over the past several years the legislature has allowed itself a staff numbering between 250 and about 270 FTEs. (FTE stands for full-time equivalent.) Some of those FTEs are divided into temporary and part-time positions.

Broadly speaking, there are two categories of staff. First there is the House and Senate staff, who serve only when the General Assembly is in session. They are mostly temporary, part-time positions, and mostly partisan (meaning Republican, at present). Second, there is the staff of the four premier service agencies that are vital to the year-round functioning of the legislative branch: (1) the State Auditor's Office — about seventy FTEs, (2) the Legislative Council — about forty-four FTEs, (3) the Office of Legislative Legal Services — about forty-eight FTEs, and (4) the Joint Budget Committee — about fourteen FTEs. These staff members are mostly full-time, professional, and nonpartisan.

The clerk of the House and the secretary of the Senate are two of the most important people under the capitol dome. They are the ones who see to the daily logistics of the legislature. *Logistics* is a military word — that branch of military science having to do with procuring, maintaining, and transporting material, personnel and supplies. A legislature has many different needs, mostly in the realm of paperwork and record keeping. Each day's action in both houses must be recorded in daily journals, and any action left for another day must be recorded in the daily calender. The journal must include roll calls, a listing of those present and absent, a record of motions, amendments, debates and final actions on bills, and more. The clerk and the secretary must be on top of all this. Furthermore, legislators need to be reminded when a particular bill will be debated, and they need some way to turn to find out the status of any bill — where it is in the legislative mill and what has happened to it so far. All these actions pertaining to bills, motions, and amendments that may happen each day must then be printed up each night without fail and distributed to all members by 9 A.M. the next morning, with copies to multitudinous other places as well. Again, the secretary and the clerk must discharge these duties promptly and efficiently. They may be the only two indispensable people in the capitol.

During a session, the clerk and the secretary are prime movers in a rampage of activity. And before the session begins they are in charge of getting ready for it — ordering supplies, hooking up phones, assigning offices and parking, cleaning and supplying committee rooms, polishing the mammoth brass chandeliers that hang over the House and Senate chambers. Most members of the staff of the legislature (those not working in the four service agencies) work for the clerk of the House and the secretary of the Senate and perform all this work. The clerk and the secretary together supervise around one hundred full- and part-time people during the session — many fewer, of course, between sessions.

LEGISLATIVE SERVICES

It is said that knowledge is power. A legislature without independent means of informing itself falls dependent upon those who do have knowledge: special interest groups and the executive branch of government. In the past fifty years legislatures in the United States have greatly improved their staff services and are now much more self-reliant in gathering the expert knowledge needed to legislate intelligently. The most important legislative services in Colorado are provided by five agencies attached to the legislature and supervised by joint committees of the legislature.

THE LEGISLATIVE COUNCIL

The Legislative Council, created in 1953, is a joint committee of the General Assembly consisting of seven legislators from each house. When one thinks of the Legislative Council, however, what usually comes to mind is the professional staff that works for the council. The council appoints a research director, who in turn appoints (with approval of the Council) such professional, technical, and clerical employees as it needs. Their job is to serve as a permanent research staff, working directly with the legislature to obtain facts for individual legislators and committees of reference during the session and to help other study committees between sessions.

The council of fourteen legislators establishes, from time to time, subcommittees to study certain problems that will be or are before the legislature. The research staff does most of the work on these special projects. This work usually culminates in published reports in the form of facts, figures, arguments, and alternatives, including recommendations for action. Such staff services are often provided for interim committees not directly under the Legislative Council. The Legislative Council also does what it can to provide research assistance to the standing committees of the legislature. In addition, within the bounds of reason, the professional staff of the council helps individual legislators acquire facts and information.

JOINT BUDGET COMMITTEE

(See p. 216 for discussion of the Joint Budget Committee).

OFFICE OF LEGISLATIVE LEGAL SERVICES

The joint rules of the General Assembly require that before any bill is introduced into either house, it must be approved as to format, grammar, and legality by the Office of Legislative Legal Services. In effect, this means all bills introduced into either house are actually put into language suitable for publication in the *Colorado Revised Statutes* (that is, they are actually drafted by the Office of Legislative Legal Services). Here we use the word *drafted* in a specialized sense. It is one thing to draft a bill on the back of an envelope during supper and another thing to draft a bill for actual introduction as a bill. The "Drafting Office" (slang for the Office of Legislative Legal Services) does the latter. The general ideas and rough drafts brought in for approval by members of the legislature must usually be recast in legalese and must be checked against laws already on the books in order to avoid duplication and in order to square the proposed new law with what is already required by law. And it is done to be sure every bill has all the pieces and parts that a properly drawn bill is supposed to have, such as the names of the bill's sponsors, title of the bill, a summary of the bill in lay language, an enacting clause, a severability clause, and a safety clause. Only a member of the legislature or the governor may request the Office of Legislative Legal Services to draft a bill.

All requests received by the office for bill drafting are held in confidence and not discussed or released outside of office staff without prior permission or instruction of the member making the request. A lawyer-client relationship exists between the office and the member.

The revisor of statutes and his or her staff are part of the Office of Legislative Legal Services. In fact, the director of the office is ex officio the revisor of statutes. Formerly, the Drafting Office and the Office of Revisor of Statutes were two separate staff agencies working for the legislature. Today they are combined because they depend so heavily on each other to get their jobs done. The basic job of the revisor of statutes is to publish the statutes, in other words, to publish the *Colorado Revised Statutes* (usually abbreviated *C.R.S.*), and keep it up to date annually, and annotate it. (See p. 314 for more on the *Colorado Revised Statutes.*) The revisor also prepares the *Session Laws* for publication after each session of the legislature. (See p. 315 for more on the *Session Laws.*) Also, the revisor prepares miscellaneous other publications that help straighten out what has been enacted into law by the legislature and the governor, what has been abolished or changed, and, in short, what the law is today.

The Office of Legislative Legal Services is also the chief keeper of legislative records. Any bill, resolution, or memorial that was drafted by the office and subsequently enacted by the legislature is kept on file in the office together with all records pertaining to each. Also, during the session the office keeps on top of the progress of such bills, resolutions, and memorials through the legislative maze. It tracks this progress on a computer that is easily accessible to members and to others who want a quick way to find out the status of these various legislative activities. And while they're about it, the office puts lots of other information on the computer to help with statutory searches and other functions. Following adjournment, the office prepares a *Digest of Bills* summarizing the major provisions of each bill passed during the preceding session.

If the legislature is sued, the Office of Legislative Legal Services coordinates the litigation. Yes, even the legislature is sometimes sued. In 1989 the General Assembly was sued (unsuccessfully) by Common Cause for alleged violation of the GAVEL amendment's prohibition against binding votes in party caucuses.

The Office of Legislative Legal Services also has responsibility for implementing the statutory provisions for legislative review of administrative rules and regulations. (See p. 181 for details of how this is accomplished.)

The Office of Legislative Legal Services is supervised by the Committee on Legal Services, a joint committee of the legislature. The committee appoints a director of the office (who is an attorney-at-law). He or she in turn appoints a professional staff.

STATE AUDITOR

The state auditor conducts post audits of all financial transactions of all agencies of the state government, conducts performance audits (helping determine whether agencies under the sunset law should live or die), and makes special audits upon the request of the governor, legislature, or any state agency. The state auditor is appointed by majority vote of the General Assembly and serves a term of five years. He or she must be a certified public accountant licensed in Colorado. The Legislative Audit Committee helps the legislature make this appointment by reviewing the qualifications of each applicant for the job. The committee also reviews the state auditor's reports relating to post audits and submits recommendations concerning those reports to the General Assembly.

(See p. 255 for further discussion of the role and function of Colorado's state auditor.)

SOME OTHER LEGISLATIVE SERVICES

Other assistance to the Colorado legislature is provided by the chief clerk of the House, the secretary of the Senate, the Supreme Court Library, and the Colorado State Library. The General Assembly is also assisted by several other services. Its Commission on Uniform State Laws promotes uniformity of law among all states with regard to matters where uniformity is practical and useful. The State Officials' Compensation Commission helps the General Assembly determine the proper compensation for state officials and employees. The Joint Sunrise and Sunset Review Committee helps the legislature with its periodic responsibility to determine whether certain agencies (especially the occupational and professional regulatory boards) shall be terminated.

FORMAL AND INFORMAL RULES OF THE LEGISLATURE

WRITTEN RULES

The rules governing the organization and procedure of the General Assembly are found partly in the state constitution (Art. V) and partly in its own enactments: The Rules of the House of Representatives, The Rules of the Senate, and The Joint Rules of the Senate and House of Representatives. The Colorado Constitution goes into much more detail concerning the procedures of the legislature than does the United States Constitution concerning the procedures of Congress. This is typical of the contrasting style of the two constitutions: one detailed, the other general. The Colorado Constitution discusses the terms of members, the times of sessions, the officers of the legislature, what constitutes a quorum, the journal of the legislature and when votes are entered into it, open sessions, adjournment, privileges of members, bills and amendments, the enacting clause, revenue bills, appropriation bills, signing bills, and other matters.

The rules adopted by each house, and the joint rules adopted by them both, are more comprehensive and detailed than the rules contained in the state constitution. Because the two houses do some things separately and some things jointly, it is necessary to have three sets of rules, one for each house and one for the legislature when it acts jointly (as when it sets up a Joint Budget Committee).

UNWRITTEN RULES

Some of the procedural rules of the General Assembly are not found in writing. This is not an attempt to be secretive but simply reflects the sociological fact that every group, whether it be a legislature, a family, a fraternity, or a card club, has unspoken and unwritten rules. No doubt there are hundreds of unwritten rules that bind the legislative group no less than any ordinary group of Americans. "You will not come barefoot to the Senate chamber" might be one, or "you will not spit on the floor of the House" — there are a multitude of these rules of decorum. Certain unwritten rules are of special importance to the legislative process. One of these is restraint in debate. Both the House and the Senate, it should be said, have written rules restraining the frequency and length of speeches. For example, the House of Representatives has set forth in its written rules that a member may not speak more than twice on a subject, nor more than ten minutes, during meetings of the House. Although that rule does not apply in committee meetings, where most of the talk goes on in the legislature, there are unwritten rules that deter members from being too long-winded. It is annoying to other members when one member talks too much.

Courtesy is expected, one form of courtesy especially: when a member opposes a bill, he or she should oppose the bill and not the author of the bill. Members should remain impersonal in debate and refer to each other in respectful terms personally, no matter how heated the debate. Sometimes members insult one another by being overly polite, the only form of insult permitted. Keeping your word is another unwritten rule that applies with particular force to the legislature and to politics generally. A politician might get away with double-crossing the public — with promising the moon and delivering nothing — but the opposite code prevails among politicians, especially among members of a legislature, in their relations with each other. There is honor among legislators; the word of a legislator is his bond, if given to to a colleague.

These unwritten rules are as forceful as written rules, perhaps more forceful, and they greatly expedite legislative business. There are sanctions against violators of the rules, whether written or unwritten. A member who constantly violates the group norms of the legislature will pay a price. His bills may be obstructed, he may be personally ostracized to one degree or another, he or she may be given poor committee assignments, and so on.

APPROPRIATIONS

If hundreds of millions of dollars are going to be spent intelligently, there has to be some knowledgeable weighing of one claim on the state's resources against another. There is no end to the amount of money each agency of the state would spend if it had it, and there is no end to the number of hungry new agencies that would be set up to spend even more money if there were no limit. One of the salient problems of government today — national, state, and local — is how to weigh one crying need against another in the face of wholly inadequate revenues to support them all. Numerous social problems, all staggering in their importance and cost, elbow each other for the attention of lawmakers. Education, for example, which already consumes two-thirds of the general fund, is apparently insatiable; more state aid is asked for junior colleges, for the state's numerous four-year colleges, for graduate education and research. Demands for money to aid other worthy causes hammer ceaselessly at the legislature: more state aid for highways, more to combat juvenile delinquency (50 percent of all crimes in Colorado are committed by juveniles), more for rehabilitating convicted criminals, more for health programs, more for seemingly everything. The tax burden is already heavy, and legislators have to maneuver within the bounds of limited state revenues.

FISCAL NOTES

It is important for legislators to know the dollar-and-cents cost of what they do. Passing a law is easier than paying for its consequences. Almost everything costs money. When a bill is introduced, legislators need to know right away what it's going to cost if they pass the bill, or, on the other hand, how much money might be saved or raised. To serve this need to know, the Legislative Council is asked to look at each newly introduced bill to determine whether it would have any significant impact on the revenues or expenditures of the state — plus, minus or nil. The Legislative Council will then prepare a *fiscal note* assessing the fiscal impact of the bill if passed. This note is attached to the bill where it is available for all to see throughout the legislative process. The note is edited from time to time as the bill is amended, changed and reshaped at various stages in its passage through the intestines of the General Assembly.

This procedure applies only to subject-matter bills. Each proposal must run the legislative gauntlet twice — once as a subject and again as an appropriation for that subject. The appropriation must be passed separately in an appropriation bill, which goes through approximately the same legislative procedure as the subject-matter bill (with the same numerous opportunities for enemy attack). Not every subject-matter bill requires an appropriation (a bill to alter the divorce laws of the state would not), but many might imply an expenditure of money — for example, a bill to start licensing all insect exterminators in the state and set up a new Board of Extermination to handle licensing.

Any bill that has a fiscal impact on the state government not only gets a fiscal note from the Legislative Council but must be considered and approved by the appropriations committees. In view of the close relationship between the appropriations committees and the Joint Budget Committee, it is unlikely that a bill would clear the appropriations committee of either house unless its chances were good for clearing the Joint Budget Committee.

JOINT BUDGET COMMITTEE

The Joint Budget Committee (JBC) is the chief author of an enormous bill every year (called the *long bill*) that appropriates money to run the state government and meet its various financial obligations. The greatest power of the legislature is the power of the purse, and the greatest power within the legislature belongs to those who control the purse. In Colorado legislative procedure, that power belongs primarily to the Joint Budget Committee. The JBC studies the programs, management, operations, and financial needs of all state agencies. It reviews money requests and holds hearings with agency managers. The JBC also reviews capital construction recommendations made by the Capital Development Committee.

COMPOSITION OF THE JBC

The committee is composed of three senators appointed by the president of the Senate and three representatives appointed by the speaker of the House. In naming three members to the JBC the president of the Senate is required to choose the chairman of the Senate Appropriations Committee (who is naturally a majority party member), plus one other majority member and one minority party member from the Appropriations Committee. The speaker of the House of Representatives follows the same procedure in picking three members from the House Appropriations Committee. These six remain members of the House and Senate Appropriations Committees while simultaneously serving as JBC members. Thus, there is an intimate, almost incestuous, relationship between the JBC and the two appropriations committees, useful for coordinating all three committees.

RELATIONSHIP OF JBC WITH APPROPRIATIONS COMMITTEES

The JBC drafts a long appropriations bill and submits it to the two appropriations committees, where in the nature of things it receives a friendly reception due to the partially overlapping membership. One may ask, why are there Appropriations Committees in the House and Senate when the JBC does all the work? Answer: the JBC does not do all the work of drafting appropriations bills. It deals chiefly with appropriations for existing programs, while the two appropriations committees spend their time pondering appropriations for new programs, which are tacked onto the long bill when it reaches the appropriations committees. The long bill proceeds along the same legislative path followed by other bills once it leaves the JBC. Occasionally, alterations are made, but the long bill is usually enacted substantially as submitted by the Joint Budget Committee.

The Joint Budget Committee works year-round and, unlike most other committees, does its work with the help of a professional staff. A staff director appointed by the committee examines in detail all requests for funds with the help of about a dozen analysts. The staff director and analysts are employees of the General Assembly and are not subject to the civil service laws of the state of Colorado.

TURNOVER AND CONTINUITY ON THE JBC

Membership on the Joint Budget Committee is considered the most important committee assignment a legislator of either house can have. Work on the committee is so demanding of a member's time that no committee member is permitted to serve simultaneously as chairman of any other committee except the appropriations committee of either house. Unfortunately, this removes several of the most competent people of the majority party from eligibility for assignment as chairmen of other committees.

Although members of the JBC are known to put in long hours and work very hard, one really wonders how they can become really familiar with the state's financial needs, agency by agency. Turnover on the committee is high. Many members serve only one year. Furthermore, the chairmanship of the committee alternates each year between House and Senate. Consequently, continuity of membership on the committee is not great.

However, continuity among the analysts who work for the

committee is strong. Recent staff directors and many analysts appointed by those directors have held their positions a long time and enjoy a high reputation for competence. It seems very likely that the real backbone of the Joint Budget Committee is its professional staff. Over time the staff becomes intimately familiar with the strengths, weaknesses, and needs of every state agency, knows where the bodies are buried, and is able to lead the yearly parade of new Joint Budget Committee members by the hand through their important work.

CAPITAL DEVELOPMENT COMMITTEE

It is uncertain whether the Capital Development Committee (CDC), created in 1985, contributes anything to the JBC's ability to keep a firm, centralized hand on appropriations. The CDC does a piece of work that used to be done by the JBC: it studies state agency requests for capital construction, maintenance, and capital asset acquisition; it holds hearings; it predicts state needs, ranks them, and sends its findings to the JBC. The JBC still has the final say, but the existence of the CDC and its recommendations cannot but suggest division of authority in the area of capital construction.

THE JBC AND LEGISLATIVE CONTROL OF THE BUDGET

The Joint Budget Committee is key to legislative control of the budget process in Colorado's state government. The amount of money spent by the state is immense, and the demand for financial support comes from many directions. It would be chaotic for the legislature to leave spending to the uncoordinated whims of its numerous subject-matter committees. That would be like letting each member of a large family freely write checks on the same bank account without consulting each other. The case for a Joint Budget Committee is strong indeed, and that need gives it great power.

Very few state legislatures in America really exercise the power of the purse, their greatest power. Most legislative bodies, from Congress down to mosquito control districts, have somewhat abandoned their responsibility to decide who should get how much money. Most state legislatures go through the motions of making budget decisions — they pretend to decide, but when one probes beneath the surface, the executive branch is making most budget decisions in most states, and legislators are following their lead. Not so in Colorado.

Most state legislatures are dreadfully unprepared, either physically or spiritually, to decide — really decide — who should receive how much money. In most states the governor, assisted by a well-staffed budget office, makes studies, balances one need against another, calculates costs, probes the efficiency of what is already under way, draws up a plan of expenditures (the budget), and delivers that budget to the state legislature. Most legislatures assume the governor and his staff of professionals know what they are doing. Legislatures normally pass with few changes the budget they receive from the chief executive. Most governors in the United States do not face a legislature like Colorado's, which refuses to abandon its power of the purse, refuses merely to pretend, and has armed itself with a sleek Joint Budget Committee with the power, the will, and the staff support to do what most other states have abandoned to the governor. The governor of Colorado, of course, also is equipped (modestly) to make a budget (see p. 265), and the governor does indeed submit a budget, but it isn't received by the legislature with the same submissive reverence that governors' budgets in most other states are received. The governor's budget in Colorado is treated no more respectfully (and no less respectfully) than suggestions from a multitude of other sources. Its main value to the legislature today seems to lie in its rather savvy estimates of projected state revenue.

Allowing the bureaucracy de facto power to enact its own appropriations bill (through an overly revered governor's budget) is not only an affront to separation of powers, but may be an affront to economy and efficiency. Separation of powers is meant to foster an adversary relationship between the executive and legislative branches, primarily to check bureaucratic power. When the legislature leaves budget making entirely to the governor and his hand-picked crew, this becomes an invitation to wanton and luxuriant growth of bureaucracy (bureaucrats seek to advance their careers through an ever-increasing apparatus with ever-increasing power to control everybody and everything in sight). Executive budgets invite bureaucratic inefficiency because no bureaucracy cross-examines itself, questions itself, or weighs itself with the same ruthlessness that a well-armed and determined legislature can cross- examine, question, and weigh. The Colorado Joint Budget Committee confronts executive power: the JBC is one of the few surviving bastions of legislative power in a world swept by bureaucratic might.

Recently, the legislature consolidated its power still more by taking away from the governor's Office of State Planning and Budgeting (OSPB) the responsibility for drafting the fiscal notes that accompany bills through the legislature. Because no bureaucracy is disposed to question itself and because the Office of State Planning and Budgeting is in the cockpit of the state bureaucracy — almost a part of the governor's personal staff — with an executive director who sits on the governor's cabinet, the objectivity of its fiscal notes was always suspect in the legislature. Therefore, the job of drafting fiscal notes was given to the Legislative Council, a reputable research arm of the legislature. The legislature does not worry so much anymore about bum steers regarding the fiscal costs or benefits of bills spawned in the bureaucracy.

Looking at the long bill, one notices that it bears footnotes, not unlike footnotes that adorn the pages of scholarly journals. In this respect, Colorado appropriation bills are somewhat unique. These footnotes and headnotes help fortify the appropriations bill against the natural tendency of administrators to pervert the budget. Nothing pleases an administrator more than to be handed one big lump sum of dough to do with what he or she wants — this is one of the greatest causes of governmental fat. Though there is much to be said for administrative flexibility, there is a difference between flexibility on the one hand and unchannelled, uncurbed, unlicensed, heedless, lawless, and profligate discretion on the other. Legislative intent concerning the goals of an appropriation are often lost when a budget confines itself to line items and dollar signs. But when the legislature adds footnotes defining its intent and outlining the standards of performance it expects, this curbs the nomadic wanderings of administrators and helps the legislature audit administrative performance.

THE MAJORITY PARTY BUDGET CAUCUS

We must not overlook one informal but vital stage between JBC action and final passage by the two houses — majority party caucuses. Members of the majority party in each house hold a caucus (meeting) to agree upon some common stand with regard to various disputes over appropriations. This is very important if the majority party is to maintain its ultimate power in the legislature. If the party dissolves into factional disputes over spending and is unable to stand together as a block, then it loses, one might say, the almighty power of the purse.

It is not necessary for the majority party caucus to be unanimous. All it needs is enough votes to assure passage of the bill: thirty-three in the House, eighteen in the Senate. Members of the majority party who stand together in the caucus are considered duty bound by their colleagues to stand by their position when the long appropriations bill reaches the House and Senate for final vote. In recent years these caucuses have been one of the very few moments in legislative procedure that a political party has acted with iron self-discipline and unity. When the majority caucus of one house disagrees with the majority caucus of the other house, a compromise is worked out in a House-Senate conference committee.

The caucus has been particularly powerful lately because both houses of the legislature have been strongly dominated by the same party. But that dominant Republican Party has been divided among moderates, conservatives, and "crazies" (the far fiscal conservative right). The latter have demanded their way — have been strong enough and willing enough to bring down the party if they didn't get it. In the interest of party unity and control, the remainder of the Republican Party in the General Assembly has let itself be yanked around.

The budget caucus is criticized for practically excluding the minority party from a voice in the final critical stages of the appropriations process. Thus, in 1988, it, too, became a target of the GAVEL (give a vote to every legislator) amendment to the Colorado Constitution. The amendment prohibited members of the General Assembly from committing themselves or other members in a party caucus to vote in favor of or against any matter pending. This part of GAVEL is, one would think, wholly unenforceable. After all, in America we do have some basic constitutional freedoms, including the freedoms of speech and assembly. If a group of people wants to assemble and talk and promise things to one another (and that's what a party caucus is), who will say this is not protected by the

First Amendment to the United States Constitution and by similar clauses of the Colorado Constitution? These clauses have always been elevated higher than other constitutional clauses because they are essential to liberty. Common Cause, a "good government" lobby discovered this in 1989 when their suit to have the long bill of that year nullified on grounds it was preceded by an illegal Republican budget caucus. The court quickly dismissed the suit, citing higher First Amendment rights.

CHAPTER OUTLINE

BILLS

A bill is the draft of a proposed law from the time of its introduction in a legislative house through all the various stages in both houses. In Colorado a bill dies if it is not passed before the end of the annual legislative session, but it may be introduced as a new bill in any succeeding annual session. An act is different from a bill. The term act means a bill that has been passed by both houses. Roughly speaking, about six hundred bills are introduced into the legislature every regular annual session, of which about two-thirds are passed. The 120-day session limitation has prompted the legislature to limit each member to six bills and each interim committee to four bills. Of course, legislatures take other actions besides pass bills. Resolutions and memorials also occupy them from time to time.

BIRTH OF A BILL IN THE COLORADO GENERAL ASSEMBLY

How do legislators fight on the legislative terrain? How do they introduce and defend bills? How do they attack and defeat bills? For the sake of illustration, let us focus our eyes on a bill we loathe, pursue it through the legislative process, and try to defeat it. And in the process let us observe the tactics of those who want that bill to pass.

SPECIAL INTERESTS AND THE AUTHORSHIP OF BILLS

Pretend it is a bill sponsored by a group called the Auto Safety Association (we are inventing a fictitious bill and a cast of fictitious characters and interest groups). Its members are service station owners. The bill sponsored by the Auto Safety Association would require motorists to have their automobiles safety checked every ninety days, for which a fee of $10 per inspection would be charged, three-fourths of which would be kept by the inspector. Inspections would be done by service station owners licensed by the state to perform inspections. Let's say we are the people opposing that bill — the League for Less Government. Our slogan is "the less government the better." We oppose making every service station manager a government inspector. Furthermore, we think an inspection every ninety days is too often and $10 per inspection is too much. Above all, we think there is conflict of interest when someone in the auto repair business is given legal power to determine whether your car needs repair.

This sets the stage for a typical battle in the legislature, a battle between special interests, pressure groups. We of the League for Less Government are a special interest. We are also lobbyists. Anyone who tries to persuade a legislator to act one way or another regarding a bill is a lobbyist. Being a special interest is not evil, nor is being a lobbyist evil — at least not necessarily. All interests are "special," whether they be business interests, religious interests, do-gooder interests, or any other interest. Here, in our pretend case, we have a clash of special interests: on one side a group called the Auto Safety Association plus their various allies; on the other side, our group, the League for Less Government, plus our various allies. Legislators are implored and cajoled by competing interests and by competing lobbyists to take a stand and to cast the "right" vote.

The Auto Safety Association has found a state representative to introduce the inspection bill. Only a member of the legislature may introduce a bill; a senator in the Senate or a representative in the House. Actually, that's only a technicality: this bill, like many bills, did not originate in the mind of the representative but in the mind and heart of a pressure group.

Let us hasten to note here that the idea for a new bill may, indeed, come straight out of the mind of a legislator, and we should not leave the impression that legislators are mere porters for outsiders. Many proposals have no outside sponsorship. Other hundreds, however, are sponsored by special interests outside the legislature and often come from associations of one kind or another or from within the state bureaucracy.

So often are bills conceived and concocted in the minds of special interests, so plentiful are the lobbyists in and around the legislature, so active are they in stage managing the progress of their bills through the procedural steps of legislation, that one may well wonder who are the real legislators. Members of the House and Senate who consent to sponsor a bill for a special interest sometimes become a little lazy about seeing to it that the bill moves along. Lobbyists for those interests are on their toes day and night during the session. They will see to every detail, arrange for witnesses at committee hearings, design legislative strategy, and do almost everything except crash the floor of the legislature and vote. With such royal help from lobbyists, a few legislators fall into a kind of lazy stupor about what this or that bill they have agreed to sponsor is all about in the first place and what its current status might be. If you are a student interning in the legislature and you want to know what's going on with regard to a particular bill, what the amendments really mean, and what its chances are, locate a lobbyist supporting (or opposing) the bill. They'll tell you all about it. (See pp. 112–16 for more on special interests and lobbyists.)

We of the League for Less Government are a special interest par excellence. We are going to kill a bill. It is going to be mainly we and our allies who do it.

FINDING A SPONSOR FOR THE BILL

Our opponent, the Auto Safety Association, has found a sponsor

for their auto inspection bill, the member of the House of Representatives who will actually introduce the bill on the floor. Finding the
right sponsors is really pretty important. The Auto Safety Association was smart enough to approach the speaker of the House and
ask him personally to sponsor it. That made good sense because the
speaker, the ultimate leader of the majority party, appoints and can
remove all the majority party members of all the committees of the
House, as well as the chairs of all those committees, and becomes
the virtual boss of the House. All the chairs of committees prick up
their ears when he talks, and he usually has meetings with them
every week or so to keep the business of the legislature's 120-day
session rolling along.

The speaker turned down sponsorship of the auto inspection bill.
Not that he was against it. But sponsoring bills is not his main job
in the legislature. Powerful as he is, he never has trouble getting
others to carry his water for him.

On top of that he is neither for nor against it. He (a Republican)
doesn't see any particular partisan advantage. After all, safety isn't
always exactly a partisan matter; he himself has had a few too many
close calls on the streets with rattle-trap cars. On the other hand,
we are the League for Less Government, and as a right-wing Republican the speaker has been habitually against big government. But
the speaker decided this was probably going to be one of those bills
that was not rigidly partisan, one that could probably be introduced
even by a minority party Democrat and be passed (or defeated)
without much appeal to party loyalty on either side, which actually
is the case with most bills before the legislature.

Still, the Auto Safety Association didn't want a Democratic Party
member to sponsor their bill. It was simple logistics. The pass rate
for bills sponsored by Democrats in a Republican legislature is
sharply lower than for Republicans. After all, the legislature is a
partisan body, and the majority party never likes to let the minority
party build up a record that is too brilliant, especially in an election
year. Also, sometimes a basically nonpartisan issue can suddenly,
out of nowhere, blow up into something intensely partisan. It could
happen in this case, considering the name of the bill's chief opponents: League for Less Government — a name that could be counted
on to pull at the heart strings of every Republican. Just to be on the

safe side, even if this wasn't going to be a partisan bill, they wanted a Republican — a well-connected one.

The Auto Safety Association prevailed on John Brouhaha to sponsor its bill. Except for being a little sensitive about his name, the constant butt of jokes, he was well liked on floor. ("Brouhaha," he insists, is derived from a medieval aristocratic name in Upper Serbia, Brouhahanovitchas. It was summarily shortened by an overworked American immigration official at Ellis Island when his father, Jacob Brouhahanovitchas emigrated in 1888.) Sixty-six-year-old Representative John Brouhaha is presently retired from his truck-stop business on Interstate 25 just north of Colorado Springs. His son now runs the business. Brouhaha limps and uses a cane because of back injuries suffered just two years ago when a teenager driving a car without brakes hit him broadside at an intersection near his truck stop. He is a living symbol of the need for auto safety inspections and is himself a member of the Auto Safety Association, which now seeks to have all Coloradoans go to service stations (like Brouhaha's truck stop) to have their vehicles safety inspected periodically (at a substantial fee).

Representative Brouhaha has been in the House for three terms already, is well connected with the majority party Republican leadership, and serves presently on the Transportation Committee, where the bill is sure to be heard. From our point of view, we don't have too many differences with Brouhaha. He's a conservative Republican, and so are most of us in the League for Less Government. It just happens that on this issue, we differ. Because this is going to be something of a Republican civil war, the Republican leadership is deterred from trying to make the bill a party issue. Also, if the bill is kept nonpartisan the door is opened for support from some Democrats.

Our opponent, the Auto Safety Association, isn't big enough or wealthy enough to hire its own full-time lobbyist, but it has contracted with one of the larger lobbying firms in Denver, which assigned an associate to hover over the bill. John Brouhaha is glad for this help because during the session he is a very busy person and not all that energetic anymore since his auto accident. Furthermore, he is an extremely sociable person, who eagerly looks forward to every annual session of the legislature as one grand outing;

endless breakfasts, lunches, dinners, and late evening parties with fellow legislators and with lobbyists who always pay the bills. Mrs. Brouhaha does not come to Denver during this period. They are loyal and devoted spouses, but she knows John loves the legislature, loves this long party in Denver, where once again he is important, happy, busy. During the four-month session, John takes an apartment near the Capitol Building in Denver (he's got the money) and does not try to drive the seventy miles south to Colorado Springs more than once every couple of weeks.

DRAFTING THE BILL

Just as soon as Representative Brouhaha has agreed to sponsor the Auto Safety Association's bill, he arranges a three-martini lunch at his favorite dive on East Colfax with two officers of the Auto Safety Association and their lobbyist. They talk of many things, including the economic benefits of this proposal for the whole lagging service station business in the state. You might, he observes, almost think of it as economic development for Colorado. After Brouhaha has downed his Reuben sandwich he searches his pockets for a piece of paper and finds an envelope. As the four table companions toss out ideas for the bill, Brouhaha scratches notes on the back of his envelope (well, wasn't the Gettysburg Address written on the back of an envelope?).

After lunch Brouhaha and the Auto Safety Association lobbyist walk back to the State Capitol Building and pay a visit to the Office of Legislative Legal Services. One of the staff attorneys in the office is assigned to draft this bill for Brouhaha and sits down patiently to decipher just what mix of ideas Brouhaha has in mind. She is only fresh law school but sharp as they come. She immediately objects to the presence of the lobbyist and points out that she is required to maintain a confidential relationship with Brouhaha concerning everything about his bill. Brouhaha understands this perfectly, having used the office a hundred times before, but he specifically authorizes her to work directly with the lobbyist during all phases of the bill drafting and subsequent amendments as the session progresses. This is acceptable to the office, which actually, in that way, spends a good part of its time working with member-designated

lobbyists. Shortly thereafter, Brouhaha departs, leaving the Auto
Safety Association lobbyist and the bill drafter to work things out.
Intermittently during the session these two rewrite and redraft the
bill as necessary along the way. (See p. 210 for more on the work of
the Office of Legislative Legal Services.)

FIRST READING: INTRODUCTION

All members of the House and Senate and all five hundred
lobbyists who hover over bills are acutely aware of the rigid
deadlines which the legislature must adhere to in order to get any
work done during a fleeting 120-day session. There is a deadline for
introduction of bills, a deadline for committees of reference to finish
their work and report bills, a deadline for passage of a final bill.
There are other similar deadlines for bills received from the other
house after being passed there. If a deadline is missed, the bill is
dead unless the speaker of the House mercifully grants late-bill
status. The speaker, who is responsible for moving things along
expeditiously, is very stingy with late-bill reprieves and is most apt
to use one to save something intensely important to the majority
party in an election year and in a few crisis situations. Nobody is
inclined to rely on being granted late-bill status, and everybody toes
the line regarding these rigid deadlines, unless, of course, they are
deliberately trying to kill the bill. The final long appropriations bill,
however, is exempt from most deadlines.

Brouhaha meets his deadline for introduction of the auto safety
bill. One snowy day late in January he hobbles with great dignity
into the House leaning on his cane to be present for his bill's *first
reading*. He personifies the need for auto safety. The bill's first
reading on the floor of the House is nothing more than the reading
of its title. The representative supplies four copies of the bill to the
speaker, who gives them to the chief clerk of the House, who
arranges to have copies of the bill printed and distributed to the
members. Bills are numbered in the order in which they are received
by the docketing clerk, who keeps a list of bills introduced.

Up to this point, we who are opposed to the auto inspection bill
have not been able to bring our forces to bear against the enemy
anywhere in the mechanics of House procedure. There is nothing to

be gained in pressuring the Office of Legislative Legal Services, the chief clerk, or the docket clerk — their work is almost entirely technical.

TO COMMITTEE

However, the speaker of the House is a worthy target for pressure at this point; his role does not end with handing over a new bill to the chief clerk. He now does a crucial thing politically: he or she assigns the bill to a committee of reference (sometimes called a standing committee because it stands session after session). Every bill goes to one or more such committees before it is considered by the whole House; in a committee of reference, the fate of a bill can be woven.

Now we who are fighting the auto inspection bill go to the speaker of the House and try to convince him that it is a bad bill and should be sent to a hostile committee. We know the bill might reasonably be sent to any one of several House committees: it concerns automobiles and could logically be sent to the Transportation Committee; it concerns safety and could be sent to the Health, Environment, Welfare, and Institutions Committee; or it could go to the State Affairs Committee, because everything the legislature deals with is a state affair; or to Business Affairs, because it concerns the service station business. And so on. It is up to the speaker to consign the bill to a particular committee or committees. We want the speaker to send it to some dark and unfriendly place from which it may never return, or if it does return, will not be recognizable.

Representative Brouhaha pays the speaker a visit. Brouhaha wants the bill referred to a bright, sunny, friendly committee — say the Transportation Committee, of which he himself is a member. Brouhaha and the speaker are simpatico fellow conservatives, but, then again, so are we. The speaker is noncommittal. He really doesn't care how this one goes. We're lucky he's not against us, because if he were, our chances of stopping Brouhaha would be close to zero, so great is the speaker's influence.

The speaker promptly decides where to send Brouhaha's bill. The speaker knows his committee chairs well. He has handpicked them all. He refers the bill to two committees. First, to the Business Affairs and Labor Committee for consideration of the substantive merits of the bill and second, to the House Appropriations Committee for consideration of the bill's financial merits or problems. This is an obligatory stop for every bill with any sort of financial impact. Before introduction, the Legislative Council has attached a fiscal note to the bill briefly outlining the purpose of the bill, the cost involved, projected future cost, proposed source of revenue, and fiscal impact on state or local finances. The bill is heard first by the substantive committee and second by the Appropriations Committee.

With regard to the substantive committee (Business Affairs and Labor), the speaker correctly sensed that the auto safety inspection bill has much to do with business — the service station business — and with labor, too, because of the thousands of auto mechanics who will be kept busy repairing autos found unsafe.

The Business Affairs and Labor Committee chair is a lawyer by trade, a slightly cynical one and something of a loner. A woman who never joined a law firm and never became house counsel for any corporation or union or organization, she was content to be in solo law practice in her home and therefore content with the lowest imaginable status in an acutely status-conscious bar. She only narrowly won her seat after refusing to accept any donations from political action committees (PACs). She is a Republican like the speaker, and a conservative one at that, for she, too, believes the republic is safer when run by people in private enterprise rather than by people employed by government. She is a "call 'em as you see 'em" chair, and the speaker who knows it very well, felt the bill would get evenhanded treatment in her committee. She is independent-minded but still a team player when it comes to things the House leadership wants, even if she can be embarrassingly obstreperous at times.

Representative Brouhaha is a little worried by "the lady," as he is prone to call her. What if the "call 'em as you see 'em" lady, who had flatly refused a service station political action committee campaign contribution, decided she didn't like the bill? But we, for our part, are worried for the same reasons: she refused our contribution, too.

THE POWER OF COMMITTEES

Reference committees of the Colorado legislature are not quite so almighty and all powerful as committees of the United States

Congress. Colorado committees are less independent, their members having a less secure hold on their committee seats than do members of Congress. Committee assignments in Congress become almost the personal property of the members assigned. In the nearly ironclad traditions of Congress, committee assignments are permanent, although a member, once assigned, may ask to be moved to another committee, or may be forced for mathematical and technical reasons to move.

Committee assignments in the Colorado General Assembly have a less permanent quality. Members of the lower house of the Colorado legislature are appointed by the speaker to serve two years. Members of upper house (Senate) committees are appointed for two-year terms by the president of the Senate (who normally is also leader of the majority party). Both houses follow a policy of giving each party the same proportion of seats on each committee of reference as it has in the house as a whole, and the minority party leader is generally allowed to name the minority members of reference committees. Reappointment to Senate and House committees is customary but by no means guaranteed. Thus, a member of a Colorado legislative committee is not quite as free to show contempt for the leadership of his house as is a member of the United States Congress.

A hierarchy of prestige exists among the committees; some (such as appropriations) are considered more influential than others. Some tend to receive more important bills than others. Obviously, the committees that control money are important. Also, the state affairs committee of each house tends to be especially close to the leadership and provides the killing grounds where bills are often sent to be bumped off (the chairman of the House State Affairs Committee is known as "Dr. Death" among members of the House). The power of a legislator is reflected somewhat in his or her committee assignments. To win good assignments a legislator finds it useful to cooperate with the leadership. Many legislators, however, prefer particular committees because of their subject matter interest, regardless of any other consideration.

COMMITTEE CHAIRMAN

The principal reason legislative committees in Colorado are slightly more assailable than congressional committees has to do with the chairmanship. The chairs of committees of reference in the Colorado General Assembly get their jobs in an entirely different manner than do chairs of congressional committees. The method customarily used in Congress is based on seniority of service and is a recipe for independence, a formula for autonomy so great that the committees of Congress have been called tsardoms and the chairs tsars. By contrast, the chairs of a committee of reference in the Colorado General Assembly is appointed for a two-year term — in the House, by the speaker; in the Senate, by the leadership. He or she is appointed like any other member, and the rules of the House say that the first member appointed to a committee of reference shall be the chair. Consequently, the leadership and the speaker take care in who is first appointed. In the Senate this is done by a committee on committees in the majority party, dominated by the leadership of that party. Once a member is appointed to the chairmanship of a committee, that member customarily retains the chairmanship as long as he is reelected to the House by the voters and as long as his party continues to hold a majority in the House. But continuance as chairman is vastly more dependent on the willingness of the leadership, and of the speaker, to reappoint than is now the case in Congress.

We should not conclude from this that the chairs of committees in the Colorado legislature are weak and powerless. That is far from the truth. It is true that committee chairs no longer have the pocket veto. Not too long ago (before the 1988 GAVEL amendment) chairs could simply kill any bill referred to their committee by putting it at the end of the committee's agenda. The chair could then successfully avoid dealing with it by never progressing that far along in the agenda (the committee chair had complete control over the agenda and over the frequency and duration of committee meetings). Members of the committee would never have a chance to vote it up or down, amend it, or have anything to say about it. GAVEL (a constitutional amendment initiated by petition and passed in 1988) required that every measure referred to a committee of reference be considered by the committee upon its merits — there must be a hearing and a vote on every bill.

But committee chairs still have a bag of tricks for bills they don't like. Removing the pocket veto from that bag makes chairs even more creative with their remaining powers. They still have power to set the agenda (as before) and power over the length and frequency of meetings. This is significant because legislative procedure is now strewn with a collection of rigid deadlines (described on p. 229). Although a chair cannot deny committee members a chance to hear and vote on a bill, they can hold bills in their pocket, so to speak, until it is too late to have a meaningful hearing and worse, until it is too late to meet any one of a number of deadlines down the road, although a chair is compelled to meet his or her own next deadline for reporting a bill out of committee.

Also, GAVEL requires a hearing on every bill in committee, but it does not say exactly what a hearing is. What if there's no time to have a meaningful hearing and still meet the deadline? Or no time to have meaningful hearings on all the bills referred to the committee? The crowding up of bills as deadlines approach (a crowding that can be deliberately plotted by a chair) justifies a quickie hearing, one shortened and hastened to practically nothing. One committee chair, when confronted by a roomful of carefully chosen witnesses primed to testify for hours on both sides of a bill, cut the hearing down to five minutes by merely asking those in favor of the bill to stand up and give their names and those opposed to the bill to do the same thing.

Committee chairs tend to stick together in defending the birthrights of chairs. There is mutuality of action and attitude among them. Further, they are all part of the leadership hierarchy, and the sum total of their influence tends to subdue those who are not part of the hierarchy. Many members hesitate to cross a committee chair too blatantly, lest their own bills and personal futures encounter difficulty in odd places. This is one reason why attempts to blast bills out of committee rarely work. *Blast procedure* (technically known as *demand procedure*) allows the whole house to vote to force a bill that has been voted down by a committee or is stuck in a committee to be removed from that committee and delivered to the house for consideration just as though it had passed the committee.

No committee chair is eager to blast a bill out of some other chair's committee.

COURSES OF ACTION OPEN TO A COMMITTEE

A committee of reference in the Colorado House of Representatives has a choice of five things it can do with a bill:

1. Lay it on the table; this delays it. Brouhaha wouldn't like that to happen to his auto inspection bill.
2. Favorably recommend the bill for consideration by the House sitting as a committee of the whole. Brouhaha and the bill's friends would love this, but it is the worst thing possible for us.
3. Recommend that the bill be amended and that it be favorably considered as amended by the House sitting as a committee of the whole. The chances of defeating the auto inspection bill seem very slim in this committee, so the best thing is to try for amendments that would curtail the scope of the bill — say, an amendment reducing inspections to once a year or reducing the fee to $1 or requiring the state patrol to make inspections. Here a member of the committee can be on both sides of the fence: he or she can go on record as being for the bill but can at the same time support enfeebling amendments. Our forces should shoot for a partial victory in this arena, for half a loaf if we can't win it all.
4. Recommend that consideration of the bill be indefinitely postponed. This is a polite way of saying the committee votes to kill the bill. No further action is taken on a bill indefinitely postponed and delivered to the chief clerk. We who hate the bill would love this most of all.
5. Recommend that the bill be referred to some other committee. For us, there are possibilities in this course of action. It gives us a new arena in which to fight, hopefully an arena hostile to the bill.

THE HEARING

Representative Brouhaha lets his lobbyist pick the witnesses to testify for the auto inspection bill at the committee hearing. Three are invited. First, a professor from the big university to tell the committee how dangerous it is, really, to drive a car. (This, of course, would be couched in deeply impressive academic obscurity.)

"Professor, keep it down to ten minutes," pleads the lobbyist. "Nobody wants to listen to anybody for more than ten minutes. Nine minutes would be better. And tell them right off the bat you've only got ten minutes. That'll put them at ease."

"But how can I delineate all this in ten minutes?"

"Don't, for God's sake, 'delineate.' Just give 'em the straight poop for ten minutes. Toss in a few long words so they know you're a professor and be on your way."

The second witness lined up for Brouhaha's bill is an auto mechanic, straight from the garage, with grease on his hands, to reveal the horrors of auto neglect he sees every day. "Remember. Ten minutes, max," warns the lobbyist.

Brouhaha himself is the third witness. When his turn comes, he looks the very image of an elder statesman, double-breasted suit, thick white wavy hair, cane. He simply tells his story about the high school kid with a rattletrap car that ran into him at a country intersection and concludes, "With the auto safety inspection we are proposing, kids like that couldn't have unsafe cars. We owe it to the kids who don't know what they are getting when they buy that first beloved old wreck."

Two cynical newspaper reporters whispered in the back row of the hearing room while Brouhaha spoke. "Whatever happened to House rule 21 (c)?" said one.

"What's 21 (c)?"

"It says a member with an immediate personal interest in a bill should disclose the fact and not vote on it. Brouhaha is a service station operator who stands to make money inspecting thousands of automobiles if this bill passes."

"Oh, dear boy, nobody pays the slightest attention to 21 (c). If they did, the House would be deserted most of the time. Anyway Brouhaha is just testifying here, not voting."

When the above witnesses are done, our turn comes. We have only two witnesses. One is the president of our League for Less

Government, who says it is an outrage to make every service station operator a government inspector who can determine whether your car needs repairs on the spot before you can drive away with an inspection sticker. This is really putting the fox in charge of the chicken coop.

Our second witness is a mechanical engineer who says the vast majority of auto accidents have nothing to do with mechanical failure. It's mostly driver error, carelessness, or recklessness.

After the hearing, a minority party member of the Business Affairs Committee offers an amendment to the bill reducing fees for the inspection, reducing frequency of inspections, and reducing the number of things inspected. These are all adopted. The committee then recommends that the bill be favorably considered as amended by the committee of the whole.

And so, we have come out of committee with some small victories but at the same time with a big loss. If only the committee had killed the bill outright! Instead, they compromised. Government is the art of compromise we are told.

"Maybe Brouhaha will turn against his own bill if there's no profit in the auto inspection fee," said the cynical reporter.

"Oh no," said the other. "The big profit is not in the fee. It's in the repairs. That's where they'll pluck the chickens."

APPROPRIATIONS COMMITTEE

Clearly the auto inspection bill has financial implications for the state simply because a fee will be charged customers for each inspection. Some of that fee will go to the state for administration of the program; some will go to the garage that does the inspection.

The Legislative Council prepared a fiscal note for this bill (as it does for all bills with financial implications for the state). The fiscal note accompanies a bill in its course through the legislative maze and is revised as various amendments are made to the bill. The fiscal note written for Brouhaha's auto inspection bill says that the state would make money on the program if enacted. The state's share of the fee would be greater than it needs to administer the program.

This being the case, the auto inspection bill aroused no tensions in the Appropriations Committee. However Representative Brouhaha saw an opportunity to increase the take of the service station operators by decreasing the state's share of the fee and increasing the stations'. Reducing the state's share does certainly relate to the fiscal impact of the bill on the state, the sort of matter the Appropriations Committee is supposed to deal with. But increasing the service stations' take has more to do with nonfiscal merits of the bill — merits with which other committees of reference are supposed to concern themselves. Nevertheless, the Appropriations Committee went ahead and adopted Brouhaha's suggestion on grounds that it was somehow relevant. In recent years appropriations committees have acquired a taste for doing this — for branching beyond pure fiscal impact into areas of substantive merit not especially involving fiscal impact on the state. Be that as it may, Brouhaha won another small victory against us.

SECOND READING: COMMITTEE OF THE WHOLE

Every bill is heard by the committee of the whole in each house before it is heard by the house itself. Each house — the Senate and the House of Representatives — has a separate committee of the whole, a committee to which every member of the house belongs. It holds its meetings on the floor of the house. A spectator in the galleries may not be able to tell whether the house is sitting as a committee of the whole or as the house itself.

Once a bill makes it successfully out of all reference committees that may be considering it, the bill is sent straight to the committee of the whole, where it is automatically docketed for that committee's attention in the order in which it was reported.

Since the GAVEL amendment in 1988, the House of Representatives has had no rules committee to interfere with or play favorites with bills as they come out of the committees of reference. The House Rules Committee was the Chamber's traffic cop and could do almost anything it wanted to do with a bill, from killing it to stalling it to speeding it along its way, and more. The Rules Committee was dominated by the House leadership, and it often finagled with a bill in such a manner as to deny the members of the House a chance to vote on the bill, even if successfully reported out of any or all committees of reference.

The GAVEL amendment, which was pushed by the League of Women Voters, Common Cause, and other so-called "good government" groups, not to mention many legislators themselves, was designed to prevent small leadership groups from bottling up bills before they could be voted on by the general membership of committees of reference or by the general membership of the committee of the whole. Thus, all bills that have successfully cleared all the committees of reference to which the speaker of the House has referred them are automatically docketed on the calendar of the committee of the whole in the order in which they are reported. Under those circumstances, there is nothing for a rules committee to do, and in 1989 such a committee was done away with in the House of Representatives. For its part, the Senate did not have a rules committee. It had practiced automatic order-in-which-received docketing in its committee of the whole long before GAVEL was heard of.

The committee of the whole follows essentially the same procedure as the house, with the exception of four or five key differences. It is these procedural differences that mainly explain why committees of the whole exist. First of all, the committee of the whole is a device that enables all the members of the whole house to exchange views and discuss and debate a prospective bill before the bill actually comes to the house. And it enables them to do this without some of the procedural annoyances of formal consideration before the house itself. Members in this forum can vote on the bill without such action being in any way binding. The committee of the whole enables all the members of the house to shape a bill, much as the smaller committees of reference do, and to do so with greater latitude in debate than is permitted when the house itself is meeting.

Members may speak more than twice on a subject in the committee of the whole; debate may go on much longer because there is no mechanism for cutting it off, (for example, no motion for the previous question may be made). Some bills, however, are not discussed or debated there to any great extent but are acted on with dispatch. Debate proceeds in the committee of the whole without wrangling over whether the parliamentary decisions of the chairman are correct: there is no appeal from a decision of the chair in the committee of the whole. Also, there are no votes taken by ayes and noes in the committee. This means no record is made of how

each member votes — voting is generally viva voce (by voice) —
speeding things up and enabling members to vote on the bill or upon
amendments to the bill as they truly choose. However, occasionally
this hiding place is exposed when a member stands up and demands
a recorded vote, as is every member's right. And finally, no motions
to reconsider a bill are in order, which also speeds things along.

The committee of the whole is an important target for lobbyists.
A number of things can happen to a bill there. The committee may:

1. Strike the enacting clause. This is an almost cynical way
   to kill a bill. The enacting clause is the first dozen words
   of every bill saying, "Be it enacted by the General Assembly of the State of Colorado." Without those words a
   bill cannot be enacted. We who oppose the auto inspection bill would love to have the enacting clause stricken.
2. Send a bill back to a committee of reference for further
   study and consideration. This might be an option for us
   to work for. Sending a bill back to a committee of reference might mean sending it to oblivion. Bills, to repeat,
   can be studied to death. At the very least, it gives us a
   new chance to attack the bill in a new forum or in the
   old forum a second time.
3. Amend a bill and recommend to the house that the bill
   be adopted as amended. Here again we are in the lush
   field of amendments, and the committee of the whole,
   where no recorded votes are taken, could be the place to
   hang some disastrous amendments on the auto inspection bill.
4. Recommend to the house that the bill be adopted as is.
   This is what we don't want.

We finally succeed in getting the committee of the whole in the
House of Representatives to recommend an amendment to the bill
reducing the number of inspections from one every ninety days to
one every six months. The committee rises and reports to the House
that the bill should be passed with the suggested amendments.
Adoption of such a report constitutes passage of the bill on second
reading. It takes a majority vote of all the members elected to the
House to adopt such a report. The bill, if adopted by the committee,

is then put on the calendar of the House of Representatives for final consideration and action.

THE READINGS

In the language of legislators, it is said that a bill has its second reading in the committee of the whole. The first reading was when the bill was introduced, and the third reading is when the bill is scheduled for a final vote by the house. It is standard practice in American legislatures to have three readings of every bill in each house — a practice inherited from early British custom. Today, bills are seldom actually read — we just continue to use the term *readings*. In the Colorado legislature a bill may be read in its entirety, but only if a member requests that it be read, a rare occurrence. In the absence of such a request it is presumed that unanimous consent exists to dispense with reading beyond the title.

The practice of reading entire bills aloud to the whole house started before invention of the printing press and before literacy was common — a time when many members of Parliament had no way of telling what was in a bill unless it was read aloud to them. There were three times when the bill was read: first, when it was introduced; second, after committee recommendation; third, just before Parliament was asked to vote aye or no on the bill. It remains so today in the Colorado legislature, except that our legislators can now read and write. They would dread such a full reading as an inexcusable waste of time. Still, one hears lots of talk about readings in the legislature because the terms *first reading, second reading,* and *third reading* are verbal shorthand for various stages of legislative procedure. If a legislator says a bill has only had its first reading, that means it is under consideration by a committee of reference. If a senator says a bill is about to have its second reading in the Senate, that means it is about to go to the committee of the whole in the Senate. If a representative says a bill will have its third reading on Friday in the House, that means it is coming to the House of Representatives for a final house vote on Friday.

ENGROSSED

When the committee of the whole is finished with a bill and recommends its adoption in one form or another, the bill is then *engrossed*. When a bill is engrossed it is printed as it stands after the committee of the whole in the house of origin is finished with it. Today we engross with a printing press; in early times it was done by hand. The word *engross* as used in this sense means literally "to copy the rude draft of a legal document in a fair, large hand on parchment" — today the "fair large hand" is a printing press. The changes and amendments recommended by the committee of the whole are incorporated into the final draft before the house finally takes up the bill. The engrossing is done by the enrolling clerk, who will also, as the title implies, enroll the bill after it is finally passed — that is, he prepares a true copy of the bill as it should read after legislative action has finished in both houses. In Colorado this is said to be the *enrolled bill* and is passed on to the governor. In some other states a bill is not considered enrolled until it has been passed on to the secretary of state after the governor has finished with it.

THIRD READING: FINAL PASSAGE

The House of Representatives of Colorado is now about to deal with our fictitious auto-inspection bill on third reading, and we shift our forces to that terrain, doing our best to have it defeated or to have it amended and curtailed in ways to our advantage. Ordinarily very little amending or debating takes place on third reading; the bill has already been discussed and amended at other stages.

TO THE OTHER HOUSE

Let us assume that the House of Representatives passes the auto-inspection bill in approximately the same form as it was received from the committee of the whole. Now the bill goes to the other house, the Senate, where it goes through essentially the same process as in the lower house. The bill could have started in the Senate and then gone to the House of Representatives. In either case, our forces have a second series of opportunities to attack the bill.

TO CONFERENCE COMMITTEE

If the Senate passes the bill in a different form from that passed by the House (or vice versa), then the two versions of the bill are turned over to a conference committee. At that stage both houses are committed to the bill, but to different degrees and in different ways. The conference committee is composed of three members of each house, appointed by the speaker of the House and president of the Senate. Members appointed often have some particular interest in the bill. For example, Representative John Brouhaha, as the auto-inspection bill's sponsor in the House, was one of the six appointed to the conference committee.

The job of the conference committee is to work out a compromise between the Senate and House versions satisfactory to both houses. The reason for a conference committee, of course, is that a bill must pass both houses in precisely the same form in order to become law. Our purpose here is to press for a conference committee report that will prove unsatisfactory to one house or the other, for if either house then fails to adopt the compromise, the bill dies. We lobby each of the six at various times in their favorite restaurants. We also have a friend on the committee itself to throw in a monkey wrench, if possible. Short of achieving a conference committee report fatal to the bill in at least one house, we will attempt to win what we consider a good compromise version of the bill, one calling for the least level of safety requirements, one with the least amount of payment by motorists, one with the least possible number of inspections, one that gives the least possible scope of discretion to service station inspectors, and so forth.

Of course, John Brouhaha wants just the reverse. In his secret dreams he imagines a Colorado in which every motor vehicle would have to come into a service station every day of the week for a safety inspection, at, say, $100 per inspection, plus parts and labor for "needed" repairs. An array of 1,663 possible safety violations would be searched for. Of course, he keeps his dream to himself but argues in conference committee for frequent, thorough and comprehensive safety inspections at a fee that would "cover the cost," et cetera. The conference committee does its job and reports a compromise — one that causes us who oppose the bill some anguish because we lost a little ground to Brouhaha.

BACK TO THE HOUSE AND SENATE

After the conference committee report, we shift our attack again to the two houses of the General Assembly and try to secure defeat of the compromise bill in at least one house. But the conference committee had correctly sensed the mood of the House and Senate. The compromise was adopted by both houses.

TO THE GOVERNOR

The bill's next stop is the governor's office. The governor may sign it into law, allow it to become law without his signature by failing to sign it within ten days, or veto it. We lobby the governor to veto it, which, to our total amazement, he does. Yes, he vetoes it, saying, "This is a bad bill. This bill leaves the door wide open to rip-offs in the form of unnecessary auto repairs."

Representative Brouhaha is stunned. "My stars, I played poker with the governor just three weeks ago! And I sat up with him in the mansion 'til 3:00 in the morning drinking hot chocolate. And just last week the governor, with his police escort, pulled into my truck stop for fill-ups (super unleaded all around). I'll be a monkey's uncle!"

But as you can imagine, we who fought Brouhaha and his bill are elated. At last our efforts are paying off. Still, we are wary. It's possible for the bill to be passed over the governor's veto. For the legislature to override a veto, each house must pass the bill again by a two-thirds majority of all members elected. We have an excellent chance to kill the bill: a two-thirds majority of all members elected is hard to get. But to our disappointment the auto-inspection bill succeeds in getting the two-thirds vote in the Senate. However, we heave a sigh of relief when it fails in the House of Representatives. We are victorious.

Governor 10

CHAPTER OUTLINE

SUPREME EXECUTIVE POWER

The Colorado Constitution begins its description of the gov-ernor's powers with a serious overstatement when it says he possesses the "supreme executive power of the state." The governor cannot possess supreme power when other elected executives not subordinate to him in any effective sense share executive power with him. These include the secretary of state, the attorney general, the state treasurer, the regents of the University of Colorado and the state Board of Education. Many governors in the United States have come to the sometimes bitter realization that the governor is not the supreme executive but only a stellar piece of the executive.

ORIGIN AND STRENGTH OF THE OFFICE OF GOVERNOR

DISTRUST OF GOVERNORS AFTER REVOLUTIONARY WAR

The office of governor in the United States had its origin in colonial times. The governor of each colony exercised authority derived from the king of England. The history of conflict between royal governors and locally elected colonial legislatures is almost legendary. The American Revolutionary War was a war against governors, against autocratic authority. Consequently the office of governor was all but abolished in the first years of the nation. Power centered in state legislatures. Governors were appointed by the legislatures and left so powerless that separation of powers could hardly be said to exist. Governors had become creatures of the legislature.

STRENGTHENING OF GOVERNORS; DIVISION OF EXECUTIVE POWER

Eventually the example set by the national government, which featured an independent executive and sharp separation of powers, prevailed in most states — but not exactly. There continued to be a distrust of state executive authority; most states vested executive authority not in a governor alone but in several elected administrative officers. Executive power became independent, yes, but fragmented: nobody had too much power. Not only was administrative power divided among various elective officers as in Colorado, but gradually dispersed among many independent or semi-independent boards, commissions, and agencies. To be truthful, governors did not always have much direct authority within their state administrations. No doubt the chaotic system worked as well as it did only because states did not have as much to do then as they do now. Today,

The governor's office before renovation in 1957.

The governor's office today.

however, states are often condemned for their failure to rise to the challenge of twentieth-century problems — this even after an era of state administrative reform. Part of the blame can be laid at the doorstep of the continuing inefficiency of weak state executives.

HOOVER COMMISSIONS AND ADMINISTRATIVE REFORM

A period of administrative reform in America began after the congressional elections of 1946. The victorious party, which had been out of power for many years, wanted to cut the executive branch of the federal government down to manageable size. Congress created a Commission on Organization of the Executive Branch of Government, headed by former president Hoover. The Hoover commission prepared and submitted to Congress in 1949 the most comprehensive analysis and report on the subject in our history. A second Hoover commission made still more recommendations in 1955. These two great national commissions gave much encouragement to state administrative reorganization. They sparked the idea in dozens of states to set up "little Hoover commissions" to study ways of making the executive branch of state government more efficient. And, in many states, including Colorado, a succession of studies was made by legislative councils, legislative interim committees, and committees set up by governors.

CONSOLIDATION OF DEPARTMENTS IN COLORADO

In 1966, a new amendment to the Colorado Constitution (Art. IV, Sec. 22) commanded that "all executive and administrative offices, agencies and instrumentalities of the executive department of state government and their respective functions, powers, and duties, except for the offices of governor and lieutenant governor, shall be allocated by law among and within not more than twenty departments by no later than June 30, 1968." And in 1970 still another constitutional amendment (also contained in Art. IV, Sec. 22) exempted heads of these principal departments from the classified civil service of the state, thus enabling the legislature to provide that nonelected department heads be appointed by the governor or by boards. Before the Administrative Reorganization Act of 1968 Colorado had approximately 125 separate state departments, bureaus, and commissions with varying degrees of autonomy from the governor. Today there are twenty departments, of which all but the departments of state, treasury, law, education, and higher education have chief executives appointed by the governor. State, treasury, and law are headed by elected officials. Education and higher education are headed by persons appointed by boards. Department heads appointed by the governor require the consent of the Senate for appointment, but the governor may remove them at any time without Senate approval.

CONTRAST WITH THE PRESIDENT

The reforms discussed above placed Colorado's governor in a position comparable to the president's in relation to the executive branch. Still, the authority of the governor over the executive branch is limited to the extent that the heads of three Colorado departments are elected and two other department heads are appointed by boards. Also, the president can appoint officials deep into the federal bureaucracy, that is, several layers down, whereas Colorado's governor can appoint only department heads.

As for budgeting, Colorado's governor has the *item veto* over appropriations made by the legislature. The president lacks this important power. On the other hand, the president, helped by a large and effective budget office, has a very strong influence over Congress in the making of appropriations. This is not at all the case with Colorado's governor, whose influence over budgeting is small by comparison.

Colorado's governor and the president both serve four-year terms, and, like the president, the governor may serve only two consecutive terms (eight years). Despite the benefits of term limitations (curbing the excess advantages of incumbents and broadening opportunities for public service), Colorado's governors are now lame ducks in their last term. A lame duck is an official who loses influence because everyone knows his or her power is coming to an end. A second-term president and a second-term governor in Colorado share this fate, and the deeper into their second term they are, the lamer they must surely become.

COLORADO GOVERNOR
COMPARED WITH OTHER STATE GOVERNORS

Because Colorado's governor serves a four-year term, he or she is stronger than governors who serve two-year terms. However, only three state governors serve two-year terms. More than half the states limit the number of terms a governor may serve or prohibit successive terms in some manner. Colorado's two-term limitation was adopted by voters in 1990. It applies to terms of office beginning on or after January 1, 1991. Governor Roy Romer, who was reelected in 1990, is presumably eligible for two more terms besides the one just previously served from 1987 through 1991. The two-term limitation, incidentally, also applies to the offices of lieutenant governor, secretary of state, state treasurer, attorney general, and members of the Colorado Senate. A member of the Colorado House of Representatives may serve four terms (which are shorter). The constitutional amendment also purports to limit the terms of members of the United States Congress elected from Colorado. Whether the United States Constitution permits a state to limit the terms of federal officers is yet to be decided by the United States Supreme Court.

Also, like the governors of forty-three other states, Colorado's governor has an item veto. But it is harder for the legislature to override an item veto in Colorado than in many other states. (It requires two-thirds of all legislators elected to override in Colorado.) On the other hand, Colorado's item veto, unlike that of some other states, applies only to appropriation amounts. The governor cannot veto items of subject matter that do not pertain to money amounts.

Colorado's governor is strengthened by the Administrative Reorganization Acts of 1968 and 1971, which consolidated agencies into twenty departments and made the heads of many departments subject to appointment and removal by the governor. Still, Colorado's governor lacks power to reorganize the executive branch (except his personal staff). Governors of nearly half the states do have some sort of power to reorganize the bureaucracy by executive order. In the area of budgeting, the Colorado governor is weaker than most other governors, for reasons to be explained. Like almost all governors, Colorado's governor gets an automobile, an airplane, and an official residence. Pay for the job is about average ($70,000 in 1990) — not as low as Montana's $52,000 and not as high as New York's $130,000.

THE TOOLS OF GUBERNATORIAL POWER

STRONG AND WEAK GOVERNORS

United States presidents are often classified as strong or weak. The same can be said of governors, and the strength or weakness of governors has little to do with whether they are good or bad governors. Good does not necessarily mean strong. A strong president or governor takes an activist role and uses the power of office to prevail on the legislature and other centers of power to move in a particular direction. A weak president or governor will not attempt to lead but will perfunctorily carry out the formal duties of office, leaving the activist role to others. Colorado governors who want to be strong have various tools at their disposal, even though in some ways, especially in budgeting, their formal powers are weaker than those of many other governors.

APPOINTMENT POWER

The authority to appoint heads of most departments gives the governor some degree of leverage over the executive branch and therefore over multitudinous interests touched by agencies and subagencies of state government. In Colorado, the governor's power of appointment is more limited than that of most American governors. This, to repeat, is largely because some form of merit system and tenure covers almost the entire executive branch, except for the heads of departments, members of most boards and commissions, and several dozen members of the governor's immediate personal staff. The governor's power to appoint and remove is severely limited by civil service rules that cover almost everybody beneath department head. Nor, to repeat, can he appoint all department heads, some of whom are elected and some of whom are appointed by boards. Those he does appoint are subject to Senate confirmation. Also, the governor's influence over the selection of merit appointees within departments is greatly limited by virtue of a constitutional provision that vests appointment power in division heads (who are themselves merit appointees) rather than in department heads, who are gubernatorial political appointees.

Furthermore, the existence of an independent Personnel Board to make rules for the merit system greatly limits the governor's ability to administer the personnel system.

Also, members of many boards (such as the Personnel Board) serve statutory terms and cannot be removed except in unusual circumstances. Quantitatively, the power to appoint members of boards and commissions is by far the greatest swath of appointive power possessed by the governor of Colorado. Scores of boards and commissions are filled by gubernatorial appointment, and hundreds of individual appointments are made. Keeping track of the ceaseless flow of expiring terms is like keeping track of stones in a rock slide. A member of the governor's personal staff has the duty of watching over this scene and informing the governor (and the press) what vacancies exist or are about to exist.

The governor also appoints judges to their initial term, but his power to fill a judicial vacancy is limited to choosing one name from among three submitted to him by an appropriate judicial nominating commission. The governor has no power to appoint anyone other than judges in the judicial bureaucracy; employees of the judicial branch (other than judges) are hired thorugh a personnel system supervised by the supreme court. Nor does the governor appoint employees of the legislative branch.

BUDGET

By comparison with governors of many other states, the budgetary power of the governor of Colorado is weak. What is a budget? What do we mean by budgetary power? What do we mean by weak? A budget is nothing but a plan — a plan submitted to the legislature suggesting how much money it should appropriate for each agency and function of government. The term *budgetary power* means, first, the sheer ability of the governor to make a budget: does the governor have enough staff to gather and analyze the mass of data that is necessary for a good budget? Second, and perhaps more important, budgetary power means the influence of that budget once it reaches the legislature; does the legislature pay any attention to it? In Colorado, the governor's equipment to make a budget is modest (not in quality, but in quantity), and the influence of that budget upon the legislature is often even less than modest. (See p. 265: Office of State Planning and Budgeting.)

The legislature in Colorado is much better equipped to make a budget than the governor. Many state legislatures are not well prepared, either in staff or in will, to make a budget and are really at the mercy of a governor's budget because it is the only intelligent analysis and systematic guide to the state's financial requirements and resources — agency by agency, program by program. The United States Congress was once in a similar woeful condition, depending heavily upon massive budget documents prepared by a large, expertly staffed Office of Management and Budget in the Executive Office of the President. Only recently has Congress taken steps comparable to those taken long ago in Colorado to acquire more legislative control of budget making.

The Colorado legislature is not by any means at the mercy of the governor's budget, nor does it wish to be. Perhaps no other state legislature receives its state governor's budget so cavalierly as the Colorado legislature. In Colorado, the governor's budget is politely received but treated no more reverentially than any other suggestion. The legislature is armed with a Joint Budget Committee of six legislators, who in turn are outfitted with an expert staff, which, working year-round, painstakingly drafts a long, itemized appropriations bill called the long bill. This elongated, interminable, and gangling bill is simultaneously a budget and an appropriations bill. The JBC delivers its long bill to the House and Senate a couple of days before adjournment, where it usually passes fairly promptly with few modifications. (The Joint Budget Committee is discussed at greater length on p. 216.)

Once the long bill passes, the bureaucracy must cope with several hundred footnotes, headnotes, and asterisks sprinkled liberally throughout the bill, instructing in detail how the money is to be spent. Line item appropriations distress the bureaucracy. Leafing through the long bill (so called because it is usually the longest bill passed by the legislature each year) one finds hundreds of these specific line items, sometimes even for small amounts of money. Administrators find the system extremely awkward because not one penny can be transferred from one line to another without permission of the legislature. Most bureaucrats wish the long bill were dramatically shorter. Some of this legislative passion for detail has resulted in recent years from a contest of power between a governor of one party and a legislature dominated by another. But some of it results from a well-founded suspicion of bureaucrats — a suspicion of what they might do with total freedom to move funds around in ways wholly unintended by the legislature.

Those who believe that the governor's budget-making machinery should have greater influence seek to reach this goal by weakening the Joint Budget Committee and producing a sufficiently high level of chaos in the legislature's appropriations process that the legislature will have to rely on the governor's budget office. In this they have allies of sorts within the legislature itself. Some of the ninety-four legislators who are not among the six JBC members grow restive at their exclusion from the budgetary process. One sees evidence of that restiveness each year in last-minute efforts of the majority party caucus to have its say about appropriations just before the long bill passes.

Getting back to the governor's budget, it is, naturally, a combined effort of the entire state bureaucracy, although coordination of its preparation is a responsibility of the Division of Budgeting (conveniently located near the governor's office). Of course, the governor has final say about what goes into the budget. The Division of Budgeting is responsible for what we call the budget cycle, but the year-long process of making a budget involves nearly everyone who works for the state. Proposals laboriously work their way up the long bureaucratic ladder.

Incremental Budgeting. The whole process is largely incremental (to use the jargon of budget making), that is, it's largely a matter of adding an increment (the word *increment* means growth) to the amount each agency received the previous year. Agencies do not generally attempt to justify what they are already doing, do not generally ask, "Should we exist at all?", do not analyze the value of their operation from the ground up. That would be *zero-based budgeting,* a form of budgeting in which no agency gets any money unless it justifies everything it is doing, every year.

Zero-based budgeting disturbs all kinds of vested interests, especially the interests of bureaucrats in keeping their jobs. Politicians in the legislature (and in the bureaucracy) much prefer incremental budgeting, which, though less scientific, is politically more workable and comfortable. Incremental budgeting is easier because it does not involve a massive annual investigation into everything the whole government is doing. Investigations under our present system of incremental budgeting are generally (though not always) limited to probing the merits of a few upward or downward adjustments of existing levels of expenditure. Zero-based budgeting probably would be impossible because no one has (or could have) enough staff to study and justify and explain everything from the ground up.

The closest thing we have to zero-based budgeting in Colorado's government is a periodic examination of some forty regulatory agencies. Colorado's so-called *sunset law* (a pioneering law now copied in several other states), passed in 1976, provides that every such board or agency automatically terminates after six years unless legislative review determines that it serves a useful purpose. Every year the legislature tackles a dozen or so regulatory agencies. The Joint Sunrise and Sunset Review Committee of the legislature, the state auditor, and the Legislative Audit Committee are in charge of studying and analyzing the worth of these agencies. Those studies then go to the legislature for its use in deciding whether to extend the agency's life.

The Colorado legislature has not abolished many boards by this procedure. Therefore, the research cost has been many times greater than any savings realized. The investigative apparatus required by the sunset law is an addition to bureaucracy greater than any deletions of bureaucracy it has accomplished. And the legislature periodically refuses to abolish some agencies, such as the state Mortuary Board or the state Abstracters Board, despite recommendations that they be allowed to die. Nevertheless, defenders of the sunset law believe that the process of investigation yields many useful innovations and reforms besides the mere abolition of an occasional board. The review process strengthens the legislature's power and improves the legislature's ability to oversee the executive branch.

Weakness in Budgeting Related to Weakness of Appointive Power. The governor's role in budgeting falters not only because of the General Assembly's determination to do its own budget making but also because of the governor's general weakness over the executive branch. As noted elsewhere, the governor of Colorado cannot control the executive branch of which he is the supposed chief officer. His power of appointment within the various departments of state government is limited to the heads of those departments. Even at that he cannot appoint the head of every department because three are elected and two are chosen by boards. Nor can the governor appoint deeper into the bureaucracy than department head. Appointees beneath department head earn their positions through the competitive civil service merit system. Nor, for the same reason, can department heads adequately control their merit-system subordinates. This translates into many troubles for the governor as chief executive. One such trouble is the inability to remove numerous agency heads who may not cooperate with the governor in terms of how much money they ask for, the manner in which they ask and press for it, and the manner in which they spend it after they get it.

Concerning the manner in which agency heads ask for money, the problem (as viewed from the governor's office) is that these people know perfectly well that the Joint Budget Committee of the legislature, not the governor, makes Colorado's real state budget. Therefore, no matter what goes into the governor's budget, agency heads can with virtual impunity make end runs around the governor and even around their department head, going straight to the legislature with requests, and they indeed do so with the encouragement of the Joint Budget Committee. This makes a mockery of the governor's budget and of the governor. Attempts by governors to prevent agency heads from making these end runs have always failed. The governor might be able to exercise better budgetary discipline over the bureaucracy by bringing division heads and other upper echelon bureaucrats more frequently and thoroughly into the decisions that appear in a governor's budget. To the extent that decisions come unilaterally from a governor and his personal staff, they will be disdained by agencies hurt by those decisions.

Weakness of Governor's Budget and Planning Staffs. No doubt the quality of a governor's budget also would improve if the budget and planning staffs of the various departments and of the Office of State Planning and Budgeting were larger. In recent years the Joint Budget Committee of the legislature has not seemed inclined to greatly expand the staff of the Office of State Planning and Budgeting.

One of the greatest shortcomings of budgeting in Colorado, whether done by the executive branch or by the legislature, is its deficiency in long-range planning. State budgeting in Colorado seems preoccupied with today, to the excessive neglect of tomorrow. But the problems of tomorrow — the perplexities of growth and how to handle it, the question of water and where to get, and use it, and many other dilemmas — loom over the future of Colorado like giant thunderheads. They are not now being adequately planned and budgeted for. The Division of Planning within the Office of State Planning and Budgeting supposedly does some of this but is too shorthanded to do all that needs to be done.

Adequately staffed executive budget offices could hand the legislature a budget that is easier for them, and the public, to understand: a budget that lucidly shows what the money is intended to buy (not only in physical objects such as a truck or computer, but in broad programs, too). A well-staffed budget office could supply the legislature with any number of other useful studies highlighting the impact of expenditures (and of taxes) on geographical areas, ethnic groups, ages, sexes, towns, counties, or other interests affected.

Perhaps it is futile to speak of budgeting in Colorado. Budgeting means planning what to do with money, and there really is not much loose money to be planned for. Most money spent by the state is committed in advance, sometimes by law, sometimes by practice and political necessity. Even where there is legal discretion to spend or not spend, it is not really as discretionary as it seems; incremental budgeting leaves little money unentangled. Furthermore, the Colorado legislature curbed its own power to spend by enacting a bill that limits the growth of tax-supported general-fund spending to 7 percent of the previous year's budget.

VETO

The veto power of Colorado's governor is stronger than the veto power of the United States president and of some state governors — the governor has an *item veto,* meaning he can veto a single item of an appropriation bill without vetoing the entire bill. If he did not have an item veto, the governor would have to veto whole appropriation bills to get at one small item, and it isn't always politic or wise to veto whole appropriation bills, as United States presidents have bitterly learned. Congress often takes advantage of the president's lack of an item veto and tacks riders to important bills, knowing they will sail through whether the president likes it or not. In Colorado there are few riders to legislative appropriation bills; the governor can simply pick them off with an item veto.

In Colorado, the item veto applies only to appropriation bills. There is some disagreement about the precise meaning of the word *item*. The Colorado Constitution does not clarify matters where it says that an item embraces "distinct items" — which is like saying a zebra is a distinct zebra. The courts of Colorado have nailed at least one thing down: the governor may not veto the salary of any single employee. That would be considered a veto of only a portion of an item, not a whole item. In other words, the governor may veto items, but not portions of items, according to the Colorado court! (*Strong* v. *People,* 200 P. 999.) Of course, the governor may veto whole bills of any type as well as individual appropriation items.

The veto procedure in Colorado is about the same as in other states. No bill passed by the state legislature may become law before its presentation to the governor. The governor has only ten days to either veto or sign. If he does neither within ten days, the bill becomes law without his signature, although if the legislature adjourns before the ten days are up, then the governor has thirty days to either sign, veto, or let the bill become law without his signature. The governor does not have a *pocket veto* to use on end-of-session bills (in which the governor puts bills "in his pocket" until the signing deadline passes).

The right of veto does not extend to measures referred to the people or to measures initiated by the people. If the governor approves a bill passed by the legislature, he signs it into law. If he disapproves, he may return it with his objections to the house in which it originated. That chamber reconsiders the bill, and if two-thirds of the total membership of the house agrees to pass it, the bill goes to the other house; if two-thirds of the total membership of the other house also passes it, the bill becomes law without the governor's signature. It is difficult to get the necessary two-thirds to override a veto, and it seldom happens. The same procedure applies whether the veto is against a whole bill or against an appropriation item. If an item, only the item goes back to the legislature, and the remainder of the bill becomes law.

Party Leader

In Colorado the party pros who make up the party committees, assemblies, and conventions are more powerful than the party pros in many other states, owing to the preprimary nominating procedure (described on p. 129). The governor, as leader of his party, draws more power by being leader than do governors of some other states, where being party leader doesn't mean as much. Governors of Colorado, by having some degree of influence upon designating assemblies of their party, can at times influence who gets on the primary ballot.

Leader of Public Opinion

The governor of Colorado is usually the best-known public official in the state other than the president of the United States. The governor is frequently in the news and becomes a celebrity. He has only to notify the press that he intends to give a pint of blood to the Red Cross or pay his personal respects to a one-hundred-year-old grandmother, and his performance will be broadcast across the state. This ability to reach the public of the whole state exceeds that of all other state politicians. When the governor speaks on issues, the people hear. When the state representative from Rio Blanco County speaks, he may speak more intelligently, more wisely, more perceptively, but what he says may not be heard outside Rio Blanco or even in Rio Blanco. What the governor says is important if for no other reason than that it is heard far and wide. The legislature, on the other hand, speaks with a hundred voices, none of which begins to match the governor's command of public attention. This fact affects legislators, who understand very well that the governor is better equipped than they to reach the voters.

Governor Roy Romer threw himself fully into the fight for Denver's new international airport now under construction and campaigned tirelessly for it. He was not alone in this but was very effective in highlighting arguments for the airport. On the other hand, Romer fought introduction of lotto in Colorado. He lost that one but very nearly stopped this form of state-run gambling, which he opposed as poor public policy.

ACCESS TO EXPERT KNOWLEDGE

Some say "might is right," but the reverse is also true: certainly power often flows naturally from those who are right. Furthermore, "knowledge is power" — we see the words chiseled over the portals of many libraries. To secure his power, a governor needs to be right; to be right, he needs knowledge. His tools in acquiring this knowledge are the entire executive branch of state government, all twenty departments and their multiple subagencies. These agencies are likely to be on top of current state problems; within them are thousands of employees who possess expert knowledge about nearly every subject in the encyclopedia. The governor can readily draw on this pool of knowledge to support his programs and can orchestrate public statements by various experts on behalf of these programs.

The points made above are by no means a complete inventory of the governor's sources of political power, but they are some important ones. Perhaps the personality of the governor is his greatest source of power.

WHAT DOES THE GOVERNOR DO?

If you ask, What does a governor do all day long?, the question would be a little difficult to answer because the governor does a variety of things officially and a still wider list of things unofficially. The official list includes signing bills, appointing people to office, making a budget, and more. Most official duties of a governor may border on the tedious; it is the unofficial activities that make life exciting, countless things in the realm of public relations and granting favors to friends and withholding them from enemies. These unofficial duties often build political influence for the governor and his friends and allies. Possibly most of a governor's time is devoted to this unofficial realm. Usually the official and the unofficial mingle. For example, it is the governor's official duty, or prerogative, to declare special days, weeks, or months in honor of this or that: salesmen's week, iron and steel month, dairy day, and so on. It is seldom bad politics to proclaim support of worthy causes such as the March of Dimes (although he must be careful not to blunder into support of a fraudulent charity). Nearly every convention held in the state asks him to bestow a letter of greetings upon them. He participates in many ceremonial functions. All this becomes good political capital.

THE GOVERNOR'S OPERATING BUDGET

For the 1990–91 fiscal year the governor's office had an operating budget of about $53 million, of which, oddly, almost 90 percent came from the federal government. But this federal percentage is deceptive. Almost all the giant federal contribution to the governor's operating budget is distributed throughout the state to support several federally funded programs administered by the governor's office. Very little of the money goes to support staff within the governor's office itself. The federal money comes mostly from the federal Department of Health and Human Services and primarily supports activities under the federal Job Training Partnership Act.

The Colorado legislature appropriated about $3.3 million to the governor's office in 1990 to support most of the governor's personal staff. This staff is now (1990) about forty FTEs (full-time equivalents), which, in the language of budgeting, means positions continuously filled full-time for an entire fiscal year. An FTE may be subdivided into part-time positions.

THE GOVERNOR'S PERSONAL STAFF

In a sense, the entire executive branch of state government is the governor's staff. All department heads are charged by the state constitution with giving him an annual report, and as head of the executive branch he may draw to some extent on the services of the entire bureaucracy. However, the governor's personal staff, properly speaking, is the collection of people working immediately near him, either directly in his suite of offices or in close, regular support of his duties.

The governor's personal staff is organized into thirteen functional groups called clusters, some of which are *core clusters,* and some of which are *initiative clusters.* The core clusters are those funded by the general fund (that is, monies appropriated by the state legislature). Funding of the initiative clusters comes from federal grants and private donations. The initiative clusters generally focus on one issue as opposed to the core clusters, which do a variety of related jobs and focus on several issues. There are four other offices that are part of the governor's office but operate as separate entities and are not considered part of the governor's close personal staff.

Most of the clusters are very small, consisting of only two or three persons. No one on the governor's immediate personal staff (especially among the core clusters) is covered by merit procedures of the civil service; anyone may be fired at any time for almost any reason. Most persons who work in the governor's office have had much practical experience in the governor's political party. It is no doubt true that governors use their personal staff to some degree as a publicly paid campaign committee seeing to their reelection, advancement, and glorification. But this is also true of legislators and of many others in government who benefit by the public information work of their staffs.

The governor's closest personal staff includes, for the most part, those in the core clusters, which are as follows:

The Core Clusters

The Administrative Cluster. The administrative cluster manages and coordinates the entire office. The chief of staff directs the cabinet and senior staff in moving the governor's agenda forward. The administrative director manages office budgeting and accounting, office personnel policies and procedures, general upkeep and maintenance of the office, purchasing for the office, and more.

The Boards and Commissions Cluster. The boards and commissions cluster helps the governor with his appointments to the more than 275 boards and commissions that are central to governing the state. The cluster maintains records on hundreds of applicants for appointment to all these various boards and commissions and conducts searches for other applicants, does background checks on applicants, and submits candidates to the governor for final selection of appointees. All in all, some thirty-five hundred individuals serve on Colorado's state boards and commissions.

The Citizens' Advocate Office. The citizens' advocate office handles constituent problems with state agencies and officials and works with individual citizens on a case-by-case basis. Lately there have been some seventeen or eighteen thousand inquiries directed every year to the citizens' advocate office.

The Constituency Outreach Cluster. The constituency outreach cluster works to assure that the governor interacts with a diversity of groups and interests throughout the state.

The Legal Cluster. The legal cluster evaluates and recommends judicial nominations made by the state's various judicial district nominating commissions, reviews applications made to the governor for clemency, handles interstate extradition cases, coordinates executive orders issued by the governor, acts as liaison with the attorney general's office, and in general provides legal guidance to the governor, the cabinet, and the staff.

The Legislative Cluster. The legislative cluster coordinates the governor's legislative agenda with all executive departments, advises the governor day by day on what the legislature is up to, and acts as liaison between the governor and the legislature.

The Mansion Cluster. The mansion cluster coordinates all public and private functions that occur at the executive residence. This includes managing staff and overseeing food purchase, preparation, and presentation. Those who hold functions at the mansion must pay the costs. The mansion is maintained both as a public building and as the private residence for the governor. Staff is there to meet the needs of both. The mansion cluster works with the advisory board of the Colorado Historical Society in preserving and maintaining the building for the citizens of the state.

The Policy and Research Cluster. The policy and research cluster analyzes policy issues, drafts speeches and briefings for the governor's public appearances, responds to citizen letters about issues, and generally serves as the governor's think tank on policy and legislative matters. Each of the four policy analysts and the director are responsible for specific issue areas.

The Press Cluster. The press cluster provides information to the news media about the governor and first lady and about happenings related to the governor's office. Other duties include issuing proclamations and greeting letters, coordinating incoming and outgoing mail (more than twenty-two thousand letters come from constituents every year), editing all documents and correspondence issued over the governor's signature, and maintaining the permanent records for the governor's office.

The Scheduling Cluster. The scheduling cluster coordinates the governor's daily and long-range schedule, handles all requests for the governor's time, coordinates the flow of paper and traffic in and out of the governor's office, and acts as a central clearing point for information to and from the governor.

THE INITIATIVE CLUSTERS

The clusters described above are the governor's closest personal staff, and most of the money used by these clusters goes to pay the staff. Additionally, there are three so-called initiative clusters, each focusing on a single subject or issue.

The Communities for a Drug-Free Colorado Cluster. The communities for a drug-free Colorado cluster organizes and supports local community teams in a statewide effort to reduce substance abuse.

The Education Cluster. The education cluster develops policies for the governor on education matters.

The First Impressions Cluster. The first impressions cluster advises the governor on early childhood issues and works with various state agencies and groups to coordinate programs affecting Colorado's children.

THE ADJUNCT OFFICES

Finally there are four adjunct offices that operate as separate entities:

The Governor's Job Training Office. The Governor's Job Training Office administers funds for the federal Job Training Partnership Act. These are federal funds appropriated to all fifty states for training economically disadvantaged individuals and others who face serious barriers to employment. The Governor's Job Training Office awards grants to counties, private industry, and others to provide various types of training. Earlier we said that close to 90 percent of the governor's operating budget comes from the federal government. This is where most of that 90 percent goes.

The Office of Energy Conservation. The Office of Energy Conservation develops, implements and monitors energy conservation programs designed to reduce energy consumption and increase awareness of its benefits. This office is supported by money distributed to all fifty states by the federal government.

The Office of Economic Development. The Office of Economic Development promotes economic growth in Colorado by helping incoming and existing Colorado businesses and by cutting through red tape and regulations.

The Office of State Planning and Budgeting. The Division of Budgeting helps the governor draft the governor's budget, a document technically known as the *executive budget,* submitted to the legislature annually on January 1. The director of the Division of Budgeting is known as the budget director. He and his staff evaluate all plans, programs, policies, and budget requests of all departments, institutions, and agencies in the executive branch of government. They try to make an accurate educated guess each year of what the state's revenue will be and to balance proposed expenditures with anticipated revenues. The division reviews construction and program planning by state agencies and develops construction standards about space, functional consolidation, and quality levels. The Division of State Planning, whose director is known as the director of state planning, coordinates and tries to stimulate the preparation of long-range master plans that recommend executive or legislative action for achieving state objectives. The governor appoints the executive director of the Office of State Planning and Budgeting with consent of the Senate. He or she serves at the pleasure of the governor.

LIEUTENANT GOVERNOR

Candidates for the office of lieutenant governor, and especially people who make speeches in support of such candidates, go overboard describing the importance of the office. It is called the second highest office in the state, second only in importance to the governor. The lieutenant governor stands next to the governor and is "only a heartbeat away" from being governor. All this is technically true. Still, the office of lieutenant governor could possibly be extinguished with no damage at all to the state of Colorado; there is almost nothing for him or her to do. Seven states have no lieutenant governor: Arizona, Maine, New Hampshire, New Jersey, Oregon, West Virginia, and Wyoming. In three, the secretary of state succeeds the governor; in four, the president of the senate succeeds.

In 1990 President of the Senate Ted Strickland, Republican of Westminster, supported the idea of a constitutional amendment to abolish the office of lieutenant governor in Colorado. Strickland

himself once served as lieutenant governor and concluded the office
was unnecessary. It now costs about a quarter million dollars annually to run the office. In addition to the lieutenant governor, who
makes $48,500, seven full-time-equivalent employees work there.
Two serve the Commission on Indian Affairs, which the lieutenant
governor chairs (the only statutory duty required beyond two basic
constitutional duties).

Where lieutenant governors exist, they customarily have three
basic duties: (1) succeed the governor if he or she dies, retires, is
impeached, or otherwise put out of office, (2) act as governor when
the governor is out of state, and (3) preside over the state Senate,
breaking roll-call ties if necessary. Colorado's lieutenant governor
fulfills the first two functions, but recently a constitutional amendment took away his function as president of the state Senate.
Senators prefer to elect their own president.

Besides lying in wait to take over as governor, the lieutenant
governor is also usually available for special assignments from the
governor. A recent candidate for the office described the lieutenant
governor as the governor's "super assistant." Just how much the
governor uses the lieutenant governor as an assistant depends on
how they get along (they may be rivals) and on the talents of the
lieutenant governor.

The governor and lieutenant governor run in the general election as a team and are chosen jointly by the voters, who cast one
vote applicable to both offices. However, candidates for governor and
lieutenant governor do not run as a team in the primaries: each has
(sometimes sadly) to take potluck for a running mate in the November general election.

HOW MANY DEPARTMENTS?

Textbooks on public administration usually teach that no boss should have more than seven to ten subordinates reporting directly to him or her; a wider span of control is said to be unmanageable. This ideal span of control is often exceeded. In 1968 there were more than 125 separate departments, bureaus, and commissions in Colorado, reporting in some fashion to the governor. No person, especially one as busy as a governor, could possibly begin to supervise all of them.

Several decades ago the state legislature put an interim committee to work on the problem. The committee studied how to streamline the administrative branch of government. A reorganization proposal was taken to the people in 1968 in the form of a proposed constitutional amendment. It passed, and today most

Table 13-1: Executive Departments of Colorado Government

1.	Administration	11.	Military Affairs
2.	Agriculture	12.	Natural Resources
3.	Corrections	13.	Personnel
4.	Education	14.	Public Safety
5.	Health	15.	Regulatory Agencies
6.	Higher Education	16.	Revenue
7.	Institutions	17.	Social Services
8.	Labor and Employment	18.	State
9.	Law	19.	Transportation
10.	Local Affairs	20.	Treasury

state agencies are organized under (crammed into) twenty major executive departments. (See Table 11–1.)

These departments, however, are subdivided into various major operating units (often called *divisions*), some of which are, in turn, further subdivided. Most of the major subdivisions are created by statute, that is, by act of the state legislature. But quite a few are simply set up by the department's chief executive. Some departments are a mixture of statutory divisions and administrative divisions, and some are all one or all the other. For example, each major subdivision of the Department of Public Safety is created by law; the chief of the department could not get rid of them without going first to the legislature. By contrast, the three major divisions into which the Department of State is presently organized are all set up by the chief of that department (the secretary of state) by administrative order and represent her concept of how the department should be organized. There are no statutory divisions. But even if a division itself is not created by law, the work it does is, of course, sanctioned by law, although not necessarily assigned to that particular division by law.

The chief executive of each department (with certain exceptions) holds the title of executive director. Some departments, however, are headed by elected officials, who are referred to by their elected titles: attorney general (Department of Law), state treasurer (Department of the Treasury), secretary of state (Department of State). And, although not elected, the head of the Department of Military Affairs is called the adjutant general.

The chief executives of fifteen of the departments are appointed by the governor with consent of the Senate (meaning that the state Senate has power to reject a governor's nominee for the job). The five exceptions are, of course, the elected officials who head the departments of State, Treasury, and Law — plus two others, the head of the Department of Higher Education, who is selected by the Colorado Commission on Higher Education, and the Department of Education, who is selected by the State Board of Education. There is not space in this book to catalog all the work of every department. What follows is a sketch.

DEPARTMENT OF ADMINISTRATION

Whether for better or for worse, the Department of Administration intrudes upon every other agency of government, sometimes with a controlling hand, sometimes with a helping hand, sometimes, perhaps, with both. Its work is so central to the entire executive branch of government that its executive director (who is appointed by the governor with consent of the Senate) might very well be the governor's most important lieutenant within the bureaucracy.

An array of centralized services (or impositions, as some see it) are laid upon other agencies of the executive branch by the Department of Administration. Among the greatest of these is its power over the manner in which money is handled in the bureaucracy. The state controller heads the Division of Accounts and Control, which manages the financial affairs of the state. The controller prescribes accounting procedures, preaudits expenditures, issues warrants for payment of state debts, determines administrative procedures for paying state employees, and has charge of distributing several state benefits.

With responsibilities of that type, it is appropriate for the department to go one step further and conduct management studies for state agencies, which it does through its Division of Management Services. There is a natural linkage between, on the one hand, the process of auditing the use of money by agencies and, on the other, auditing the efficiency with which the agency is managed.

The department also provides a number of conveniences, such as centralized printing, mail-messenger, office supplies, motor pool, and microfilm. On the whole, the state finds it cheaper to provide these things centrally than to let each individual agency struggle with them. The department also handles surplus state property on a centralized basis and purchases (or monitors the purchase of) supplies and equipment by state agencies.

Somewhat related to all this is the department's responsibility for maintenance of buildings, grounds, and parking in the capitol buildings area, the governor's residence, and the computer center. The department's responsibility for state buildings extends to overseeing state capital construction projects, negotiating leases, and keeping an inventory of the state's real estate.

The computer revolution has not neglected Colorado's government, and the Department of Administration has been put in charge of navigating the state through these upheavals. The department oversees acquisition and use of computer equipment by the state and studies computer needs. Also, through its General Governmental Computer Center, the department provides services to over forty state agencies. The department also is in charge of the state's long-range telecommunications network — it runs the state's microwave relay system, which relays radio and telephone communications.

The state's pool of hearing officers has found a home in the Department of Administration, although one may wonder why they might not be more appropriately housed in the Department of Regulatory Agencies. Hearing officers are people who act much like judges in cases that are heard within administrative agencies rather than in courts of law. It is important that these administrative judges be independent and free from threats by agencies whose cases they adjudicate. Thus the Department of Administration is probably as safe a haven as can be found, because the department itself, being chiefly an internal staff agency, is not as likely to be involved in many controversies of the type requiring the services of a hearing officer.

DEPARTMENT OF AGRICULTURE

"When tillage begins, other arts follow. Farmers therefore are the founders of human civilization." The truth of that statement (spoken in 1840 by Daniel Webster) is one of the reasons why we have a Department of Agriculture. The department is an affirmation of the economic importance of agriculture to Colorado. Many actions of this department are designed to make agriculture (which is much more than tillage) a thriving and safe business. The department does countless things to help farmers: everything from controlling coyotes to helping farmers market their products. A veterinary inspection agency tries to minimize the incidence of animal diseases such as brucellosis. Another agency tries to prevent jackrabbits, prairie dogs, ground squirrels, gophers, and rats from destroying crops. Another tries to protect farmers from being swindled into buying seed that won't germinate or is high in weed content. Another section tries to fight insects with insects: the so-called "insectary" (located in Palisade) develops and releases beneficial insects in the hope that this will provide an alternative to chemical pesticides. Other subdivisions of the department try to promote and advertise Colorado agricultural products. The market news service helps farmers keep abreast, almost on an hourly basis, of the prices their commodities will bring. The department serves as a base of operations for numerous trade associations, whose basic purpose is to promote the sale of some particular product: the Colorado Beef Council, for example, and the Colorado Sheep and Wool Board.

Another basic purpose of the Department of Agriculture is to protect the public — the consumers of agricultural products — and to protect those who work in agribusiness by licensing and inspection programs touching many aspects of agriculture, including dairies, frozen food processors, fruit and vegetable markets, plant nurseries, pesticides, farm product warehouses, apiaries, seeds, livestock, brands, fertilizer, poultry, eggs, and weights and measures. The department makes many rules and regulations pertaining to these things and employs a platoon of inspectors to keep an eye on nearly every aspect of Colorado agriculture — to insure safety, health, and honesty. It is perhaps worth mentioning that the department also tries to protect animals; looks into their care when necessary; pays special attention to animals that have been abandoned, injured, or have strayed; and inspects animals used in rodeos.

The Department of Agriculture is one of those departments that is more or less run by a governing board — in this case the nine-member state Agriculture Commission appointed by the governor. The commission makes general policy for the department, designs the departmental budget, appoints an array of advisory committees touching many aspects of the department's work, and approves (or disapproves) each rule and regulation made by the department. The commissioner of agriculture, appointed by the governor with consent of the Senate, is the chief executive (or executive director) of the department.

DEPARTMENT OF CORRECTIONS

Criminologists debate whether jails and prisons really succeed in "correcting" their inmates. Thus it may be excessively optimistic to label the department that runs prisons a Department of Corrections. There is no question that Colorado does try to correct, and no doubt this is the ultimate, theoretical, and humane purpose of our prisons, even if detention of lawbreakers serves other purposes as well.

Colorado's prison system is very expensive. An agonizing question repeatedly troubles the legislature: whether to spend more dollars correcting and detaining lawbreakers or more dollars on things like cancer research and education. It is in making such hard choices that members of the general assembly earn their pay. To those who say it should be sufficient to house lawbreakers in open fields and tents, the answer is sometimes offered that detention in and of itself is a very unpleasant experience and that prisoners (many of them young people) are not always solely to blame for their behavior — family, friends, and surroundings may have had something to do with it — and that, in any case, prisoners are human beings and we are supposedly a humane society. At very least, there is a prohibition against cruel and unusual punishment written into the United States Constitution — a provision that courts tend to think prohibits certain oppressive conditions in prisons, such as massive overcrowding.

Colorado's prisons are classified into various levels of security: (1) maximum security, (2) close security, (3) medium security, and (4) minimum security. There are also some pre-release centers and some residential community corrections programs. Colorado's three **maximum security** prisons are all located in or around Cañon City (pronounced like canyon). These include the Territorial Correctional Facility, the Centennial Correctional Facility, and the Women's Correctional Facility. Also in Cañon City are some **close security** institutions, including the Fremont and Shadow Mountain

Correctional Facilities. Certain parts of the maximum security Women's Correctional Facility in Cañon City are also devoted to close security purposes. And the State Reformatory, located at Buena Vista, is classified as close security and used primarily for young offenders who are at least eighteen years old. There are no separate prisons for **medium security** purposes but only special areas set aside in the Women's and Territorial Correctional Facilities in Cañon City. **Minimum security** correctional centers, as they are called, exist in Golden, Rifle, and Delta. They attempt to provide work-training experiences with emphasis on outdoor maintenance and conservation projects. Also, there are several **prerelease centers,** such as those at Mesa and Fort Logan. Prisoners are released for certain periods to go to school or to work at certain jobs. And finally, the **community corrections centers** are intended to serve as alternatives to prison for certain offenders.

A Division of Correctional Industries within the department runs an assortment of offender-staffed industries as part of its responsibility for training offenders in work habits and skills that increase their employment prospects when released. The industries are self-supporting, profit-oriented, and provide forty hours of work each week for all able-bodied offenders. The industries generate revenue, which partially reimburses the state for the expense of correctional services.

These facilities do not, of course, constitute the entire correctional system within Colorado. There remains the system for juvenile corrections, managed by the Department of Institutions. Also, there are the city and county jails and miscellaneous attempts at correction run by local governments.

The state Parole Board is attached to the Department of Corrections and may have more success with actual correction than prisons have. Of course, its success depends in part upon the threat of prison. The Parole Board is composed of four full-time state employees appointed by the governor with consent of the Senate. The board has power to grant (and revoke) parole. Parole is a conditional release, generally under supervision of a parole officer, of a prisoner who has served part of the term for which he or she was sentenced. It may be revoked and the prisoner sent back to prison if he or she fails to observe the conditions provided in the parole order. There is a separate Juvenile Parole Board attached to the Department of

Institutions to deal with youthful offenders under the age of eighteen who have been sentenced to one or another of the state's juvenile facilities. The executive director of the Department of Corrections is appointed by the governor with consent of the Senate. Headquarters of the department is located in Colorado Springs, the only department situated outside the Denver metropolitan area.

DEPARTMENT OF EDUCATION

The basic function of the Department of Education is to help local school districts do their job. It does this in two ways: (1) by distributing state financial aid to school districts and (2) by trying to provide leadership and support services to school districts.

The state government spends nearly a billion dollars on elementary and secondary (high school) education. The Department of Education parcels this money out to school districts according to elaborate formulas set forth in the Public School Finance Act of 1988. This law attempts to provide at least minimum financial equality among school districts. The department also distributes money to support transportation of students to and from school (under the Transportation Fund Act of 1975).

The Department of Education financially supports a long list of special programs, many federally funded: bilingual education; civil rights; programs for the economically disadvantaged; technical assistance for deaf, blind, and multihandicapped children; early childhood education; library improvement; educational services to refugee children; and the national School Lunch Program.

The department is also involved with an array of other matters pertaining to such things as food service equipment, nutrition education, delinquency prevention, adult education, individually guided education, home study, education for gifted and talented students, and education for students who are exceptionally deficient in health, hearing, sight, emotion, et cetera. And, very importantly, the department oversees teacher education and certification.

Library development is one of the department's favorite interests. It runs the state library and furnishes library services to state officials, to state departments, and to state correctional and medical institutions. It operates a special library for the blind. The department tries to encourage resource sharing among Colorado libraries.

The state School for the Deaf and the Blind is run by the Department of Education. Located in Colorado Springs, the school serves children who, by reason of the impairment of their sense of hearing or of sight, cannot be advantageously educated in other schools.

The Colorado Constitution provides that "The general supervision of public schools of the state shall be vested in a board of education whose powers and duties shall be . . . prescribed by law" (Art. IX, Sec. 1). The state Board of Education is composed of one member elected from each congressional district, but if that is an even number, then one additional member is elected at-large. The board currently has seven members, one of whom is elected from the state at-large. They serve six-year terms, without pay. The Board of Education appoints a commissioner of education, whose job is to do the executive work of the board and of the department. Obviously, the board, the department, and the commissioner are all independent of the governor.

Among the duties of the commissioner is to submit a consolidated annual report to the governor and to the General Assembly tabulating the receipts and expenditures of each school district in the state for the regular school year. The commissioner also submits a report documenting such things as dropout rates, teacher-pupil ratios, number of courses offered, teacher turnover rates, reading and achievement levels, and such other statistics as may be required to show the quality of education offered in each school district. Also, because school districts must submit countless reports on countless things, the Department of Education does what it can to help them survive this agony. The commissioner of education is ultimately a kind of lobbyist and spokesman for the educational needs of the state. The commissioner maintains contact with all sorts of people, especially with members of the legislature, regarding public school matters.

DEPARTMENT OF HEALTH

The Department of Health spends two-thirds of its annual appropriation on health care. But the department's greatest contribution to Colorado may be in regulating the delivery of health care by others. In large measure, the department is a regulatory agency.

It protects the public health by making rules and setting standards for a number of health-related activities. For example, it does not actually run hospitals, but it regulates how they do their job.

One of the department's health-care activities is the delivery of treatment, in cooperation with several other departments, to alcoholics and drug addicts. Also, the department provides various family health services, such as prenatal and maternity care. It carries on a program of immunization of children that reaches most children in the state.

But, to repeat, the department is a regulator. It makes rules to protect the public from air pollution, water pollution, radiation, and hazardous wastes. Colorado's automobile owners in populous counties are apt to encounter the department's air-quality control regulations when they have their annual auto emissions tests. Although the tests themselves are generally made at private garages by individuals licensed to do so by the Department of Revenue, the standards applied are made by the Air Quality Control Commission, which is attached to the Department of Health. Any gasoline- or diesel-powered motor vehicle that fails to meet the standard must be adjusted.

Power to make rules also usually implies power to enforce them. The Department of Health employs many inspectors to enforce rules in dozens of areas — water quality, for example. One reason why you can turn on a tap and get a glass of water that won't put you in the hospital is the department's regulatory program to ensure safe drinking water. Numerous very important inspectors in the Department of Health are forever testing samples of drinking water to protect our health and survival. "Detectives" in the Department of Health keep a sharp eye on disease outbreaks in the state. They investigate the causes and give advice to local health departments for diagnosis, prevention, and treatment.

The department licenses all sorts of health-care facilities, makes endless rules governing their operation, inspects to see that the rules are obeyed, and revokes licenses where gross noncompliance is found. Nursing homes are among the facilities so regulated, which is fortunate for many helpless patients whose only defenders may be the Health Facilities Regulation Division of the Department of Health.

The department keeps statistics on numerous subjects pertaining to health, as well as records of all births, deaths, marriages, and divorces (the so-called vital statistics). If you are writing a term paper on almost any topic pertaining to health, you might want to see whether the Health Policy Planning and Statistics Division of the department has any information tucked away that might be useful to you.

DEPARTMENT OF HIGHER EDUCATION

The Department of Higher Education is for the most part a loose confederation of boards that collectively govern many state-supported institutions of higher education in Colorado. The programs of academic instruction offered by all these institutions are more or less coordinated and supervised by the Colorado Commission on Higher Education (CCHE), which has numerous powers over higher education in the state. However, each board retains a high degree of autonomy in the management of institutions under its control. The executive director of the CCHE serves simultaneously as executive director of the department.

Also, the Department of Higher Education has some other important components. The state Council on the Arts and Humanities gives grants and does what it can to stimulate the arts and humanities in Colorado. The state Historical Society runs a library, has control of the state's historical monuments, keeps a register of historic properties, and gives permits for excavations of historic locations. Also, the department runs a student loan program.

THE GOVERNING BOARDS

Each of the governing boards, except one, is composed primarily of members appointed by the governor with consent of the Senate. The one exception is the University of Colorado Board of Regents, an elected body. Most of the boards also include a student member and a faculty member chosen by student and faculty groups; they generally serve in an advisory capacity without vote for terms of one year. Under the state's sunshine law, the boards are required to conduct all their deliberations in public, except when they are in executive session for personnel actions.

The **Regents of the University of Colorado** supervise four campuses of the University: Boulder, Colorado Springs, Denver, and the Health Sciences Center (also located in Denver). The board is composed of nine elected members, each of whom serves a six-year term. One regent is elected from each of Colorado's six congressional districts, and three regents are elected at-large (by the whole state). No student or faculty representatives serve as members of the board; however, the board has for many years routinely invited student and faculty representatives to participate in its meetings. Unlike the other governing boards, the Board of Regents (and the University of Colorado itself) is established by the Colorado Constitution. Although the university is largely dependent upon the legislature for appropriations (and for good will), the board, and much of its activity, is technically beyond the official authority of the legislature. Thus, it has been said that the University of Colorado is a state within a state.

The University of Colorado has now more or less divested itself of the University Hospital and drawn a bright line between the Health Sciences Center on the one hand and the University Hospital on the other, at least as far as financial responsibility for the two is concerned. Prior to this, the hospital was a constant threat to every part of the university budget, chiefly because of its responsibility for indigent patients and the unpredictability of income and outgo for that function. The hospital is now a nonprofit corporation that has to sink or swim financially on its own sources of revenue. But the corporation is controlled by the Board of Regents of the University of Colorado, which appoints its governing board. There is an extremely snug and cozy relationship between the University Hospital and the University of Colorado Health Sciences Center: all (or most) of the doctors who work in the hospital are faculty members of the University's Heath Sciences Center.

The **State Board of Agriculture** (not to be confused with the state Agriculture Commission in the Department of Agriculture) supervises Colorado State University in Fort Collins, Fort Lewis College in Durango, and the University of Southern Colorado in Pueblo. The board is composed of fifteen members, nine of whom are appointed by the governor with consent of the Senate for four-year terms. The other six (three students and three faculty) are selected by students and faculty at each of the aforementioned institutions and serve only in an advisory capacity without vote for one-year terms.

The **Board of Trustees of the Colorado School of Mines** supervises the Colorado School of Mines located in Golden. The board is composed of eight members, seven of whom are appointed by the governor with consent of the Senate for six-year terms. The eighth is elected by students at the School of Mines and serves a one-year term in an advisory capacity without vote.

The **Trustees of the Consortium of State Colleges in Colorado** supervises Adams State College in Alamosa, Mesa College in Grand Junction, Metropolitan State College of Denver, and Western State College of Colorado in Gunnison. There are nine trustees, seven appointed by the governor with consent of the Senate. An additional member representing students serves a one-year term in an advisory capacity without vote. Another member representing faculty also serves a one-year term, but unlike faculty members on other governing boards, this faculty member is a full voting member. Each year, a different college selects the faculty trustee.

The **Board of Trustees for the University of Northern Colorado** supervises the University of Northern Colorado in Greeley. Seven of the nine trustees are appointed by the governor with consent of the Senate. One member representing students serves in an advisory capacity without vote for a one-year term, and an additional nonvoting advisory member represents faculty for a one-year term.

The **Board of Directors of the Auraria Higher Education Center** (known as the Auraria Board) links the Community College of Denver, Metropolitan State College of Denver, and the University of Colorado at Denver into a comprehensive higher education center in downtown Denver. The board is composed of nine members, four of whom are appointed by the governor with consent of the Senate for four-year terms. Additionally, one member is appointed by each of the three boards that supervise the three participating institutions. One student representative and one faculty representative also serve as members of the board for one-year terms in an advisory capacity without vote.

The **State Board for Community Colleges and Occupational Education** has eleven members. Nine are appointed by the governor with consent of the Senate for four-year terms. The board must have at least one member from each of Colorado's six congressional districts, and no more than five members may be affiliated with the same political party. One student representative and one faculty representative also serve as members of the board for one-year terms in an advisory capacity without vote.

The board supervises twenty-three institutions, including Aims Community College in Greeley, which also has a Loveland Center and a South Campus in Fort Lupton; Arapahoe Community College in Littleton; the Boulder Valley Area Vocational Technical Center in Boulder; Colorado Mountain College, with four campuses — Alpine Campus in Steamboat Springs, Roaring Fork Campus and Spring Valley Campus, both in Glenwood Springs, and Timberline Campus in Leadville; Colorado Northwestern Community College in Rangely; the Community College of Aurora; the Community College of Denver, with separate campuses in Aurora, Westminster, Golden, and Denver; Delta-Montrose Area Vocational School in Delta; the Emily Griffith Opportunity School in Denver; Front Range Community College in Westminster; Lamar Community College in Lamar; the Larimer County Center in Fort Collins; Mesa State College in Grand Junction; Morgan Community College in Fort Morgan; Northeastern Junior College in Sterling; Otero Junior College in La Junta; Pikes Peak Community College in Colorado Springs; Pueblo Community College in Pueblo; Red Rocks Community College in Lakewood; the San Juan Basin Area Vocational School in Cortez; San Luis Valley Area Vocational School in Alamosa; Trinidad Community College in Trinidad; and the T. H. Pickens Technical Center in Aurora. Some of the aforementioned institutions are community and technical colleges, and some are local junior colleges. The state Board of Community Colleges and Occupational Education has direct supervision of the community and technical colleges but has only limited authority over local junior colleges, which are set up as described below.

Junior college districts in Colorado may be organized in any area approved for organization by the state Board for Community Colleges and Vocational Education. The area to be approved must have a 12th-grade school population of 400 or more and a valuation for assessment of $60 million or more. Junior college districts are organized in somewhat the same fashion as special districts (petition followed by vote on the proposition). The districts are run by a five- or seven-member board of trustees elected for four-year terms. A junior college is a two-year institution of higher education.

THE COLORADO COMMISSION ON HIGHER EDUCATION

The Colorado Commission on Higher Education was greatly strengthened by law in 1985. In so doing, the legislature was no doubt motivated by a desire to shield itself from intense pressures continuously exerted by the state's numerous institutions of higher education, each ambitious to realize its full potential, each wanting to offer degrees in almost everything, each guarding what it has like a dog with a bone, and each mobilizing alumni and clientele to fight politically for dollars to do all these things. The CCHE protects the legislature by guarding it from the need to finance duplicative and/or wasteful programs. In its first year of operation, the new CCHE commenced examining the whole system of higher education in Colorado, evaluating each of the many degree programs and cutting a number of them. The goal is to maintain a well-weeded academic garden, to spare the legislature the burden of fertilizing that which is not necessary, and to promote the cause of higher education in Colorado.

The legislature continues to appropriate money, of course, and continues to be lobbied. Appropriations are made to each governing board, which then distributes the money among the institutions it governs. Thus, the CCHE does not have direct financial control of individual colleges and universities. But it does make annual systemwide funding recommendations to the legislature and governor. In so doing, the CCHE recommends formulas by which the legislature can decide how much each governing board should be given. These funding formulas are based on the roles and missions of the various institutions, some of which are inherently more expensive than others. Also, the CCHE must give its approval to all capital construction (new buildings, et cetera) before construction may begin on any campus.

Perhaps the greatest powers of the new CCHE are its duties with respect to approval, review, reduction, and discontinuance of degree programs. No new degrees may be offered at any state-funded institution of higher education without prior approval of the CCHE. Furthermore, the CCHE may direct the discontinuance of any degree program. Also, the CCHE establishes admission standards for each of Colorado's colleges and universities. To help it in these duties, the CCHE has a very influential staff of employees. Also, it has a thirteen member advisory committee chosen in a rather complex manner designed to represent the Senate, the House, the students, the faculty, and other interests.

DEPARTMENT OF INSTITUTIONS

This rather curiously named department is certainly not the only department of state government that maintains institutions. Be that as it may, the Department of Institutions does run about fifteen institutions across the state where care and treatment for the mentally retarded and the mentally ill are provided and where certain juveniles are given care and/or held in custody. The executive director of the department is appointed by the governor with consent of the Senate.

MENTAL HEALTH

The primary function of the Division of Mental Health is prevention and treatment of mental and emotional disorders. It runs two psychiatric hospitals: the Colorado State Hospital at Pueblo and the Fort Logan Mental Health Center in Denver (which have a combined caseload of about seven thousand per year) and a number of centers and clinics throughout the state (with a combined caseload of more than sixty thousand per year).

Following a trend begun some years ago, more state resources are being directed to community-based mental health operations. In the future, primary mental health treatment will probably rest on the shoulders of community services. Instead of prolonged and costly treatment provided by state hospitals, community programs are developing alternatives to hospitalization treatment in which citizens are able to carry on much of their normal daily life and remain with families in familiar surroundings while receiving high quality treatment. This philosophy permits state hospitals to commit a greater proportion of their resources to specialized services that can't be effectively or efficiently handled in community-based centers. State hospitals will be essentially concerned with intensified or specific treatment for the mentally ill who for some reason cannot or should not be treated in an open, close-to-home setting.

DEVELOPMENTAL DISABILITIES

The Division for Developmental Disabilities provides services for individuals with disabilities attributable to mental retardation, cerebral palsy, or epilepsy; or are related to mental retardation and require treatment similar to that required for the mentally retarded. Developmentally disabled people are assisted to realize their ultimate capabilities and to live productive lives, either in an appropriate community living situation, within a community residential facility, or within a state home and training school. Programs are constructed to assure every developmentally disabled individual the maximum care, treatment, education, training, and habilitation. The division maintains three regional centers — in Wheat Ridge, Pueblo, and Grand Junction — where over a thousand profoundly disabled persons are served. Those who are less severely handicapped are served in community programs. Typically, about seven thousand persons annually receive treatment for developmental disabilities.

YOUTH SERVICES

If a juvenile court determines that a child between the ages of ten and eighteen is delinquent or in need of supervision, the court may commit such a child to the Department of Institutions for a period not to exceed two years (five years in the case of repeat or violent offenders). The department will place newcomers in either the Lookout Mountain School or the Mount View School, its two receiving centers, where a further determination will be made concerning placement of the child. Other institutions used by the Youth Services Division include the Adams County Juvenile Detention Center, the Closed Adolescent Treatment Center, the Golden Gate Youth Camp, the Lathrop Park Youth Camp, the Gilliam Center for Juvenile Justice, the Jefferson County Youth Center, the Zebulon Pike Detention Center, and the Pueblo Detention Center. About eight thousand youths are in detention at one time or another during a typical year. A Juvenile Parole Board of seven members appointed by the governor has power to grant paroles to children committed to the department's institutions or to defer, suspend, or revoke such parole.

DEPARTMENT OF LABOR AND EMPLOYMENT

The Department of Labor and Employment is one of those agencies of state government that is primarily financed by the federal government to carry out federally inspired programs. By far the greatest part of the budget goes to a variety of programs designed to help the unemployed. Among other things, the department helps job seekers find employment. Special efforts are made to find jobs for disadvantaged youth, disabled veterans, and recipients of Aid to Families with Dependent Children. Some degree of job training is provided, including the training of apprentices for skilled trades. Another major service is unemployment insurance, which provides payments for a short period of time to persons who have been terminated from their jobs involuntarily and who are ready and willing to work.

Workers' compensation is administered by the department. Under workers' compensation laws, injuries suffered by workers on the job are considered to be a cost of production. Employers are made liable for these injuries, whether at fault or not, and are required to insure themselves privately or with the state. This insurance program is carried on under rules and regulations of the state Industrial Commission, which is attached to the Department of Labor and Employment. In recent years the cost of workers' compensation insurance has grown burdensome beyond the endurance of those who must have it and need it. Costly as it is, benefits seem inadequate. The General Assembly perceives workers' compensation as a crisis area that must be addressed.

The Industrial Commission's authority extends far beyond its role in workers' compensation. It makes rules for the health and safety of workers engaged in a number of occupations. It is a quasi-judicial body that adjudicates citizen-state disputes that arise with regard to application of the various rules and laws within its sphere of authority. The commission is an independent agency in that its three members, appointed by the governor with consent of the Senate for six-year terms, cannot be removed by the governor except for cause — failure to report to work or do their jobs.

DEPARTMENT OF LAW

The Department of Law spends most of its money providing general legal services to all parts of state government. Its duties include looking at state contracts to make sure they are legally sufficient and providing written legal opinions to the state auditor and members of the legislature. Of course, the department provides lawyers to represent state agencies when they are suing or being sued and in various criminal prosecutions. In the field of criminal prosecution, the department does what it can to help local governments detect, investigate, and prosecute such things as organized crime, Medicaid fraud, and consumer fraud. A separate Office of Consumer Counsel attempts to represent certain affected interests in matters before the Public Utilities Commission — an agency that regulates (among other things) gas, electricity, and telephone rates. The Department of Law is headed by an elected attorney general, but he or she appoints a solicitor general, who might best be described as the state government's chief practicing lawyer.

DEPARTMENT OF LOCAL AFFAIRS

Most of the money that comes to the Department of Local Affairs goes out again in the form of grants to local governments to help them improve their knowledge and performance in a number of areas, such as land use planning. The department administers several programs that channel federal dollars to local governments.

The department has a number of responsibilities regarding housing. For example, (1) it applies uniform safety construction standards for hotels, motels, and multifamily dwellings in areas with no locally adopted codes and (2) it administers loans to local housing authorities to provide low income housing.

The department makes a considerable contribution to local and regional land use planning by providing advisory assistance and grants of money. Also, it generates a good deal of geographic and demographic information and maintains a library on planning matters.

Much is done by the department to help local government administer the property tax. This form of taxation is heavily relied on by most local governments as a source of revenue. To apply this tax fairly and intelligently requires a great deal of knowledge, which many local officials do not possess. The department issues manuals of instruction for assessors, holds meetings of assessors, and reviews methods used by assessors in appraising property. And because the property of public utilities is especially difficult to assess, this job is done by experts in the Division of Property Taxation. The division also decides which property owned by churches, schools, and charitable institutions is exempt from the property tax. The state Board of Equalization (attached to the department) sees to it that property is valued equally among the various Colorado counties so that state aid to local governments based on property values will be fairly distributed. The board consists of the governor, the speaker of the House, the president of the Senate, and two persons appointed by the governor. It has power to order sweeping revisions of property assessments in any county found to need such revisions. A separate body, called the Board of Assessment Appeals, consists of three members appointed by the governor. It is a quasi-judicial body to which one may appeal the decisions of county boards of assessment appeals (the county boards hear appeals from assessment decisions made by county assessors).

The department has a role in promotion of economic development in the state. It promotes tourism in Colorado, tries to talk movie and television producers into using Colorado locations, gives all sorts of advice to business firms wishing to locate in Colorado, and works at developing rural Colorado.

Anyone interested in Colorado's local governments will find the Department of Local Affairs to be a gold mine of information.

DEPARTMENT OF MILITARY AFFAIRS

More than 90 percent of the money spent by this department goes to the five thousand–member Colorado National Guard — the remaining small fraction goes to the one thousand–member Civil Air Patrol. Those two functions constitute the work of the Department of Military Affairs.

Before the United States Constitution was written, each state was considered sovereign and had its own army. The Constitution now forbids states to keep troops but allows them a militia (something between troops and police). During World War I, Congress formed the active militia of each state into the National Guard. The governor is commander-in-chief of the state's National Guard except when it is in actual service of the United States. The governor appoints a military chief of staff, called the adjutant general, who is also executive director of the department. The National Guard, which has two components, the Army Guard and the Air Guard, receives substantial federal funding. In most ways, National Guard units are identical to their counterparts in the United States Armed Forces. The National Guard is occasionally used by the governor to cope with emergencies within the state. But most of the guard's time is spent training for the day when they might be called into federal service.

There is also an organization existing only on paper called the Colorado State Guard, separate from the National Guard. It has never been activated in modern times but might be called into existence at some future time when the National Guard is occupied elsewhere. The state guard would consist entirely of volunteers.

The Civil Air Patrol (CAP), an auxiliary of the United States Air Force, is composed entirely of volunteers. The CAP makes air searches for downed aircraft and helps transport supplies and personnel to disaster areas.

DEPARTMENT OF NATURAL RESOURCES

When Colorado was admitted to the Union in 1876, Congress gave the state a generous gift of land to be retained as a continuing source of income for schools — millions of acres of surface lands and mineral rights. To make the utmost and best use of these lands, the Board of Land Commissioners was established directly by the Colorado Constitution and is now attached to the Department of Natural Resources. The board sells and leases land, grants rights-of-way, manages timber, and collects royalties and rents. Revenue from these activities is used primarily for public schools. The board administers a multimillion-dollar Public School Permanent Fund.

Also within the department, there is a Soil Conservation Board, which coordinates some eighty soil conservation districts in Colorado. The overall objective of the board and of the districts is to conserve soil resources by controlling soil erosion and reducing flood damage.

Concerning minerals, the department's basic job is to enforce safety and health laws that relate to extraction of minerals, to prevent wasteful practices in their extraction, and to promote maximum output. The Geological Survey inventories and analyzes the quantity, quality, and location of these resources, collects geological data relating to them, and gives geological advice to the general public, to industry, and to other government agencies.

Colorado is an arid state, and as such it is important to conserve water and promote its greatest utilization. That is the function of the Water Conservation Board, a function that it fulfills with the help of the Division of Water Resources.

The department spends a very large chunk of its budget on programs to prevent the decline of wildlife, to facilitate public use and enjoyment of wildlife, to operate Colorado's state parks, and to develop new parks. A considerable part of the department's revenue comes from fees and miscellaneous sources, such as hunting licenses and park permits.

DEPARTMENT OF PERSONNEL

About sixty thousand people work for the state government of Colorado. Of these, about half are part of a formal merit system by which employees are hired, fired, paid, and so forth. These merit system employees are part of what we call the *state personnel system* — sometimes referred to as the *classified system* (because all the jobs in the classified service are put into classes of similar jobs for similar treatment). The Department of Personnel runs the personnel system.

Perhaps we should take a look at who is not a merit system employee. Half the jobs in the state government may be filled without competitive tests and without regard to any specified standard of merit and fitness — temporary employees, for example. This does not necessarily mean that persons outside the merit system are without merit. By no means. A number of jobs are deliberately left outside the merit system for a variety of reasons. Faculty members of state colleges and universities, for example, are outside the merit system. It is to be hoped, of course, that professors are appointed with some regard for merit, but they are not included in the personnel system of the state. Nor are college administrators, students employed at state educational institutions they are attending, or inmates employed at various state institutions. In addition, members of the many boards and commissions who serve without pay are outside the personnel system, as are employees in the offices of governor and lieutenant governor. Also outside the personnel system are all the members, officers, and employees of the legislative and judicial branches of government. Each of the three elected members of the executive branch (treasurer, attorney general, and secretary of state) may appoint one deputy outside the personnel system. The Department of Personnel has almost nothing to do with these individuals. The department confines itself to those within the system; it administers the system and enforces standards.

The Department of Personnel is headed by the state personnel director, appointed by the governor with consent of the Senate. The director is responsible for classifying jobs, establishing pay plans, making salary surveys, setting procedures, and in general doing work necessary to administer a merit system.

The state Personnel Board adopts rules implementing the personnel system described above and hears appeals from disciplinary actions. The board was created by the state constitution and consists of five members, three of whom are appointed by the governor with consent of the Senate and two of whom are elected by classified employees of the personnel system. All members serve five-year terms. None of the members may be employees of the state or employees of any state employee organization.

In making appointments under the system, the *rule of three* is used. That is, examinations are given for each position, and the names of those who pass the exam are arranged on an *eligible list* according to how well they did on the exam. When a vacancy occurs, the top three names on the list are submitted to the head of the division where the job opening exists. When one of the top three is actually appointed, the other two hopefuls remain on the list and are submitted again (together with a new third name) for the next job opening. Once appointed, the new appointee remains on probation for a certain period of time and, if found satisfactory, will be given *tenure* and cannot be terminated except for certain specific causes such as failure to perform duties.

If an attempt is made to dismiss, suspend, or discipline any merit system employee, the employee must be given written notice stating how he or she has failed to comply with standards of efficient service or what else has been done to justify the action. The employee ultimately has a right to appeal to the state Personnel Board, where he or she has a right to be heard in person or through an attorney.

The civil service system was first established in 1907 by the state legislature but in 1918 was cemented into the state constitution. The 1918 amendment put the whole system under a civil service commission, but in 1970 another amendment abolished the commission and replaced it with the Personnel Board and the Department of Personnel. Also, the 1970 amendment provided that division heads, not department heads, are the appointing authority. It was feared that department heads (who are politically appointed) might show some political bias in making appointments, whereas division heads (who themselves are merit system appointees) might not be so politically motivated.

The current system has been under attack in recent years. Critics think the system is too awkward. They want to abolish the Personnel Board and let the personnel director, who is appointed by the governor, make rules for the merit system as well as administer the system. The rules, of course, would have to conform to the constitutional requirements, such as the rule of three and veterans' preference. This scheme would put the governor in a better position to manage the executive branch of government — a job he is elected to do. Critics of the present system also want to change the appointing authority from the division head to the department head. This, too, would give the governor more influence over the personnel system, because he appoints most department heads. Critics would also like to use arbitrators rather than the Personnel Board to hear and decide labor-management disputes in the classified service. Arbitrators, it is said, have no vested interest in the outcome of an appeal, nor does arbitration require the services of attorneys.

Defenders of the present system believe the governor has quite enough authority over the personnel system by virtue of the fact that he appoints the personnel director and three of the five members of the Personnel Board. Many classified state employees are partial to the Personnel Board, partly because it includes two members whom they elect. Also, defenders of the present system claim that shifting the appointing authority from the division head to the department head could lead to an intrusion of illegal political patronage. Furthermore, many people fear that a system of arbitration for settling labor-management disputes might make collective bargaining agreements between the state and its employees necessary and strengthen the role of public service unions.

DEPARTMENT OF PUBLIC SAFETY

Without much rhyme or reason the various agencies now constituting the Department of Public Safety were, until 1984, scattered elsewhere in the government. The purpose of this newest department is to organize those scattered agencies under one hat.

Its biggest component is the Colorado State Patrol, which uses about two-thirds of the department's annual appropriation. Most of the money to support the 725-member patrol comes from the state tax on gasoline. The patrol consists of commissioned officers, noncommissioned officers, and patrol officers. It is proper to address them all as "officer." The chief of the patrol is appointed by the executive director of the department. Obviously, the main job of the patrol is to enforce state laws relating to motor vehicles — their equipment, weight, cargoes, licenses, operators, and so on. The patrol also keeps an index of stolen vehicles, deals with abandoned vehicles, investigates traffic accidents, and helps collect motor vehicle taxes. The patrol more or less confines its enforcement of traffic laws to state highways, leaving county roads and city streets chiefly to local officers.

The Colorado Law Enforcement Training Academy offers basic training courses for peace officers from throughout the state. All newly appointed police officers, deputy sheriffs, and town marshals are required to have fulfilled certain minimum standards of training, which they may get from this academy if the local government that employs them does not maintain its own academy. Incidentally, all full-time investigators for the attorney general or for district attorneys also must have this training. The chief of the Colorado State Patrol is superintendent of the academy, and he works with an advisory board appointed by the governor. The advisory board has power to certify peace officers who have met the minimum standards of training. Also, incidentally, the Department of Public Safety is interested in firefighters too, especially in seeing to it that all firefighters in the state have at least a minimum level of training.

The Colorado Bureau of Investigation (CBI), a "little FBI," is within the Department of Public Safety. It receives hundreds of requests for assistance every year from local police agencies. The bureau provides technical services, such as analysis of physical evidence, and assists in the investigation of crime as well as in the prosecution of cases. It also maintains a statewide criminal identification system that includes fingerprints, which is available to local police agencies as well as to law enforcement agencies nationwide. The Colorado Crime Information Center is part of the CBI. Its job is to maintain a computerized system for locating fugitives, missing persons, and lost, stolen, or recovered property. Likewise, the Colorado Organized Crime Strike Force is part of the CBI. It coordinates a statewide intelligence network about organized crime and advises how to combat organized crime.

The Department of Public Safety has within it a rather intriguing academic arm, the Division of Criminal Justice, that keeps the entire Colorado criminal justice system under scrutiny and recommends whatever improvements it thinks best. It examines the entire law enforcement, judicial, and corrections system.

Thinking the unthinkable and planning what to do about it also occupies the department. Its Division of Disaster Emergency Services tries to foresee various kinds of disasters that might strike the state and keeps plans on file detailing how to handle disasters when they happen. The governor has a Disaster Emergency Council on continuous standby to advise him or her how to respond to disasters. The executive director of the Department of Public Safety is appointed by the governor with consent of the Senate.

DEPARTMENT OF REGULATORY AGENCIES

The Department of Regulatory Agencies actually consists chiefly of a whole collection of regulatory agencies. One might think of the department as a bag into which all these bureaus are thrown simply because they do approximately the same type of work. Each regulates some occupation or business, and each goes about it in roughly the same way. Typically, a regulatory agency will consist of an independent board plus a staff. Board members are usually appointed by the governor for a certain number of years and cannot be fired except for cause — failure to attend meetings, et cetera (which is why they are called independent). A typical regulatory board is the State Board of Accountancy. It gives examinations to people who want to be accountants and licenses those who pass, makes rules for the practice of accountancy, investigates and adjudicates alleged violations, and imposes penalties. About two dozen occupations, including doctors, nurses, dentists, plumbers, and electricians, are regulated by similar boards.

Five great financial industries are regulated by separate divisions of the department: banking, savings and loan, insurance, securities, and real estate. The Division of Insurance, for example, checks into the solvency of insurance companies and their ability to pay claims, sees to it that claim processing is fair, insures that the company's representatives are qualified, and provides consumers with a complaint mechanism. In general, the Division of Insurance regulates the whole insurance industry in Colorado: the companies, the agents, the brokers, the agencies, the adjusters, and so forth. The Division of Banking has similar control over banks, the Division of Securities over the securities business, the Division of Savings and Loan over those companies, and the Division of Real Estate over the realty business.

The powerful three-member Public Utilities Commission (PUC) is also attached to the department. Public utilities are what economists call natural monopolies because competition within such industries is impractical. In the water business, for example, it is impractical to have competing water lines running up and down the streets. Therefore, to prevent a water company or other utility from charging sky-high prices for a product people simply must have and can't get from any competitor, the Public Utilities Commission was established to regulate rates and keep prices reasonable while still allowing the utility to make a reasonable profit. And in the process, the PUC makes many other rules and regulations governing each utility business under its jurisdiction — gas, electricity, telephone, telegraph, water, and pipeline companies.

The Civil Rights Commission, which investigates employment discrimination, and the Colorado Racing Commission, which regulates pari-mutuel wagering on horse and greyhound racing, are also contained within the Department of Regulatory Agencies.

DEPARTMENT OF REVENUE

The Department of Revenue has so much to do with motor vehicles that it could justifiably be called the Department of Motor Vehicles. It handles driver licensing and titling and registration of motor vehicles, and it administers state laws pertaining to financial responsibility, accident reporting, record maintenance, and driver schools. The department runs the ports of entry, which truckers encounter when they cross into the state. It helps collect the ton mile and passenger mile taxes and assists in a variety of inspection and enforcement activities in collaboration with the Department of Highways and other agencies that have an interest in what is being brought into or taken through Colorado. Most of these motor vehicle activities involve collecting fees and taxes and are, therefore, perhaps logically administered by the Department of Revenue.

Collection of revenue is, of course, the overarching mission of the department. The state's thousands of income tax payers mail their returns to the Department of Revenue, which audits them and takes the money (for ultimate deposit with the Treasury Department). Besides income taxes, the department oversees collection of several other taxes, including sales, use, withholding, and motor fuel taxes. Liquor taxes are also collected by the Department of Revenue. In conjunction with this, the department licenses all liquor and 3.2 beer establishments, as well as distributors and importers of liquor.

The state lottery is run by the Department of Revenue, which is logical because the purpose of the lottery is to make money for the state. A state Lottery Commission decides what games are offered and makes policy for administration of the lottery. The money earned goes to various state projects: half for capital construction and the other half mostly for park and recreation projects.

DEPARTMENT OF SOCIAL SERVICES

One of the most expensive things Colorado does is provide public assistance to those in need, but about half the cost is borne by the federal government. The department administers close to a dozen programs to supplement the income of needy people, including the food stamp program and aid to families with dependent children. The department also provides an array of helpful services to the very old and the very young who need many varieties of assistance, including such things as foster home care; protection from neglect, abuse, or exploitation; health care to the home-bound; nutrition programs including home-delivery of meals; and advocacy services. The department also carries on an extensive vocational rehabilitation program for the benefit of people who are physically or mentally handicapped. Various services for veterans are also provided by the department, most of them directed at helping aged veterans and their spouses, including help with the process of applying for benefits. Nursing-home care is provided in some cases, as well as rehabilitation services. Finally, the most expensive service the department provides is medical care to the poor through the Medicaid Assistance Program. Some of the department's programs, including assistance payments to the needy, are administered by county governments but supervised by the department.

DEPARTMENT OF STATE

The Department of State is headed by an elected secretary of state. Perhaps the department is best known for its responsibility to incorporate businesses and to administer elections. To start a corporation, the first step is to send a letter to the secretary of state asking for the pertinent blank forms. After the department receives the articles of incorporation and verifies them, it then declares the corporation to exist. The department maintains miscellaneous records of such corporations on file and available to the public. Besides its work with corporations, the department also administers the Uniform Commercial Code and the Limited Partnership Act. It also maintains a suitable collection of public records.

If you want to be a notary public, run a dance school, be a fireworks manufacturer or wholesaler, or operate raffles and bingo games, you must obtain a license from the secretary of state and post a bond.

As the chief elections official of the state of Colorado, the secretary of state administers a collection of rather detailed laws designed to protect the integrity of elections and political party activity. These laws include the Colorado Election Code, the Voter Registration Law, and the Campaign Reform Act. There is a very interesting statewide voter registration list in the Department of State.

The department has a few other fascinating duties. One is to administer the Sunshine Act, which requires elected bodies to hold public meetings. Also, the department is the records depository for many state agencies.

The Department of State is the only department that costs the state almost nothing to operate: its revenue is derived chiefly from the fees it charges for miscellaneous services.

DEPARTMENT OF TRANSPORTATION

Colorado has more than ten thousand miles of state highway planned, built, maintained, and improved by the Department of Transportation. About half the money for all this comes from the federal government, and the other half comes from the state. Both governments collect most of their highway money from highway user taxes on gasoline, new cars, tires, parts, lubricating oil, and so forth. Colorado makes doubly sure that all the highway user tax money actually goes to highways, and is not diverted to other interesting purposes, by earmarking the taxes, which means that the revenue automatically goes to highways without the legislature having to pass huge highway appropriations every year. The federal contribution to Colorado highways comes with conditions attached; a growing collection of federal regulations pertaining to such things as design of roads and the manner of their use governs how federal money is spent by the state. The fifty-five-mile-an-hour speed limit on interstate highways was a glaring example: if states did not enact that speed limit and enforce it, their federal highway money was withheld. Congress now requires states to limit speed to sixty-five miles per hour if they want their highway money. Colorado's highway user tax money is shared with cities and counties according to a complicated formula, and some also goes to support the Colorado Highway Patrol.

The Colorado State Transportation Commission dominates almost everything done by the Department of Transportation. The commission has nine members appointed by the governor, who serve overlapping terms of four years each. By law, the governor is required to appoint one member from each of the eight highway commission districts into which the state is divided by the legislature; the ninth member may reside anywhere in the state.

The executive director of the department is appointed by the governor with consent of the Senate and reports to both the governor and the Transportation Commission — has two bosses, which is never altogether fun.

In addition to highway construction and maintenance, the department tries to plan rail service and does what it can to assist the transportation needs of handicapped people and the elderly. Its budget for these activities is very limited.

DEPARTMENT OF THE TREASURY

When it is said that the main job of the treasury is to keep the state's money, that does not mean they put it into boxes and hide it in the basement of the capitol. Actually, the state treasurer (an elected official who heads this department) should be someone who knows something about investing, because his or her job is to invest the state's money (except that of the University of Colorado) in banks, in stocks and bonds, in savings and loan companies, or in other places where it will bring a good rate of return. Millions of dollars are available for this purpose, because the state does not spend all its money the instant it is collected but accumulates wealth from taxes and other sources in a continuous stream. Furthermore, the treasury is responsible for investing various special funds, such as those in the judges' retirement program. An issue that often surfaces in elections for the office of state treasurer is whether the treasurer should always seek the highest rate of return on money, even if that means depositing it in New York, or whether the money should be invested in Colorado, possibly at a lower interest rate, where it would profit local bankers and hopefully support local development. The Department of the Treasury also has the massive duty of keeping records of all money received and paid out by the state. When the controller (an officer in another department) writes checks to pay the state's bills, those checks are ultimately cashed by the Treasury Department.

Money   12

FISCAL MATTERS

This chapter describes how state and local governments in Colorado get their money and how they spend it. In other words it is about fiscal matters. Things pertaining to fiscal matters are discussed in various places throughout this book (see index headings such as appropriations, assessor, auditor, budgeting, caucus, Department of Revenue, Joint Budget Committee, long bill, planning and budgeting, school finance, and treasurer). This chapter does not attempt to repeat everything relating to those subjects said in prior chapters. For example, the process by which the state of Colorado decides how much money to spend, and on what, is discussed at several locations, to be found principally under the index heading "budgeting." This present chapter ventures merely to spotlight the main sources of state and local income and roughly what that income is spent for, accompanied by a few observations along the way.

PECULIARITIES OF COLORADO FINANCE

Probably the most startling thing to be noted is that the state government of Colorado collects and spends less money than most states. In fact, at last report Colorado was seventh from the bottom in the amount of tax revenue it raises per capita. Mississippi, New

Hampshire, South Dakota, Tennessee, and Texas were beneath us in per capita tax collections by the state government. (Texas and South Dakota have no individual income tax.)

Obviously, many states have bigger populations and spend more money and raise more money. But we are not talking total amounts. We are talking per capita (by heads, for each person). Some forty-three state governments of this Union raise more tax money per capita than Colorado raises. On the other hand, Colorado local governments (cities, counties, school districts, special districts) are high-tax governments. They raise much more tax revenue per capita than the local governments of most other states. We are a high-tax state when it comes to local taxes, especially property taxes. Therefore, when all is averaged out, Colorado taxpayers pay about as much per capita as the taxpayers of other states.

Still, when tax burdens are shifted away from the state government to local governments, a few important things change. One change is the impact of those taxes on various groups of taxpayers. Local governments in Colorado do not use the individual income tax because such a tax is too complicated to administer; Castle Rock and Crested Butte and all the other hundreds of local governments don't have the bureaucracy to run an income tax. So local governments have to rely mostly on property taxes and on sales taxes with low administrative costs. Those two taxes (sales and property) happen to be highly regressive. The word *regressive* is used by tax experts to signify that the tax burdens "have nots" more than "haves." Let's call them the poor and rich for convenience. The poor have more of their total wealth tied up in a home than the rich. A rich person may have a condominium in Aspen and a $3 million apartment on Manhattan Island (New York City) and may pay high property taxes. But by comparison with that person's total wealth, the amount tied up in the condominium and the $3 million apartment is probably a very small proportion of his or her total wealth. On the other hand the poor own hardly anything but a car and a tract home. But that home is an enormous fraction of a poor person's total wealth. The property tax therefore hits that person harder, much harder, than the rich. The same is even more true of the sales tax. Therefore, shifting the responsibility for raising revenue from the state government in Denver to local governments throughout the state means shifting it away from the progressive income tax used by the state.

The state income tax is called *progressive* because it has progressively higher rates for progressively higher incomes. It is said to be a fairer tax.

High local property taxes in Colorado may have something to do with recurrent attempts to put a tax limitation amendment into the Colorado constitution. Such amendments are almost always poorly thought out and often end up doing monumental harm to government. Therefore, it may be wise for the state legislature to overhaul Colorado's tax system so that state revenue collections are more evenly balanced with local revenue collections per capita.

STATE REVENUES AND EXPENDITURES

THE GENERAL FUND AND EARMARKED FUNDS

The state government of Colorado recently has been spending (and collecting) in the neighborhood of $5 billion per year, but the legislature has discretion over only about half that amount, the other half being earmarked in advance. You will remember that an earmarked fund is money generated by taxes or fees levied for a specific purpose and must be spent for that purpose, whereas revenues not earmarked go into the general fund. Most of the debate over the budget every year in the legislature concerns how to spend the general fund (although for all practical purposes, large kingdoms of the general fund itself are virtually beyond debate simply because any attempt to make major cuts would lead to fierce legislative rows). Earmarked funds are not, of course, totally beyond discussion: there is often a good deal said about what revenues ought or ought not to be earmarked. But some funds are earmarked by the state constitution itself, and this makes it doubly difficult to make changes. Article X, Section 18, for example, earmarks all license fees and other charges with respect to operation of motor vehicles in the state, as well as money collected from the state gasoline tax. The proceeds of those fees and taxes must be used exclusively for the construction, maintenance, and supervision of public highways in the state. Neither the governor nor the legislature has much at all to say about how that money is spent.

PRINCIPAL SOURCES OF STATE REVENUE

The principal sources of revenue flowing into the general fund are income taxes and sales taxes. In Table 12–1 the major sources of these general revenue funds are listed with the approximate percentage of the general fund contributed by each source in recent years.

Although these sources of revenue go entirely into the general fund and therefore supply most of the money spent by the legislature every year, they do not represent 100 percent of the state's income by any means — only a little over half. Sources of income to the state government in recent years are broadly categorized in Table 12–2.

Much of the federal money appropriated annually by the legislature in recent years is committed to specific purposes by Congress; the state legislature often has little control over how it will be used,

Table 12–1: Sources of General Fund Revenue in Recent Years

Source of Revenue	Approximate Percentage of General Fund
Individual Income Tax	56.75
Sales Tax	27.88
Corporate Income Tax	6.21
Insurance Taxes	3.23
Use Tax	2.09
Cigarette Tax	2.00
Other (Other Excise Taxes, Pari-mutuel Racing, Court Receipts, Interest, and Miscellaneous Other Sources)	1.03
Estate Tax	.06
Liquor Tax	.75

Source: Office of State Planning and Budgeting

Table 12–2: Sources of State Income

Source of Income	Percentage of Total State Income
General Fund Sources	50
Cash Receipts, Tuition, Earmarked Receipts, etc.	28
Federal Sources	22

Source: Office of State Planning and Budgeting

although, technically, federal funds received by the state are appropriated by the Colorado legislature every year. We consider federal funds to be substantially earmarked. (Keep in mind, however, that some federal money bypasses the state and goes directly to local governments. Such money is not appropriated by the legislature.)

A sizable portion of federal money comes to Colorado in the form of matching grants: the federal government supplies a certain number of dollars for a particular purpose if the state in turn will provide a certain percentage of that amount. The federal aid project for interstate highways, for example, is financed 90 percent federally and 10 percent by the state. Most federal payments to Colorado go for education, welfare, health, and highways, although most departments of the state government (all but three) get some federal money (as do many cities, counties, and school districts).

Federal aid has its advantages and its disadvantages. Federal grants often attempt to equalize the states in certain areas of endeavor, such as health, education, welfare, and highways. Perhaps this is good. On the other hand, when federal aid is given on condition that the state match it, this sometimes motivates a state to spend money on things favored by the federal government but not of first importance within the state. Also, federal grants sometimes encourage state agencies to begin a project that later may become a drain on state revenues after federal support for that project ceases. Once a program is in existence, hardly anything can kill it.

A new and exciting source of state revenue was found in 1983: the state lottery. Tickets selling for $1 apiece yield millions annually in state revenue. Half of all money collected by the sale of tickets goes back to the players in the form of a variety of prizes, 15 percent goes to administration of the lottery, and the remaining 35 percent is profit to the state. Half of that profit is earmarked for capital construction (buildings, and so forth) and half for parks and open space. The lottery is criticized by those who feel it encourages gambling and entices poor people to throw away their money on a very slim chance of winning anything very big. On the other hand, the lottery is, in some ways, a painless method of raising revenue. Furthermore, much of the money spent on lottery tickets might otherwise be spent on private gambling.

In 1991 the state of Colorado will enter further into the gambling business because of a 1990 amendment to the state constitution legalizing limited gambling in the cities of Black Hawk, Central City, and Cripple Creek. Up to a maximum of 40 percent of the adjusted gross proceeds of this gambling is to be paid by the licensee (in addition to any license fees) for the privilege of conducting a gaming business. Such percentage is established annually by a state Gaming Control Commission appointed by the executive director of the department within state government into which the commission is placed. Such proceeds are paid directly into a limited gaming fund established in the Treasury Department. First claim on proceeds paid into the gaming fund goes to the state agencies involved in administration of the system to pay their related expenses. The remainder of the proceeds will be divvied up in various percentages to the state of Colorado and to the governing boards of the various county and city governments wherein the gaming is to occur, plus some to the state historical fund. Just how profitable this will be to the state and to the various city and county governments involved will depend on such interesting variables as what percentage of the profits of gaming the Gaming Control Commission wishes to levy against licensees each year for the privilege of doing business, on how high the license fees are, on how many customers partake of the gambling made lawful by the amendment, and on how profligate the players are with their money.

STATE EXPENDITURES

Most of the departments and branches of Colorado state government receive money from a variety of sources: usually most is in the form of appropriations from the general fund, but generally some, at least, is in the form of federal aid, earmarked funds, or cash funds (meaning cash received for services — such as tuition at state colleges). Table 12–3 pertains only to the general fund: it lists the percentage of each department's appropriation that has been received in recent years from the general fund (and only from the general fund) and does not include cash funds or federal funds.

As you can see, almost two-thirds of the money appropriated by the legislature goes to education, and that is why the legislature is sometimes called the "great school board in the sky." The figures in Table 12–3, to repeat, do not include money given to the state by the federal government, which can be considerable. For example, the Department of Labor and Employment receives about 60 percent of

Table 12–3: Distribution of General Fund Appropriations in Fiscal Year 1990–91

Agency	Percentage of General Fund Appropriation
Department of Education	41.13
Department of Higher Education	19.24
Department of Social Services	16.38
Department of Institutions	5.26
Department of Corrections	5.10
Judicial Branch	4.16
Capital Construction	1.93
Department of Public Safety	1.01
Department of Revenue	.97
Department of Health	.92
Legislative Branch	.71
Department of Administration	.51
Department of Natural Resources	.59
Department of Local Affairs	.57
Department of Regulatory Agencies	.35
Department of Law	.33
Department of Personnel	.33
Department of Agriculture	.21
Governor and Lieutenant Governor	.12
Department of the Treasury	.09
Department of Military Affairs	.07
Department of Labor and Employment	.02
Department of Highways	00.00*
Department of State	00.00**

*The Department of Highways is financed almost entirely from the highway users tax fund and federal funds.

**The Department of State is generally self-supporting by fees and charges.

Source: Colorado General Assembly Joint Budget Committee

its money from Washington. The departments of health, military affairs, and social services all get about half their money from Washington, and most other departments get at least some fraction from federal sources. Nor do the figures in Table 12–3 include earmarked funds: the Department of Highways (to mention a glaring example) gets a very large portion of its money from

Table 12–4: Distribution of Total State Expenditure in Fiscal Year 1990–91

Agency or Branch	Percentage of Total State Expenditure
Department of Education	23.73
Department of Social Services	20.48
Department of Higher Education	17.40
Department of Highways	8.16
Department of Institutions	5.95
Capital Construction	4.75
Department of Corrections	2.90
Department of Health	2.64
Judicial Branch	2.10
Department of Local Affairs	1.76
Department of Revenue	1.55
Department of Natural Resources	1.44
Department of Public Safety	1.42
Department of Administration	1.34
Department of Labor and Employment	1.31
Governor and Lieutenant Governor	.98
Department of Regulatory Agencies	.61
Legislative Branch	.39
Department of Law	.37
Department of Agriculture	.27
Department of Personnel	.25
Department of State	.09
Department of Military Affairs	.07
Department of the Treasury	.04

Source: Colorado General Assembly, Joint Budget Committee

earmarked funds. Nor, to repeat, are cash funds included. The various institutions within the Department of Higher Education in Colorado receive roughly 40 percent of their revenue from payments of tuition.

To see what percentage of total state expenditure, rather than simply general fund expenditure, each agency has received in recent years, see Table 12–4.

PAY OF ELECTED STATE OFFICIALS

And perhaps you would be interested to know the 1987 pay of elected state officials (see Table 12–5):

Table 12–5: Pay of Elected State Officials

Governor	$70,000
Lieutenant Governor	$48,500
Attorney General	$60,000
Secretary of State	$48,500
State Treasurer	$48,500
Regents of the University of Colorado	no pay
Members of the State Board of Education	no pay
Members of the General Assembly	$17,000*

*Legislators also receive $99 daily ($45 for Denver-area legislators) in living expenses during the regular 120-day session and for committee or official business between sessions. They also get $.20 per mile travel money for one round-trip per week to their districts.

Source: Colorado General Assembly

REVENUES AND EXPENDITURES OF COUNTIES

Counties get most of their money from two principal sources: (1) the property tax and (2) state aid. Statewide, on average, counties receive about as much in state aid as they raise in property taxes. State aid to counties is used primarily for welfare and highways. Of those two, welfare consumes by far the greatest amount in the more populous counties. In a small county such as Hinsdale, the least populated in the state, with about six hundred people and about one mile of county road for every inhabitant, almost all state aid goes to support highways, and much less is needed for welfare.

Highways and welfare are not only the largest consumers of state aid, but they also represent the largest total expenditures for many counties. El Paso County, for example, has recently devoted about 45 percent of its expenditures to welfare and about 20 percent for highways (including roads, bridges, capital outlay, and operating expenses). The remaining 35 percent is for all other purposes.

REVENUES AND EXPENDITURES OF CITIES

Cities have four main sources of revenue: (1) the property tax, (2) the sales tax, (3) state aid, and (4) charges for utilities and services. Of these, the greatest source is the sales tax. Colorado Springs revenues are a typical example. In 1991 the city of Colorado Springs expects to collect about $115,528,887 in revenue from the sources shown in Table 12–6, and in roughly the percentages indicated.

Table 12–6: Colorado Springs: Approximate General Fund Revenue in 1991

Source	Percentage of Revenue
General Sales and Use Tax	43.29
Intergovernment Revenue (county, state, and federal)	11.56
Property Taxes	14.54
Other Taxes	2.89
Other Revenue	4.10
Rebudgeted from 1990	6.15
Charges for Services	3.53
Transfers (chiefly from utilities in lieu of taxes)	13.94

Source: City of Colorado Springs

Federal grants to cities have declined sharply in recent years. In the early 1980s about 10 percent of the revenue of Colorado Springs came from federal sources. But in more recent years that has dropped to about 1 percent. Such money as still comes to Colorado Springs from Washington is largely in the form of Department of Transportation urban mass transit operating and capital assistance and monies from a community development block grant.

The state of Colorado, however, supplies about 10 percent of the total revenue of Colorado Springs, mostly in the form of state shared revenue, including such things as cigarette tax revenues, state severance tax distribution, highway users tax, and fee revenue. The state also provides a small amount of grant money. As one can see by looking at Table 12–6, money from other governments is a large source of Colorado Springs city revenue.

The approximate general fund expenditure of the city of Colorado Springs in 1991 is projected to be $115,528,887. The percentage of each expenditure to the total is shown in Table 12–7.

Table 12–7: Colorado Springs: Approximate 1991 General Fund Expenditures

Expenditure	Percentage of Total
Public Safety	46.11
Public Works	20.30
Parks and Recreation	11.00
General Purpose	10.13
Administration (city council, manager, auditor, attorney, controller, clerk, treasurer, etc.)	8.34
Community Development	3.07
Capital Improvements	.59
Museum	.46

Source: City of Colorado Springs

REVENUES AND EXPENDITURES OF SCHOOL DISTRICTS

Many people do not realize that it often costs more to run public schools than to run the cities or counties they are in. In general, school districts are the most expensive form of local government in Colorado. Most of the money to support elementary and secondary schools in Colorado comes from two great sources: (1) the local property tax and (2) state aid.

It is remarkable to note the variations among school districts in their ability to support schools. If you take the total assessed value of all the property in Denver and divide it by the number of children going to school, you get, perhaps, about $3,000 per student. But in a place such as El Paso County School District 8, that figure might be only around $300.

PUBLIC SCHOOL FINANCE ACT OF 1988

In 1988 the Colorado General Assembly (and one of its interim committees) made a great effort to reform the state's aid to public schools. Their purpose was to fine-tune that aid so that it did more than in the past to equalize the financial inequalities of school districts. Ultimately, the Public School Finance Act of 1988 was passed.

Basically, what that law does is categorize all of the state's school districts into one of eight classifications for purposes of determining their need for state aid. These classifications are intended to recognize all sorts of differences among school districts that affect not only their ability to raise money but also how much it costs per pupil to run schools. The eight categories of districts have been designed to take into account population size and density, geographic size and population sparsity, regional economic relationships, location of economically important cities or towns within districts, and cost-of-living factors.

The number of dollars in state aid a particular school district receives each year is based on a complex mathematical formula tied to the aforesaid eight categories. A number of different elements are involved in the cost of running a school. For example, there is class size. Each of eight categories assumes a different class size (seven in the Small Attendance category; seventeen in the Urban-Suburban category). Each of the eight categories assumes a different number of students in each instructional unit. Another calculation is a flat per-pupil payment from the state to each district. Each of the eight categories assumes a different per-pupil payment. Other calculations are made for such things as capital reserve, insurance reserve, purchased services, school site funding, and so forth. Each of the eight categories sets a different payment for each funded need. To make all these calculations is a job for experts with computers. But one thing is clear. The category a school district is placed in will greatly affect the amount of state aid it receives.

One cannot help wondering what political battles lie ahead as this or that school district among the 176 tries to get the legislature to transfer them out of their present category of funding to another that is more favorable. And how many members of the General Assembly will try to cement relations with school teachers and their families and their education associations by campaigning to get this or that district into a more favorable category? How many dollars will be donated to the campaigns of such candidates by political action committees representing this or that element among school employees?

DEBT

The Colorado Constitution practically forbids the state to contract any significant amount of debt. In recent years the state legislature has been forced to take severe economizing steps to avoid debt. Each year the Colorado General Assembly carefully calculates

Categories of Districts under the Public School Finance Act of 1988

Category I — Core City: composed of large urbanized districts with district and city boundaries that are coterminous. Core city districts are characterized by large enrollment declines over the past twenty years, high concentrations of low-income students, students with special needs, high dropout rates, and total pupil enrollments in excess of forty thousand. Denver County School District Number 1 is the only school district in this category.

Category II — Denver Metro: composed of districts located within the Denver-Boulder standard metropolitan statistical area that are primarily suburban in nature, compete economically for the same staff pool, and reflect the regional economy of the area. Denver metro districts are characterized by a more homogeneous pupil population and generally smaller numbers of special needs pupils than core city districts. Example: Arapahoe County School District Number 1.

Category III — Urban-Suburban: composed of districts that comprise the state's major population centers outside of the Denver metropolitan area and their immediate surrounding suburbs. Urban-Suburban districts are found within population centers of thirty thousand persons or more. Example: El Paso County District 11 (Colorado Springs).

Category IV — Outlying City: composed of districts in which most of the pupils live in population centers of more than seven thousand, but fewer than thirty thousand, persons. Example: Fremont County School District Number Re–1 (Cañon City).

Category V — Outlying Town: composed of districts in which most of the pupils live in population centers in excess of one thousand, but fewer than seven thousand, persons. Example: Garfield County School District Re–1 (Roaring Fork).

Category VI — Rural: composed of districts with no population centers in excess of one thousand persons and characterized by sparse, widespread populations and do not meet the enrollment criteria for Category VIII — Small Attendance. Example: Teller County School District Re–1 (Cripple Creek–Victor).

Category VII — Recreational: composed of districts that contain major recreational developments that impact the cost of property values, community income, and other cost-of-living components. Example: Pitkin County School District Number 1 (Aspen).

Category VIII — Small Attendance: composed of districts that are rural in nature and have pupil enrollments of less than one hundred fifty. Example: Mineral County School District Number 1 (Creede Consolidated).

Source: *Colorado Revised Statutes*, 22–53–105

what revenue will be collected by the state during the next fiscal year. The legislature then declares a ceiling beyond which it will not permit its appropriations for that fiscal year to go. This has kept the state largely debt free, except for debts contracted for capital construction. The Colorado Constitution permits the state to contract debt for the erection of public buildings, and, in fact, the state of Colorado has acquired considerable debt for that purpose — at last report around $2 billion. (See *Council of State Governments, Book of the States, 1990–91,* p. 309.) Almost all of Colorado's state debt is nonguaranteed, meaning it is in the form of bonds, which are not guaranteed by the full faith and credit of the state. Most of these bonds are revenue bonds paid off by money earned by the project they finance. If the revenue from the project is insufficient to pay off the bond, the owner of the bond has no claim against the state. A government bond is an IOU that you get from the government to which you have loaned money by buying the bonds. They may be purchased through stockbrokers or directly from the government (local, state, or national) selling bonds and are paid off with interest at maturity.

The federal government has no constitutional debt limitation comparable to Colorado's. For that reason, and also because the federal government has emergencies to meet (such as war and depression) unlike anything states are faced with, the federal government finds itself trillions of dollars in debt.

The Colorado Constitution also strictly limits the power of local governments to contract debt. First, it prohibits local governments (except home-rule cities) from creating any debt at all unless the question of incurring it is submitted to, and approved by, a majority of the electors voting on the question. (Home-rule charters may provide for the creation of debt without vote of the people.) Second, if any local government does create a debt, it must levy a tax and/or pledge specific assets, revenue, or funds sufficient to pay the interest and principal of the debt, and such levies or pledges are not repealable until the debt is fully paid. These measures were introduced into many state constitutions early in the twentieth century, after a period of fiscal recklessness and corruption that left many state and local governments overwhelmed with debt.

Epilog

It is presumptuous to point to one problem and say, "That is the greatest problem of the state of Colorado, that is the greatest challenge to overcome." People do not agree on what the greatest problem is, nor do they even agree on what is a problem. Some might say the disease of, say, colon cancer is a worse problem in Colorado than environmental pollution. But desecration of the environment seems to be the most popular problem, so to speak, in Colorado today. Dirty air, heavy traffic, ugliness are among the problems most people mention at once when asked to identify Colorado's greatest headaches.

Smog lies over the cities, even over the ski lifts and mountainsides; condominiums have appeared in cow pastures, motels along mountain roads. Tires, wrecked cars, and beer cans lie in the beds of wilderness streams. One of the most polluted square miles on earth — where plutonium triggers for atom bombs are made — sits on the edge of Denver like a festering boil.

The future of Colorado, its economic development, lies in its spectacular beauty. Perhaps nothing is more important than protecting that beauty and magnifying it. Let us become the Switzerland of America. Let every square mile be a work of art.

Sources

Abbot, Carl, Stephen J. Leonard, and David McComb. *Colorado: A History of the Centennial State.* Boulder, Colorado: Colorado Associated University Press, 1982. 324 pages. Chiefly a social and economic history interlaced with related political information.

Annual Reports of the major departments of state government, including the judiciary. These reports are produced at the end of every fiscal year (July 1–June 30) for benefit of the legislature and others. They may be accompanied by supplements, such as the statistical supplement to the annual report of the Colorado Judicial Department. Annual reports provide an overview of what each department does, together with observations about miscellaneous needs and problems pertaining to the department and its functions. Annual reports and most documents published by Colorado state agencies are available in the State Library in Denver but can also be obtained from each department.

Appropriations Report. Colorado Joint Budget Committee. Published at the conclusion of each fiscal year. It summarizes the actions of the General Assembly relative to fiscal matters during the fiscal year to which the report pertains. The appropriations act and all other acts containing appropriations are included in the tables and accompanying narratives.

Book of the States. Lexington, Kentucky: Council of State Governments, published every two years. Each edition runs approximately 500 pages. Available in the reference department of most sizable libraries. Each volume contains a large collection of tables comparing the fifty states regarding many aspects of their state governments.

Colorado and United States Constitutions. State of Colorado. Available from the Department of State. Brought up to date periodically. Just the two constitutions. No notes citing judicial decisions or related law review articles. The state constitution with such annotations is to be found in the *Colorado Revised Statutes.*

Colorado Election Laws: Primary and General. State of Colorado. Available from the Secretary of State. A convenient compilation in paperback of state laws pertaining to the general, primary, and congressional vacancy elections; initiative and referendum; and election campaigns.

Colorado Legislator's Handbook. Colorado Legislative Council. This is a handy loose-leaf paperback distributed to legislators every year. It contains the rules of the House of Representatives, the rules of the Senate, and the joint rules of the House and Senate. The formal mechanics of getting business done in the General Assembly are set forth in these rules. The handbook also includes many provisions of the Colorado Constitution relating to functions of the legislature and a section on legislative services.

Colorado Revised Statutes. A hardcover collection of about twenty large volumes comprising all the state laws that are in the form of statutes, including the state constitution. The laws are codified, that is, arranged by subject matter. There are more than forty titles, each title being a major subject. Title 43, for example, pertains to highways and roads. Titles are subdivided into articles, sections, et cetera, refining each major topic into a myriad of subtopics. The *Colorado Revised Statutes* (cited as *C.R.S.*) do not include rules and regulations made by state agencies. (State regulations are to be found in the *Code of Colorado*

Regulations, comprising some nine or ten loose-leaf volumes). New pocket parts for each volume of the *Colorado Revised Statutes* are prepared each year after the regular session of the legislature and distributed to libraries and other owners of the *C.R.S.* There is a large index in the last two volumes. Periodically, new volumes of *C.R.S.* are made so that all the changes previously in the pocket parts are incorporated into the printed volume itself. Ultimately the entire set of books is reprinted in that fashion. *C.R.S.* is annotated, meaning it contains countless notes throughout the text referring mainly to judicial decisions that have interpreted each statute. Occasionally, the annotations take up much more space than the statutes to which they pertain. The *Colorado Revised Statutes* and the pocket parts thereto are compiled under supervision and direction of the Joint Committee on Legal Services by the Revisor of Statutes and the Office of Legislative Legal Services. The *Colorado Revised Statutes*, of course, tells the researcher only what is, not what ought to be, in Colorado's government. "What is" in these statutes is limited to formal organization and procedure. But it is important to know what is, before going on to what ought to be. Incidentally, much the same information is available in *West's Colorado Revised Statutes, Annotated*, which also runs about twenty volumes, plus index. The chief advantage of *West's* is that it is hooked up to the West Publishing Company's key-number system — a system for indexing case and statutory law throughout the United States. This is useful to lawyers, and to researchers who want to compare any point of law in Colorado with similar points of law and similar statutes across the nation.

Colorado Springs Gazette Telegraph. Daily newspaper in Colorado Springs with good coverage of local governments in the vicinity. Cited here as a source chiefly because I am a resident of Colorado Springs, and have found the *Gazette* to be a prolific source available at the front door every morning, together with other newspapers.

Colorado: The State We're In. Denver: League of Women Voters of Colorado, 1988. 116 pages. Chiefly, a thin overview of the three branches of state government and of the political party and election system. Oriented toward active citizens who need a practical guide. Does not attempt to include much analysis, discussion, or criticism.

The Colorado Statesman. Published weekly in Denver. An independent journal that covers state politics and government. It usually runs about sixteen pages, with heavy emphasis on the doings of Democratic and Republican political figures in the state.

Denver Post. Denver's largest newspaper. Circulates statewide. A good source of news and editorial comment about government in the Denver metropolitan area, including the state government.

A Directory of Colorado State Government. Colorado Legislative Council. Published periodically. Briefly describes the structure, functions, and financing of the various departments of Colorado government and gives names and addresses of key personnel.

Governor's Budget. Colorado Office of State Planning and Budgeting. In this thick book the governor suggests to the legislators how much money they should appropriate for each function. Good overview of state finance. To see what the legislature actually appropriates, see the long appropriations bill set forth in the *Session Laws of the Colorado General Assembly.*

Know Your Denver Government. Denver: the Denver League of Women Voters, 1985. 80 pages. A description of the organization and functions of the City and County of Denver.

Martin, Curtis W., and Rudolph Gomez. *Colorado Government and Politics* (3rd Ed.). Boulder, Colorado: Pruett Publishing Co., 1972. 220 pages. This is a sophisticated study of Colorado government by Martin, a University of Colorado at Boulder political science professor, and Gomez, who is also a political scientist. Unfortunately, the book is now badly dated but remains a good source of discussion about many features of Colorado's government that have not changed for decades.

Monthly Checklist of State Publications. Published monthly by the United States Government Printing Office. Helps get a fix on what is published by Colorado state agencies.

The Municipal Year Book. Published annually by the International City Management Association. Available in most large libraries. Much statistical data about American cities and their governments, including Colorado cities. Useful for putting Colorado cities in context with the general picture of American cities.

The Rocky Mountain News. Denver's second largest newspaper. Circulates statewide. A good source of news and editorial comment about government in the Denver metropolitan area, including the state government.

Session Laws of the Colorado General Assembly. After each regular session of the legislature, the revisor of statutes prepares these books (usually two volumes), which include all the statutory changes (new laws and changes in old laws) and any other action taken by the General Assembly during the session, such as passing memorials and resolutions. Good books to skim through when you want to refresh your memory on what the legislature did in a certain year. Each edition of the *Session Laws* also includes other information useful to the researcher on Colorado government. Each lists (for the year you are looking at) the elected officers of the state and their terms and pay, the state supreme court justices and their terms and pay, the state court of appeals judges and their terms and pay, the members of the Colorado General Assembly (Senate and House) and their terms, district judges by district, and county officers by county. It takes the revisor of statutes a few months after the session to produce the *Session Laws.* Meanwhile one might consult, *West's Colorado Legislative Services,* which is a series of pamphlets issued periodically even while the legislature is still in session setting forth the laws passed up to date of publication.

Shoemaker, Joe. *Budgeting is the Answer.* Privately published, 1977. 152 pages. Mr. Shoemaker was elected to the Colorado State Senate in 1962 and served three terms. He was an active member of the Joint Budget Committee. Shoemaker describes in a lively, thorough, and perceptive way how the Joint Budget Committee of the Colorado General Assembly works. He defends the committee and its mission as a unique contribution to state government that puts control of budgeting back into the hands of the legislature where it belongs, and takes it away from the executive branch, particularly from the governor.

State of Colorado Telephone Directory. Division of Central Services. This three-hundred-page telephone directory includes the name, address, and phone number of every state agency and all permanent state employees. The organizational listings include the name of individuals in key positions. Also listed are the Colorado congressional delegation, county officers and elected officials, and school districts. This phone book not only reveals a great deal about the organization and structure of the state government but also makes it easier for researchers to contact any state office for needed information. Incidentally, if you want to phone agencies and offices in other states for information, the Council of State Governments publishes two volumes of value every year for that purpose: *State Elective Officials and the Legislatures,* which gives names, addresses, and telephone numbers for such officials in all fifty states, and *State Administrative Officials Classified by Function,* which also gives names, addresses, and phone numbers for such officials by function in all fifty states. Two other publications also have a similar fifty-state function: *State Executive Directory,* published by the Carroll Publishing Company of Washington, D.C., and *State Yellow Book,* a directory of the executive, legislative, and judicial branches of the fifty state governments published by Monitor Publishing Company of New York.

Straayer, John A. *The Colorado General Assembly.* Niwot, Colorado: University Press of Colorado, 1990. 340 pages. A masterful discussion and analysis of the Colorado legislature. In process of discussing the legislature, Straayer (a political science professor at Colorado State University) probes other aspects of Colorado's government, such as the workings of political parties and elections. Many fascinating and illuminating references to personalities in the legislature.

Acknowledgments

Photographs courtesy of the State Historical Society of Colorado. Maps: (1) Colorado area before 1900, by Kenneth A. Erickson and (2) Colorado Senate Districts and Colorado House of Representatives Districts, courtesy Colorado Legislative Council and adapted by cartographer Kathy Ingraham. Photo of Supreme Court Chamber courtesy RNL, Inc. and Chief Justice Edward E. Pringle.

Index

incremental, 254, 257
Joint Budget Committee, 208, 216–
20, 253, 254, 256
Office of State Planning and, 220
zero-based, 254–55
Busing, 87

Campaign
finance, 141–42
money, 141
Reform Act, 141
Campaigns
cost, 141
reporting expenses, 141
winning, 142–46
Candidates
independent, 127
write-in, 136
Capital Development Committee, 218
Carroll, John, 193
Cash funds, 303, 305
Cattle, 31–32
Caucus, budget, 220–21
Community and Junior Colleges
Aims Community College, 280
Arapahoe Community College, 280
Colorado Mountain College, 280
Colorado Northwest Community
College, 280
Community College of Aurora, 280
Community College of Denver, 280
Delta-Montrose Area Vocational
School, 280
Emily Griffith Opportunity School,
280
Front Range Community College,
280
Lamar Community College, 280
Larimer County Center, 280
Mesa State College, 280
Morgan Community College, 280
Northeastern Junior College, 280
Otero Junior college, 280
Pikes Peak Community College,
280
Pueblo Community College, 280
Red Rocks Community College, 280
San Juan Basin Area Vocational
School, 280

San Luis Valley Area Vocational
School, 280
Trinidad Community College, 280
T. H. Pickens Technical Center, 280
Certiorari, 161
Chief Clerk of the House, 229, 230
Chief Justice, 160, 187
City, 52–64 (*see also* Municipal)
abandoned, 54
attorney, 167
council, 55–61
council, vacancy on, 140
disincorporation of, 54
expenditures, 307–08
incorporation of, 54
in state constitution, 51
City-county, 63–64, 83
City-state, 84
Citizenship requirement, 120
Citizens' Advocate Office, 262
Civil Air Patrol, 286
Civil case, 156–57
Civil procedure, 176–77
Civil Rights Commission, 293
Civil service, 251
county, 75, 76
legislative confirmation, 184
Claim clubs, 19, 151
Clerk, city, 55
Clerk, county, 71
Clerk of the House, 208–09
Colony Towns, 32
Colorado, history of, 3–34
Colorado Bureau of Investigation, 292
Colorado Commission on Higher Edu-
cation, 281
Colorado Revised Statutes, 178
Colorado School of Mines, 279
Colorado Springs, 52, 62–63, 86, 88,
91, 307–08
Colorado State Guard, 287
Colorado State Hospital, 282
Commission on Judicial Discipline,
166
Commissioner
of Agriculture, 272
of Education, 81, 275
Commissioners, board of county, 69–
70, 75, 81